Herbert Metford Thompson

**Russian Politics**

Herbert Metford Thompson

**Russian Politics**

ISBN/EAN: 9783337078898

Printed in Europe, USA, Canada, Australia, Japan

Cover: Foto ©ninafisch / pixelio.de

More available books at **www.hansebooks.com**

# RUSSIA.

## RUSSIA.

By D. MACKENZIE WALLACE, M.A., Member of the Imperial Russian Geographical Society. Large 12mo. $2.

CONTENTS: *Travelling in Russia; In the Northern Forests; Voluntary Exile; The Village Priest; A Medical Consultation; A Peasant Family of the Old Type; The Peasantry of the North; The Mir, or Village Community; How the Commune has been Preserved; Finnish and Tartar Villages, Towns, and Mercantile Classes ; Lord Novgorod the Great; The Imperial Administration; The New Local Self-Government; Landed Proprietors of the Old School; Proprietors of the Modern School; The Noblesse; Social Classes; Among the Heretics; The Dissenters; Pastoral Tribes of the Steppes; St. Petersburg and European Influence; Moscow and the Slavophils; Church and State; The Crimean War and its Consequences; The Serfs; Emancipation of the Serfs; Consequences of the Emancipation* (a. For the Landed Proprietors ; b. For the Peasantry); *The New Law Courts; Territorial Expansion and the Eastern Question.*

"One of the stoutest and most honest pieces of work produced in our time; and the man who has produced it, . . . even if he never does anything more, will not have lived in vain."—*Fortnightly Review.*

"Excellent and interesting, . . . worthy of the highest praise. . . . Not a piece of clever book-making, but the result of a large amount of serious study and thorough research. . . . We commend his book as a very valuable account of a very interesting people."—*The Nation.*

## A WINTER IN RUSSIA.

By THÉOPHILE GAUTIER. Translated by M. M. Ripley. 12mo. $1.75.

CONTENTS: *Berlin; Hamburg; Schleswig; Lubeck; Crossing the Baltic; St. Petersburg; Winter; The Neva; Details of Interiors; A Ball at the Winter Palace; The Theatres; The Tchoukine Dvor; Zichy; St. Isaac's; Moscow; The Kremlin; Troïtza; Byzantine Art; Return to France.*

"As little like an ordinary book of travel as a slender antique vase filled with the perfumed wine of Horatian banquets is like the fat comfortable tea-cup of a modern breakfast-table."—*New York Tribune.*

"The book is a charming one, and nothing approaching it in merit has been written on the outward face of things in Russia. . . . He sees pictures where most people find mere dead surfaces, and where common eyes find the tint of a picture he constructs a complete work of art."—*The Nation.*

*Catalogue of Henry Holt & Co.'s works in general literature, with over twenty portraits, free.*

**HENRY HOLT & CO.,**      **29 W. 23d St., New York.**

BY

# HERBERT M. THOMPSON, M.A.

*WITH FIVE MAPS.*

NEW YORK
HENRY HOLT AND COMPANY
1896

# PREFACE.

———o———

THIS book attempts to put the English reader in a position to understand the conditions of life and the problems of government that exist in the Russia of to-day. Some knowledge of the aspects of the country, the ethnological descent of its inhabitants, and the story of the rise and maintenance of their autocratic form of government, seems necessary as a preliminary to such understanding, and the first three chapters of the volume are devoted to an exposition of these matters; but since *modern* political life is the subject of the book, they have not been allowed to expand into greater detail than will be helpful to the object in view.

The reforms of the early years of Alexander II. have been treated much more fully, for almost all the political questions of the day in Russia are intimately connected with them and with their subsequent partial abrogation witnessed during the reactionary period of the last quarter of a century.

Finally the chief forces now in operation on the Russian political stage are described, and their relations to each other discussed; the phenomena of government at present observable are portrayed, and the question is debated as to whether in Russia good government is compatible with autocracy (aggravated by officialdom), and if not, what chance there is in the near future of the overthrow of the bureaucracy and the introduction of constitutionalism.

Chapters supplementary to the main theme of the book have been added to discuss the subjects of the extradition of prisoners to Russia by other states, and the attitude towards questions of Russian internal politics which should be observed by inhabitants of freer countries.

A rather full index at the end of the volume will it is hoped serve in some measure as a small dictionary of the subject of Russian politics. Most of the headings likely to occur to the mind in connection with it will be found there, and if the pages indicated in the text are referred to, the student of the subject will frequently find further references to various authorities on particular points.

A list of many of the books used by me will be found in the index of authors, but I have very generally treated as my principal authorities M. Anatole Leroy-Beaulieu's encyclopædic work on Russia, and the oral evidence of my friend Mr Felix Volkhovsky, who has been kind enough to read the book in manuscript and in every chapter to suggest out of the wealth of his knowledge (gathered both from personal experience, and a wide acquaintance with Russian historical and sociological books) notable additions and improvements.

I consider myself fortunate therefore in having had as my two principal guides, men of divergent views, who are yet, both of them, so instructed and so conscientious, that in their accounts of matters of fact hardly any divergence occurs.

The reader may differ widely from me in the conclusions I have drawn from the facts portrayed, but will understand that my object has been to place them fairly before him so that he shall be in no less good position than myself to draw the deductions from them which appear to him appropriate.

A word must be said on the difficult subject of the spelling of Russian names. Like Mr Kennan and others I have attempted to follow phonetic rules though my interpretation of them has not completely coincided with his; (for example where he uses the final *f*, I have used *v*). In the numerous quotations I have made from other writers, I have considered it right to preserve the spelling they have adopted though it has sometimes resulted in the inconvenience of the same name's being spelt in two or three ways, possibly within as many pages. Like Mr Kennan I have not attempted to alter the spelling of names familiar to English readers through long usage (such as Moscow, Cossack, etc.), nor the signatures that have been deliberately chosen by Russian writers in Roman letters (such as that of Madame Novikoff).

In my quotations from M. Leroy-Beaulieu's book, I have not used Madame Ragozin's English version, but have translated directly from the French edition. The frequent curtailments in the English edition make this desirable, and in the case of the third volume it has been necessary, as that part of the book has not yet been published in its English form.

My thanks are due to my brother Dr A. Hugh Thompson for having helped me to revise the proofs of the book.

HERBERT M. THOMPSON.

*September 9th*, 1895.

# CONTENTS.

## CHAPTER I.
THE PHYSICAL ASPECTS OF RUSSIA, AND THE RACIAL DESCENT OF HER PEOPLES . . . . . . . . . **1**

## CHAPTER II.
HISTORICAL SKETCH UP TO THE DEATH OF PETER THE GREAT . **31**

## CHAPTER III.
HISTORICAL SKETCH FROM THE DEATH OF PETER THE GREAT TO THE CRIMEAN WAR . . . . . . . **59**

## CHAPTER IV.
THE PEASANTRY: THEIR EMANCIPATION FROM SERFDOM, AND SUBSEQUENT TREATMENT AND CONDITIONS OF LIFE . **87**

## CHAPTER V.
PENELOPE'S WEB: AN ACCOUNT OF OTHER REFORMS UNDERTAKEN IN THE 'SIXTIES, AND THEIR SUBSEQUENT PARTIAL UNDOING . . . . . . . **125**

# CONTENTS.

## CHAPTER VI.

RELIGIONS AND RELIGIOUS PERSECUTIONS . . . . 147

## CHAPTER VII.

DRAMATIS PERSONÆ ON THE POLITICAL STAGE OF MODERN RUSSIA . . . . . . . . . . 177

## CHAPTER VIII.

"HOW LONG THE MANY MUST ENDURE THE ONE?" . . . 215

## CHAPTER IX.

THE QUESTION OF THE EXTRADITION OF PRISONERS TO RUSSIA . . . . . . . . . 247

## CHAPTER X.

PLEA FOR SYMPATHY WITH THE CAUSE OF FREEDOM IN RUSSIA . . . . . . . . . . 265

---

APPENDIX . . . . . . . . . . 273

INDEX OF NAMES AND SUBJECTS . . . . . . 277

INDEX OF WRITERS, AND BOOKS TO WHICH REFERENCE MADE . . . . . . . . . . 288

# CONTENTS.

## MAPS.

|  | PAGE |
|---|---|
| RUSSIA. SHOWING ETHNOGRAPHICAL DISTRIBUTION OF POPULATION | *face title* |
| RUSSIA. SHOWING THE ZONES INTO WHICH THE COUNTRY IS NATURALLY DIVIDED | 13 |
| RUSSIA. SHOWING PALE OF SETTLEMENT TO WHICH THE JEWS ARE CONFINED | 28 |
| RUSSIA BEFORE THE TIME OF PETER THE GREAT | 32 |
| GENEALOGY OF THE RUSSIAN IMPERIAL FAMILY | 36 |
| MAP TO ILLUSTRATE THE FINAL PARTITION OF POLAND, 1795 | 72 |

# CHAPTER I.

## THE PHYSICAL ASPECTS OF RUSSIA, AND THE RACIAL DESCENT OF HER PEOPLES.

A

## Chapter I.—*Contents.*

HUGE extent of the natural features—Singular approximation of the climate of the southern, to that of the northern parts: reasons for this—Country naturally divided into zones, viz. the Arctic or barren zone, the forest and swamp zone, the black earth zone, the steppes, the saline steppes and south-easterly regions, and Transcaucasia—The river system.

Much ethnological homogeneousness amongst inhabitants of Russia—Rapid increase of population and peopling of south Russia—The homogeneousness of the central portions (*i.e.* of Great Russia) does not extend to the border territories.

Ethnological descent of the Russians—The Uro-Altaic group of peoples, including the Finns, the Tatars, and the Mongols—The blood of the Finns and the Tatars commingles with that of the Slavs to form the modern Russian nation, but the importance of the last predominates—The Slavs, a purely Aryan stock.

The Great Russians, the Little Russians, the White Russians, the Lithuanians, the Letts, the Finns, and the Poles.

The Jewish and Teutonic elements.

Hindrances in the way of complete Russification.

# L

## PHYSICAL CHARACTERISTICS AND ETHNOLOGY.

It would be difficult to give a better account of the physical characteristics of the Russian Empire than that contained in the opening chapters of M. Anatole Leroy-Beaulieu's "The Empire of the Tsars and the Russians."[1] They are the chief source of information for the contents of this chapter.

Humboldt has remarked that the part of our globe governed by the Russian sceptre is larger than the area which the moon exhibits to us at its full. In proportion with the huge extent of the country are its natural features. Its plains (steppes) are the vastest of our planet; whilst the characteristic of the great bulk of the European and much of the Asiatic parts of the empire is extreme flatness, at the south the gigantic barrier of the Caucasus springs from below the level of the sea, its summits overtopping Mount Blanc by 800 metres; the lakes of north-east Russia, Ladoga and Onega, are the largest in Europe, and the Siberian lakes of Baikál and Balkash are the largest in Asia; whilst the Caspian and Aral Seas form the largest lakes of the world. The rivers are in proportion to the plains. The most remarkable of these in the place it

---

[1] This book is referred to in future pages as "Leroy-Beaulieu."

takes in the national life (though, if we include the Siberian rivers, not the longest), is the Volga. It seems almost an accident that from the point where it so nearly approaches the Don it does not, like its brother river, flow into the sea of Azov. But as M. Leroy-Beaulieu remarks, this accident has "considerable influence on the destinies of the Russian people," for this great artery of trade and intercourse "turns its back on Europe," and empties itself into the Caspian, a vast salt lake with surroundings that are Asiatic.

A very large proportion of Russian territory is still uninhabited, and already the population numbers 120,000,000, of whom only about 20 per cent. dwell in Siberia and the rest of Asiatic Russia.

M. Leroy-Beaulieu regards the conventional geographical distinction between the continents of Asia and Europe as a somewhat arbitrary one. He would rather distinguish in this huge expanse of the world's surface three main divisions, viz. Europe proper, Asia proper, and the Empire of the Tsars. The last must be distinguished from Europe proper, for it is not, like what is ordinarily called Western Europe, invaded on all sides by arms of the sea, so as to form a congeries of peninsulas, and consequently it does not enjoy the same temperate climate. The seas which wash its shores are too far off or not large enough to serve, as ours do, in turn as reservoirs of warmth and sources of refreshing coolness. Another distinguishing feature is the absence throughout the great bulk of Russia of mountain ranges and deep valleys. The geological strata lie evenly superimposed the one on the other, and over them stretch the interminable steppes. If one described these as being saved from perfect flatness by gradual undulation, one would be using a figure more strongly suggestive of variety in landscape than the facts allow. Rather one might say that there is a *swell* on the steppes as there may be on the surface of a smooth sea. Nothing then stands in the way of the ice-laden polar winds which sweep right across the country from north to south freezing the ports of the Azov, and even the river mouths of the Black Sea itself during the winter season as they do the harbour of Archangel, though for a considerably shorter time.

The Urál Mountains are marked on the maps with more emphasis than their actual importance quite justifies. One expects to find them comparable in dignity and altitude to the Alps; in reality they may be more fittingly compared with the mountains of Scotland. The highest summit on the rounded ridges of this range is only 4875 feet—not much higher than Ben Nevis. The Uráls serve rather to mark the boundary between Europe and Asia than to make any very formidable barrier between them. Indeed they are not permitted to fulfil even this humbler office consistently, for the European province of Permia juts out to the eastward far beyond their slopes. They however have their importance, for volcanic action has here disturbed the even lie of the strata enough to make great mineral wealth accessible to mining enterprise. But regarded as a screen to shield the country from the freezing air currents, they are unimportant; what little protection they might give in this way is lost from the fact of their running north and south: the screen is placed edgeways to the draught.

Another point to observe is that over the huge expanse of Russia and Siberia, the fertilising rainfall is very small compared to what it is in Europe, and especially is this true of the central portions of the former.

But if Russia is climatically so unfortunately distinguished from Europe, it is also distinguished from Asia. For the Russian sun does not waste away the cultivator of the soil, nor does it threaten with degeneracy the race that works under it. Man encounters but two obstacles to his progress there, coldness, and immensity of space. Now coldness is less difficult to overcome than extreme heat, and it is an enemy that our races and our civilisation need dread less. As for the difficulties of immense extent of territory they have already been partly overcome; whilst the very fact of immensity has advantages which promise much for Russia in the future.

We have now enumerated the main reasons for the singular uniformity of climate which obtains throughout almost the whole of European, and a great part of Asiatic Russia. Of Russia in Europe it is almost true to say that if we cut off the northern limbs of Finland and Lapland, and the southern mountain-protected excrescences of Transcaucasia and Southern Crimea, the winter coldness of the south is comparable to, though less intense than that of the north, whilst the scorching summer heat is felt hardly less in the north than it is in the south. In each case there is of course some degree of moderating influence exercised both by the difference of latitude, and in some parts, by the neighbourhood of the sea, but not nearly as much as one would expect from reflection on the fact that Archangel is about as much north of Odessa as Christiana is of Naples. There is of course a difference in the respective lengths of the cold and of the hot seasons; the ports of the Azov are not frozen for so long a period as those of the Baltic.

The effect of these mitigations and intensifications becomes apparent in the next feature of the physical conditions of Russia which has to be described. Nature has divided the country into great belts or zones, running east and west, or in the more southern parts of the country, north-east and south-west. The most northerly of these zones in consequence of the intense rigour of the climate has no forest trees, and hardly any vegetation of any sort except lichen. But at about the 65th degree of latitude there begins to spread southwards the enormous forest region or zone of Russia. The map tells one that in mere extent of territory it embraces more than half of the European part of the empire; nor is it confined by the rather feeble barrier of the Urál mountains, but it stretches away eastwards into Siberia. Its southern boundary runs from as far down as the province of Kiev in the west, to the far more northern province of Kazán as it gets eastwards, crossing the Volga near where the great water highway joins the Káma and begins to run south.

The proportion of this forest zone that is actually covered with wood varies considerably. In the comparatively populous south-west it is about a third only, so that one must not picture what is called the forest zone as anything like a continuous stretch of wood; but in the north-east it much more nearly becomes so, for there the wood covers as much as three-quarters of the land. In the northern parts the trees are almost exclusively the fir, the larch, the pine, and the birch; but the further south one travels the more variety of species one encounters. Throughout there is but little brushwood and undergrowth, so that in this respect these great forests present a contrast to those of South America. To give a more vivid idea of what these forests are like, it may be interesting to quote a Russian's account of a ride through the forest region between Viatka and Nízhni Nóvgorod in winter. The passage is taken from Alexander Herzen's "My Exile":—

"The following day I arrived at Soransk.

"From this point, the road runs through endless pine woods. The nights were moonlight; the ground was frozen; the small sledge glided quickly over the narrow road. Such woods I have never seen again. They extend, without interruption to Archangelsk, whence reindeer sometimes pass through them, to the district of Wiatka. Most of the trees are suitable for building. The pines, wonderfully straight, flew past my sledge like soldiers, tall and snow-covered, and their pointed pinnacles looked out of the snow like upraised daggers. You fall asleep, you awake, the regiments of pine-trees pass uninterruptedly with a hurried step past the sledge, shaking off the snow from time to time; and then comes the post-station in a small space cut out of the wood. There stands a little house behind the trees, seeming to have lost its way hither. The horses, tied to a pile, ring their little bells; some Tcheremiss boys rush out of the house, in their embroidered shirts, still half asleep. The Wiatka postillion begins in a hoarse voice to quarrel with his companion; then he exclaims, 'Aida! aida!' ('Quicker! quicker!') commences a song of two notes, and again the eye meets with snow and pines, pines and snow."

South of the forest zone is the black earth zone, in many respects the most remarkable region in Russia. It owes its name to a layer of soil which covers its surface to a thickness differing from half a yard to a yard and a half. This soil is formed of decayed vegetable matter and is of marvellous fertility so that this part of the Empire is one of the natural granaries of the world and is the most thickly populated part of the country though the population is as yet very largely condensed in the south-western portions. With a thickness about equal to the length of the province of Podolia it forms a broad band to the south of the forest region crossing the Volga near the Samára horse-shoe.

Below the black earth zone the country is occupied for another broad belt by the zone of the steppes, the Russian prairie. In the black earth zone the inhabitants are settled on the land, and follow the three-years rotation system of cultivation. Most of the prairie zone is now becoming settled in the same way, but in the north-easterly regions the inhabitants are still nomad; they cultivate the land till it is exhausted and then move on to another position. The soil here is not unpromising. It is in fact a modification of the black earth, though without its extraordinary richness. The principal disadvantage of the steppes compared with the black earth zone itself, is that they are less well watered by rivers. The features which formerly characterised the latter region alone are gradually being found over a larger area than was the case a few decades ago; to the north the felling of the neighbouring forests, and to the south the occupancy of the prairie land, less fertile though it be, with settled cultivation, are both bringing about this result.

To the south of the steppes, entering Europe as a great wedge which has its thickest end in Asia, is a still less fertile region. Part of it is the Urál-Caspian depression, which forms the desert region of South Russia. It in fact includes the bed of the vast prehistoric inland ocean, of which the Caspian and the Aral are the shrunken remnants. The line which bounds the region in question enters from the north-east, near Orenburg, crosses the Volga where it neighbours the Don at Tsaritsin, and by following the lower part of the valley of the Dnieper, arrives at the Black Sea at Khersón. Whilst its southern boundary returns to Asia along the range of mountains which first becomes visible along the south coast of the Crimea from west to east, and beyond the Strait of Kertch develops into the mighty Caucasus. This part of Russia includes some of the saline steppes which have still vaster extent in the Asiatic than in the European part of the domain. These quasi-desert parts, like the most northerly (the polar) zone, can support but a few wandering tribes. In some respects the two regions are comparable, the reindeer being replaced by the camel. But speaking generally of the south-easterly regions, there are large portions which are not only habitable but fairly fertile. Such are most of the Kuban, and the parts directly watered by the Ural, the Volga, and the Don rivers. Speaking generally of the whole region, we may say that the greater part of it is settled.

As our final and southernmost division of the country we have Transcaucasia and the southern coast of the Crimean peninsula. Here, in consequence of the protection of the mountain barrier, the climatic conditions of the rest of Russia are at last shaken off. There is a fertile land, with a sub-tropical climate, where the olive, the vine, the mulberry, cotton, and the sugar-cane grow, and where we once more find forests—forests that are far more luxuriant in their growth than those of northern Russia.

Let us now for a moment consider the water system of Russia. In the province of Novgorod, five degrees south of St Petersburg, rise the Valdai Hills. They may seem at first sight hardly worth mentioning, for they are only about 1000 feet high. But all things are comparative, and in the great flat expanse of European Russia, whether we take the sweep from the Carpathians to the Urals, or that from the Caucasus to the Baltic, this is the highest ground to be encountered between. In this part then are to be found the head-waters of the Volga and of many others of the largest rivers of Russia, which leisurely flow hence north, south, east, and west to one of the far distant seas. In consequence of the extreme flatness of the country there is often but little to determine which way the rivers shall flow, and in the course of their dilatory meanderings they form countless lakes (the two largest specimens of which are Onega and Ladoga), or still more often vast expanses of swamp and marsh which, especially in the forest region, occupy a large part of the surface of the country. The actual lakes are for the most part found near the beginnings of the river-courses, and the lake region is mostly in the near neighbourhood of the Valdai Hills, or in the part of the country stretching from thence northwards to the White Sea.

Speaking broadly, we see Russia divided into two great regions, the upper half covered with forest and marsh, with large clearances made habitable here and there by the hand of man, in which sometimes towns or villages are built; the lower half devoid of wood and suffering from a continual dearth of moisture, but compensated in great measure for these drawbacks by the marvellous fertility of its soil in its more northerly parts. The broad physical distinctions thus marked out between upper and lower Russia are not followed by fundamental distinctions between the national characteristics of their respective populations. There is on the other hand an amount of homogeneousness which is rather remarkable compared for instance with what we should find in a survey from north to south of the populations of India. The natural features of the country to some extent account for this. The great water-highways provided by the rivers form continual lines of communication; by them the north is constantly sending its timber to the south; and they are for ever carrying the grain of the south to feed the people of the north. Again the absence of important mountain ranges has saved the country from the interposition of natural boundaries which would check unifying intercommunication between the northern and the southern parts. An even more important factor in the case is that the southern half of Russia is to all intents and purposes a colony; a colony from the westerly and partly too from the northerly portions, and one that has been but comparatively recently settled. In a country where industrial and manufacturing development is in its infancy, where the great-town movement is only beginning to be felt, and where eight or nine out of every ten of its inhabitants are peasants who spend their lives in agriculture, it would be natural to find the lands presenting the most fertile soils those which were supporting the thickest populations. If we examine a map showing the modern distribution of population we find this to be largely the case. But natural conditions are settling where the centre of gravity shall be, now for the first time. History settled the early Russians amidst their forests where they were more secure from their fast-speeding enemies who scoured the open plains, the fertile soil of which is now opening up to the rest of Russia a new land of promise comparable to the fields for colonisation offered to England, Germany, and Scandinavia by the Western States of America and North-West Canada.

A surprisingly rapid increase of population has been the analogous consequence. The present population of the Empire is about 120 millions and to these it adds yearly about a million. Yet in 1723 it was computed at only about 14 or 15 millions, in 1782 at 28 to 30, in 1815 at 45, and so recently as 1851 at 68 millions. Even when we remember that these statistics take into account the populations added to the subjects of the Tsar in consequence of territorial annexation, the natural increase is on a scale that we are used to associate with newly opened up colonies rather than with old settled countries. With a newly-peopled region so enormous then, and with a population increasing at this rate, it is clear that there must be material changes in political conditions. It is one of the grounds of hope that the Liberals of the second Nicholas's reign can possess with more confidence than those of the time of Nicholas I., that developments so prodigious should help to break through the sombre political cloud that spreads its monotonous shadow over at any rate three out of the four reigns which have partitioned the present century.

As we might expect, the present population of Russia is by no means evenly distributed over its surface. Only about one-sixth of it dwells in the Asiatic part, beyond the Urals and the Caspian. Of the remainder, two-thirds are to be found in a part of the European territory not more than three times as large as France. The most thickly peopled regions are the south-western part of the black earth zone and the adjoining parts of the forest and prairie zones; Poland and some of the neighbouring provinces which enjoy the advantages of a good geographical position, an older civilisation, and a more advanced manufacturing and industrial development; the industrial region of Moscow, with its central position between the two great waterways of the Volga and the Oka, and its neighbourhood both to the most splendidly wooded countries of the north, and the black earth lands of the south; and finally the near neighbourhood of St Petersburg. The immediate future developments of population may be looked for principally in the black earth and fertile prairie zones. The north-easterly portions of these are as yet most scantily peopled.

We have observed that the physical characteristics of the country tend to promote its homogeneousness and solidarity to a rather remarkable extent. The further question now remains to be asked. Do we actually find homogeneousness and solidarity in the peoples who inhabit it? For we must remember that tendencies seemingly as potent have for ages been in operation calculated to bring about a contrary result. Across the broad plain of Russia has swept each invading nomad wave as it has swarmed across from Eastern Asia to Western Europe. Not only so, but in many cases the tide has turned again upon its level woods and plains, and the races along its western borders and seas, after having undergone the process of differentiation in the various countries that they have found marked out for them by nature, have sent back invading hosts into Russia, there perhaps once more to undergo a process of assimilation.

Within the bounds of the empire, the races of sufficient importance to be taken into account number more than a score. If we include the numerically less important ones, and those that differ less markedly from other represented specimens, they amount to fifty or sixty. All round the borders of Russia the utmost diversity of race, language, and religion are to be found. As Stepniak says, in his "Russian Peasantry" (Vol. I. p. 124-5):—

"A Russian *Moujik* presents of course as many varieties as there are tribes and regions in the vast empire. There is a wide difference between the peculiarly sociable open-hearted Great Russian peasant brisk in mind and speech, quick to love and quick to forget, and the dreamy and reserved Ruthenian; or between the practical extremely versatile and independent Siberian, who never knew slavery, and the timid Beloruss (White Russian), who has borne three yokes. But through all the varieties of types, tribes, and past history, the millions of our rural population, present a remarkable uniformity in those higher general, ethical, and social conceptions, which the educated draw from diverse social and political sciences, and the uneducated from their traditions, which are the depositories of the collective wisdom of past generations.

"This seemingly strange uniformity in our peasants' moral physiognomy is to be accounted for by two causes; the perfect identity of our people's daily occupation, which is almost exclusively pure husbandry, and the great similitude of those peculiar self-governing associations, village communes, in which the whole of our rural population, without distinction of tribe or place, have lived from time immemorial."

In the centre of Russia in fact nature's ordinance of unification has been obeyed not only in assimilation of the peasants' character, but in producing racial uniformity, and speaking broadly, there is to be found one enormous assimilated mass, the great Muscovite Russian nation.

About two-thirds of the whole population of the Empire may be included in this category; sixty or seventy millions of Russians proper occupy the whole of the central portions of the country. This great mass, the same in language and religion, is varied only by occasional isolated communities of Finnish and Tatár race. These tend ever to become less; to merge themselves in the surrounding populations who talk the Slavonic tongue and worship in the orthodox church. Accordingly on the ethnological maps all this part is coloured as Slavonic. Whatever the stock may have been, the Slav graft has undoubtedly taken thereon; but language and religion tell us but very imperfectly about the actual racial descent. To find out about this we must call in to our aid anthropology. We shall then learn that the process which we see going on before our eyes of the gradual absorption of the Turanian villages, has been taking place with many races for numbers of centuries under the unifying bond first of Christianity, and afterwards of that religion united with the Muscovite domination. We have now then to try and unravel the riddle of the racial descent of the great mass of the Russians. Is the stock mainly Slav, or is it mainly Turanian? Are we considering the fortunes of a people who are in origin the same as the inhabitants of Western Europe? Or are they more akin to the non-progressive races of Asia? On our answer to this question must depend a large measure of the reasonableness of our hope of seeing European civilisation and European culture quickly and firmly established amongst the Russian people.

When considering the ethnology of Europe, one

seems to have but little concern except with one large group of peoples amongst which a family relationship has been satisfactorily established. The Indo-European or Aryan family includes the Greco-Italian races; the Keltic races, (many of the Scotch and of the Irish, the Manx, the Welsh, the Cornish, and the Bretons); the Teutonic races, (including to a large extent the English, and more unmixedly the Flemish, the Dutch, the inhabitants of the German Empire together with those of some of the Austrian provinces, the Norwegians, the Swedes, the Danes, etc.); and the Slavs (including the Poles, the Chekhs of Bohemia, to a large extent the Russians, and the inhabitants of Servia and of others of the kingdoms which now divide the north of the Balkan peninsula, etc.). The inhabitants of France, Spain, and Portugal, are of mixed blood. The Teutonic strain probably prevails, but the Kelts who forestalled them in occupancy of these countries, and the Romans from Italy, the conquerers of the Kelts, make important contributions to their racial origin. The last of course have left a dominating mark in their languages.

Side by side with the Aryan, one hears of another well-made-out group, viz. the Semitic. But the races which form this family live for the most part in the south-west portions of Asia, and in Egypt, the only important representatives in Europe being the Jews scattered through every land.

Philologists and anthropologists alike when going outside these two well-formulated and well-studied family groups, are prone to throw everything else into a great miscellaneous class which they label Turanian (*i.e.*, having to do with darkness). One great group of these Turanians may however be distinguished as having a common origin from one particular stretch of the Asiatic continent; some traces of kinship too may possibly be distinguished between them, and they appear to be destined to play a more important part in the history, or at any rate in the progress, of the world than for example the fossilised Chinese.

The group referred to is the Uro-Altaic, and it had its cradle on the plains of Asia, which stretch between the Ural and the Altái mountains. In this group we distinguish three great families; the Finnish, the Tatár, and the Mongolian. The Finns were destined for the most part to become Christians, the Tatárs, Mohammedans, and the Mongols, Buddhists.[1]

First as regards the Finns. This race is divided into innumerable peoples, showing great divergence of type, of advancement, and of capacity for civilisation. Perhaps its most distinguished example is the Magyar people of Hungary, with their brilliant historical record and high type of physical comeliness. But the Finns of Finland, "the Finnish Finns," are another branch which show great intelligence and capacity. There are many Swedes scattered amongst them, and these Scandinavians seem to take the lead in matters of organisation and government; it is they who occupy most of the important positions in the large towns. Nevertheless the inhabitants of purely Finnish blood show a capacity and an inclination to follow an excellent lead, and the rank and file of the Finnish peasantry certainly contrast favourably with the bulk of the people in Russia proper, and take a place beside other nations of Northern Europe (which like themselves have embraced Protestantism) of which they have no reason to be ashamed. Of the Finns still distinguished as such

---

[1] It is interesting to note that some authorities now consider the Japanese also to have sprung from this Uro-Altaic group of peoples.

which remain in Russia proper the most numerous are to be found in the basins of the Kama and the Viatka, by the upper waters of the Dvina and Petchora, and on the banks of the Volga to the south of Kazán. They are of a very much lower type than either the Hungarians or the Finns of Finland; they more resemble those of Lapland. It has already been remarked that they are gradually being absorbed in the surrounding Russian population, and there is reason to think that this process has gone on so extensively in the past that the real admixture of Finnish blood in the assimilated Russian race is one of its principal constituents. But seeing what a good account peoples of purely Finnish race can give of themselves under favourable conditions we need not necessarily see in this fact any serious grounds for discouragement as to the prospects of Russian civilisation and progress.

Moreover the Finns, whenever they have been placed in near relations with races more advanced than themselves, have always shown a singular aptitude for assimilating themselves to them.

Now let us consider to what extent the Tatárs partake in the composition of the Russian race. Historically they have played so conspicuous a part that we may be inclined to expect to find that they are a more important ingredient in the ethnological formation of the Russians, than is actually the case. The Tatárs occupied the southernmost regions of the Uro-Altaic plains, whilst the Finns came from the more northerly parts. In fact the point of departure from which the Tatárs were to overrun Turkey in Asia and a large part of eastern Europe was so far south as Turkestan.

From thence the Ottoman Turks came and subjugated the Balkan peninsula; from thence too the Tatárs, who might aptly be called the Russian Turks, so closely akin are they to those who more generally bear the name,[1] overran Russia and subjugated its inhabitants. The middle of the 13th century saw their invading hosts devastating with fire and sword as far north as Novgorod, and far further west than the present western boundary of Russia. When in the latter part of the century the subjection of the Russian principalities seemed complete, they entered upon occupancy of the great steppe regions. Their principal settlements were at first on the east bank of the Volga, south of Samára, but in the course of the following two centuries the territory occupied by them increased till it covered most of the south of Russia. Warlike expeditions against the Russian towns (built in large clearances amongst the forests to the north and west) became infrequent except when the Tatár suzerainty was called in question, or the tribute exacted by them was withheld.

But a little consideration will show us that from this historical record we need not expect so much admixture of blood from the Tatárs in the south as undoubtedly took place from the Finns in the north. In the first place, the Tatárs were not governing the Russians of the steppes; the two peoples were in fact living in separate regions. At this time it might almost be said that there were no Russians of the steppes; the prairie regions were abandoned to the Tatár hordes. In this way there was less opportunity for admixture of blood than there was for instance between the Ottoman Turks and the Slavs of the Balkan peninsula. Religion too was another barrier. The Ottomans were Mussulmans before they invaded Europe, and the Tatárs became so soon after they invaded the Russian steppes. Mussul-

---

[1] Indeed the Tatárs of Kazán and Astrachan do actually call themselves Turks.

mans hardly ever apostatize, and but few of the Christian Russians were converted to Mohammedanism. Finally in the sixteenth century the domination of the Tatárs over the Russians was reversed, and ever since that time, even up to the years which have passed since the Crimean war, there has been a constant stream of emigration of the Mussulman Tatárs out of, and away from Russia to neighbouring countries where their race and religion are still dominant. On the whole then we may conclude that the ethnological influence of the Tatárs on the Russian people in the south has not been nearly so important as that of the Finns in the north.

Still less are the Mongols to be taken into account except so far as the Russian Tatárs themselves are considered to be partly of Mongol origin. At a remote period there was probably a certain amount of *rapprochement* between the Tatárs and the Mongols; how much the Tatár blood suffered admixture is a point of controversy amongst the authorities, some saying that it was of but little importance, others on the contrary maintaining that the Tatárs should properly be regarded as being more Mongol than anything else; that there was important admixture seems to be shown by the Tatár physiognomy; the ascending eye-corner for example and the ogee curves of the eyelids are quite unlike the almond-shaped eye of the Ottoman Turk. The Tatárs however became distinct from the Mongols proper, and at a later period showed more inclination in some instances to enter into close relations with the Finns. Of the latter tendency we find examples in some of the tribes of mixed Finn and Tatár race that inhabit the banks of the Volga, which though perhaps mainly of Finnish blood have come so much under the influence of the Tatárs that they have adopted their religion and language, and are even commonly taken for, and talked about, as Tatár tribes.

In south Russia, on the other hand, there is an example of a tribe of mixed Tatár and Mongol blood. With this exception the Mongols hardly appear in European Russia except in the case of the people known as the Kalmuks. A great host of these migrated in the 17th century from the north-western frontiers of China to establish themselves in the desert region of the Uro-Caspian depression where they led a nomad life till the year 1770. In the winter of that year the large majority of them, 200,000 to 300,000 in number, being discontented with the way they were treated, returned to whence they had come, making a gigantic march across Asia with fearful loss. This is the incident of which De Quincey has written such a picturesque account.[1] Some remained behind in consequence of their being prevented from crossing the rivers by the break-up of the frost. Their descendants are the Kalmuk tribes who are found on the lower Volga to-day.

Of the three races which have commingled their blood to form the Russian nation, the Finn, the Tatár, and the Slav, the last is certainly much the most important. Of the exact amount of ancestry that each can claim to have contributed it is difficult to make even an approximate estimate, but one knows that amongst the Little Russians, and the White Russians, the Slav element is largely predominant; and that amongst the Great Russians also its importance is probably greater than that of the other elements. How-

---

[1] De Quincey, who probably hardly distinguished between Mongols and Tatárs, called his account of this matter "The Revolt of the Tatárs."

ever this may be it has everywhere been the dominating influence; that which has imposed on the other constituent parts its language, its religion, and its national feeling and sentiment, so that the Russians delight to alk about themselves, and to think about themselves as a Slav nation.

Who then were the Slavs? and how have they come to dominate the Russian nation as they have done? The Slavs have as ancient and as indisputable a title to be recognised as a branch of the great Aryan family as have for example the Teutons or the Kelts. Their settlement in Europe too was at about the same period as that of those races. In very early times they occupied the valleys of the Dnieper and the Vistula. From this fatherland they spread through the forest zone of northern Russia which they found sparsely occupied by Finns. They made their way up the great rivers, gradually driving the Finnish aborigines before them, or cutting them into isolated communities. These Finns with the faculty of adoption of customs and language and religion not their own, characteristic of their races, gradually allowed themselves to be assimilated to the circumambient invaders of their country. From the same cradle there emerged other Slavonic tribes which peopled Poland, Bohemia, south-west Russia, and Gallicia. The Slavonic races soon divided into two main families. The western group, including the Poles and the Bohemians, joined the Roman communion. The eastern group, including those which are now embraced in the Russian Empire, the north Balkan principalities, and the north-eastern states of the Austrian Empire, acknowledged the Eastern Patriarch as the head of their church.

Amongst the Russian Slavs we distinguish the Great Russians occupying the centre of the empire with

Moscow as their venerated city. Their blood is un doubtedly largely mixed with that of the Finns who occupied the country before them. The Great Russians constitute more than half of the population of the whole empire. The admixture of blood seems to have given them a toughness of fibre which renders the race able to encounter immense physical difficulties.

What Moscow is to the Great Russians the holy city of Kiëv is to the Little Russians. The Little Russians call themselves Ukrainians. Ukrain means "borderland," and whilst it is used as being synonymous with Little Russia by the inhabitants of that country, by those who are not Little Russians, it is sometimes given a more general signification, for example to designate the states of the Russian western frontier. Kiev is about the middle of the Little Russian population which occupies the south-west provinces of Russia. The Little Russians are more purely Slav than are the Great Russians. What admixture of blood they have suffered has been rather with the Tatárs than with the Finns. They preserve better than their Muscovite brothers many of the qualities that we consider characteristic of the Slavs, such as their slighter frames, their dreamy poetical temperaments, and their instinctive desire for individuality and for freedom. They are a more refined race, but on the other hand it may be doubted whether they have as much enterprise or power of endurance. They really form one race with the subjects of Austria who inhabit Gallicia (the ancient Red Russia), Bukovine, and parts of Northern Hungary. They speak a dialect so distinct from that of the Great Russians that it may be considered a different language, and in it they have recorded quite a rich literature which was first printed as a distinct literary language during the present century. From the time of

Nicholas I., censorship questions have made it doubtful how far its development would be allowed, and by a tyrannous stroke, aimed presumably at the greater unification of the empire, the whole of this literature except its novels was finally suppressed by the Government in 1876; and this people, or by far the greater portion of them, were forbidden books and periodicals printed in the language which was especially their own, and understood more perfectly by them than Great Russian which they may have been taught to read in the schools. Thus an enormous hindrance was placed in their path, and the publications that could be smuggled in from Lemberg across the Austrian border, though eagerly welcomed, have been able to do but little to alleviate the situation. During the last reign the regulations were but slightly modified. The Little Russians who are subjects of the Tsar number about eighteen millions.

Of the Cossacks, the military colonists who are scattered over the Russian steppes, and supply the Russian army with its irregular cavalry, those in the Kuban (between the Sea of Azov and the Caucasus) are Little Russians; but the large majority, including those of the Urál and the northern part of the Don, are Great Russians. It is therefore of course a complete mistake to think of the Cossacks as being in any way a distinct racial constituent. They form however a separate element in the Russian populations, and it will be interesting to quote Mr Eugene Schuyler's account of their origin. He says:—

> "It is in the 16th century that we must fix the rise of the Cossacks as a class. In the middle of that century they made their appearance on the outskirts of Russia in most opposite localities:

on the confines of Poland, on the Don and the southern border, and in the extreme east. They were at first nothing but the vagabonds and men not bound to the soil by the fixed ties of serf labour, such as were to be found in every village. . . . They made their way to the confines of the empire to get rid of compulsory work for the lords of the soil, and to be free in the widest sense of the term. The word Cossack, or Kazak, is of Tartar origin, meaning, first, a free, homeless vagabond, and then one of the partisans and guerilla warriors formed out of such vagabonds. This signification of the name was never quite lost, and even when the Cossacks were pre-eminently the military colonies and brotherhoods on the frontiers, their name was in popular parlance given to robber bands. The Cossacks were a characteristic manifestation of the time,—a national protest against the governmental forms which did not satisfy the Russian ideal. The ideal of the Cossacks was full personal freedom, unconditional possession of the soil, an elective government, popular justice administered by themselves, complete equality between the members of the society, contempt of all privileges of rank or birth, and mutual defence against external enemies. The neighbourhood of the Tartars and of the other hostile tribes compelled the Cossacks to preserve a military organisation. The fact that their enemies were non-Christian only increased their own love of religion and orthodoxy. That they themselves were discontented with the form of government in Russia made them always more or less hostile and suspicious of the central administration, even where they admitted its authority" ("Peter the Great," chap. xiv. pp. 117-118).

The provinces of Vitebsk, Mohilev, Grodno, and Minsk, constitute what is called White Russia. The people here are of very pure Slav blood, but rather curiously their language assimilates more closely to that of the Great than to that of the Little Russians. Their political sympathies however, are more with the Little than with the Great Russians. But the political experiences which they have undergone, first under the yoke of the Lithuanians, and afterwards as being the continued stake for which the Poles and the Muscovites on either side struggled, seems to have crushed all spirit out of them. Of the three Russian Slav races they are the most backward and the poorest. They number about four millions.

To the north of the White Russians lie the Lithuanians and the Letts. These are not properly to be considered Slavs at all. They rather constitute an independent branch of the great Aryan family, though one doubtless more akin to the Slavonic than to the more western branches of Aryans. The Lithuanian language approaches more nearly to Sanskrit than do any other of the Aryan languages. The provinces of Vilna and Kovno constitute the Russian part of the country of the Lithuanians. To the north of them, in Courland and in South Livonia, are the Letts, in whose descent Lithuanian is perhaps crossed with Finnish blood.

Homogeneous as has now become the middle portion of the Russian population, it is engirdled, or at all events partially engirdled, by races that have not been in any way assimilated. In Siberia on the east races of Turanian origin are encountered. On Russia's western frontiers, besides the Finns of Finland, the same race inhabit Esthonia, and the northern part of Livonia. To the south of them we find first the Letts and then the Lithuanians. And east of Lithuania are the annexed provinces of Poland. None of these provinces can be said as yet to have undergone the process of Russification. Whilst considering the western frontiers there are two other racial elements that must be taken into account.

The Jews are found in great numbers throughout what is known as the "Pale of Settlement." This includes Poland, Lithuania, White Russia, and the most important and populous part of Little Russia. Then there is the Teutonic element. This is so important in the three Baltic provinces of Esthonia, Livonia, and Courland, that they have sometimes been called the German provinces. This is a misnomer, for the Germans constitute but a tenth of the population. They have however been accustomed to dominate everything. The 160,000 Germans form in fact the landed aristocracy and the bourgeois classes; they have been the governing part of the community, and have imposed their ideas of civilisation, culture, government, and even of religion on the Finns and Letts amongst whom they live. German has even been the official language. In Poland the Germans are also strong, but Roman Catholicism is there the prevalent religion. In South Russia the Germans though not numerically strong have their importance. Some of their colonies have had a very marked influence on the inception and the spread of reformed religious sects, especially those known as the Stundists.[1] In White Russia and the adjacent parts of Little Russia there has also been a considerable infusion

---

[1] See chapter vi.

both of Germans and Poles, in fact in White Russia the Poles take pretty much the same position that the Germans do in the Baltic Provinces.

There are considerable obstacles in the way of the Russification of the western chain of non-Russian peoples. Firstly there intervenes between Great Russia and them Little Russia and White Russia, which are themselves from the point of view of the Great Russian, not completely and unmixedly Russian. They are therefore less calculated to bring about the Russification of the border states than Great Russia itself would be if it were in direct geographical contact. This aspect of the matter is further emphasised by the fact that the southern part of White Russia is very sparsely populated. The marshes formed by the river Pripet till the work of reclamation (at which something has been done) is complete, will not support anything but the scantiest population. The Poles and the Lithuanians are thus still further cut off from Russifying influences. Finally the great wave of emigration in Russia is not from east to west, but from west to east. The Great Russians are always pouring eastwards to Siberia, or southwards to the Caucasus where they can obtain land; they do not press so much on the already occupied territory to the west so that these do not experience the Russianising influence that the immigrants bring with them. The Russian Government has recently shown itself most anxious to overcome these natural difficulties by artificial means, by attacks on the Lutheran religion in the Baltic Provinces, and on the Roman Catholic religion in Poland; by suppressing German as the official language in the former, and Polish in the latter, and by attacking what political rights of local self-government the Germans had created in the provinces under their influence. But Russia will hardly gain the hearts of her non-Russian subjects by persecuting their religions, outlawing their languages, and depriving them of the scanty political privileges enjoyed by some localities.

The following may be read in amplification of the contents of this chapter:—

> Anatole Leroy-Beaulieu:—"The Empire of the Tsars and the Russians"—Vol. I. Books I and II. (This book is referred to in future pages as Leroy-Beaulieu.)

# CHAPTER II.

## HISTORICAL SKETCH UP TO THE DEATH OF PETER THE GREAT.

## CHAPTER II.—*Contents.*

NINTH century : incursion into Russia of Rurik and his Scandinavian companions — From middle of eleventh to middle of thirteenth century—Russia divided into independent yet related states, betwixt whom petty wars are waged—Thirteenth century : establishment of Tatár domination — Fourteenth century : amongst the Slav states the Prince of Moscow obtains position of predominant importance — Fifteenth and sixteenth centuries : establishment of Muscovite supremacy : waning of the Tatár's power.

The "Golden Horde," after the defeat of the Tatárs on the Oka, breaks up into three Khanates, two of which are conquered temp. Ivan IV. ("The Terrible") [reigned 1533-84]—1598-1605 : reign of Borís Godunóv—1605-13 period of turmoil and confusion—1613 : Michael Románov elected Tsar.

1689 : Peter the Great's effective reign begins and lasts till 1725 —His visit to the Netherlands and England—Social and political reforms—Aim of Russia to become a great maritime power ; consequent collision with Sweden, 1700-9—Battles of Narva (1700) and Dorpt (1702) : the founding of St Petersburg (1703)—Charles XII. invades Russia (1708) ; battle of Poltáva (1709).

Peter invades Moldavia and is defeated by the Turks on the Pruth (1711), but utter disaster averted—Further war with Sweden: naval victory (1714)—Peace of Neustadt (1721), securing Russia's position on the Baltic—Expedition against Persia (1722).

Story of Alexis : his death (1718)—Estimate of Peter's work.

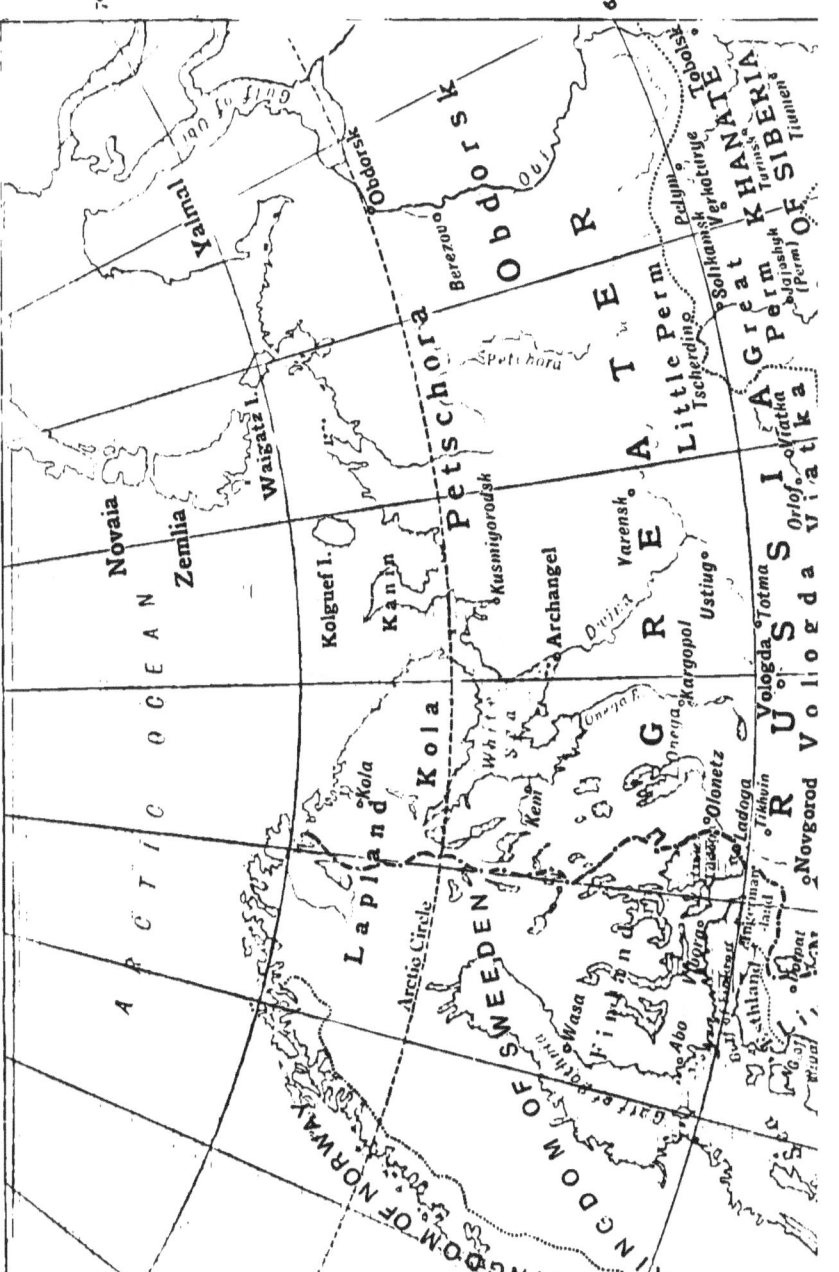

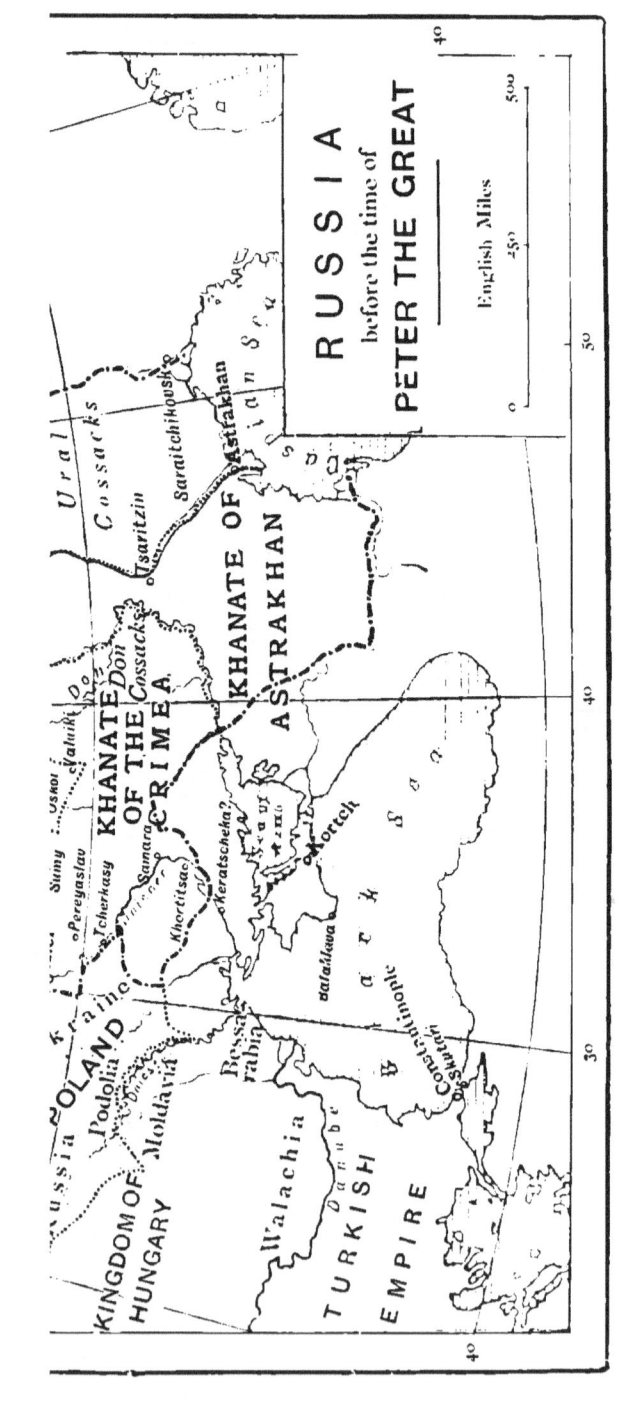

## CHAPTER II.

### HISTORICAL SKETCH UP TO THE DEATH OF PETER THE GREAT.

HAVING examined the foundations as it were of the Russian people, I now propose to summarise in the briefest possible way their history.

The earliest legendary incidents relate to a period rather more than a thousand years ago. A.D. 862, a few years before the time of our King Alfred, is the date given of the year in which Rurik with his brother Scandinavian adventurers invaded Russia and settled at Novgorod. (The Novgorod here referred to, is of course Novgorod the Great, the ancient city situated a little off the route from St Petersburg to Moscow, not Nizhni [*i.e.* Lower] Novgorod.)

The Scandinavian family which made this incursion into Russia soon found itself at the head of a number of states, the subjects of which were Slavonic, with a substratum of Finnish blood; this last element however being almost absent towards Kiev and in the south-west, but getting more and more marked the further one went to the north-east. The blood of the ruling family quickly became mingled with that of the subject peoples, and the language adopted by rulers and ruled alike was Slavonic.

When Rurik and his companions came to Russia

they found established there many important Slavonic city-states, notable amongst them Novgorod, Smolensk, and Kiev. Not a great deal is known of the rise of these cities, but Kiev is said to have been founded as early as 430. The growing territory which the Prince and his descendants acquired, stretched far enough south to include it within its bounds, and the southern city figures even more prominently than Novgorod in the subsequent annals.

Of Rurik's immediate descendants Vladimir is remarkable for having introduced Christianity. He went to Constantinople to be baptized in 988, and on his return caused his people to undergo the same rite. He and his son Yaroslav too are to be remembered as the first legislators, Yaroslav promulgating the first code of laws.

The princes of the House of Rurik became a ruling class. Each was supposed to have a domain to govern as prince, but the hegemony lay with the "Great Prince" to whom all the others were subordinate. The Great Princeship was to go to the senior in age amongst the princes, and the other princedoms in like manner were transferred as death made vacancies, according to their reputed desirability on the one hand, and to the standing of the princes in seniority on the other. It is easy to see how numerous the causes of quarrel might be under such a method of government. The princes of the ruling house multiplied rapidly, and it was difficult to carve out new domains for all of them; a father knowing that if he died he would (if the custom were observed) be succeeded by a brother or cousin, might very probably view the prospects of his own children with dissatisfaction; he would often try to establish them during his own life as heads (though subordinate to himself) of parts of the domain he governed. On his death a struggle would very naturally arise between the princes who had thus acquired an established position and the collateral heir. After a time attempts were made to limit the fierceness of the competition amongst the princes, and it was ordained that no one should succeed to a princedom of greater dignity than had been enjoyed by the one governed by his father.

During this appanage period Russia is thus divided into very numerous states bearing these curious relations to each other, and the middle of the 11th to the middle of the 13th century is taken up by petty wars. Amongst the Slav cities, Smolensk, Chernigov, and Kiev became three of the most important of the principalities; at the beginning of the 13th century however the last was subjugated by Suzdal. The republics of Novgorod, of Pskov, and of Viatka the daughter city of the latter, were also important.

> "The absolute power of the princes was, in some measure, controlled by the popular assemblies which existed in most of the larger towns. Pskov and Novgorod had already been greatly developed, and Russia seemed to have entered early that path of progress which would in time have rendered her a free and constitutional country. Trade, especially with the west of Europe, through Novgorod and the Hanse towns, had received a great impetus, and the court of Kiev displayed a high civilisation."[1]

But at the end of the first quarter of the 13th

---

[1] Introduction to Schuyler's "Peter the Great."

century the Tatár hordes began to sweep into southern Russia, and by the end of the century they had established the domination which was to last two hundred years. They established themselves on the southern steppes and by ferocious expeditions against the cities of the west and those in the forest region of the north-west, everywhere established a suzerainty. With the exception of Novgorod, hardly one of the chief cities escaped pillage and burning, with slaughter of many of its inhabitants. Finally each princedom and each republic acknowledged the supremacy of the Tatárs and sent tribute to them on their distant plains.

Meanwhile the hegemony amongst the little Slav states dwelt first with one and then with another of the cities. For some time it seemed to waver between Novgorod and Kiev; then Vladimir overshadowed them both; and finally Moscow began to come to the front, and in the middle of the 14th century the Prince of Moscow attains a position of predominant importance.

"The effect of the Mongol supremacy was not felt in mixture of race and very little in corruption of language, but chiefly in the arrest of all political and commercial development, and in the introduction amongst the Grand Dukes of new maxims and methods of government..... The greatest positive effects produced by the Tartar supremacy were the separation of Russia from Europe and its withdrawal from western influences, the gradual union of the whole country under the Grand Dukes of Moscow and the establishment of autocracy, which was indeed necessary to this union and to the expulsion of the Tartars. One state after another was swallowed up by the Grand Duchy of Moscow, and even the free cities of Novgorod and Pskov were mulcted of their privileges and received the tyrant. After the autocracy had justified its existence by unifying the country and freeing it from the Mongol yoke, it reached its highest development under Ivan the Terrible."[1]

The real establishment of the Muscovite ascendancy, and the growth of its territory took place during three reigns contemporary with those in England of Edward IV., Edward V., Richard III., Henry VII., Henry VIII., Edward VI., Mary, and more than half the reign of Elizabeth.

Ivan III. reigned 1462-1505.

Basil reigned 1505-1533.

Ivan IV. "the Terrible" or "the Cruel" reigned 1533-1584.

When Ivan III. came to the throne he had on his west the great Lithuanian principality joined in a sort of confederation with Poland;[2] to the east and south was the great Tatár khanate; and nearer at hand were the Slavonic republics and princedoms, amongst the former of which were Novgorod, Pskov, and Viatka. The chief conquests and acquisitions during his reign were Permia (1472), Novgorod, a city which formed one of the great Hanseatic League and now a place of very great size and importance (1478), Tver, and Yaroslav (in 1482), and Viatka—a Slavonic republic which had been colonised from Pskov—(in 1489).

In the reign of Basil there were the further annexations of Pskov—like Novgorod a Slavonic republic and

---

[1] Introduction to Schuyler's "Peter the Great.'

[2] In 1386 a Lithuanian prince had married a Polish princess.

like it one of the Hansa cities—(1510), Riazan, and Smolensk.

In the reign of Ivan IV. too the conquest of Siberia was begun by the Cossacks and the territory which they thus brought under Russian influence was annexed. The acquisition of this first part of Siberia was actually accomplished by a powerful merchant named Strogonov. His position in regard to the Muscovite government may be compared to that of one of the chartered companies in Africa in the present day, to the home Government of Britain. To accomplish his purpose, he engaged in his private army a band of Cossacks as mercenaries at the head of whom was Yermák of the Don.

The waning of the Tatár power is a very important feature of this period. In 1478 Ahmed, the khan of what was still the great united horde, sent to Ivan III. demanding homage. It was refused and two years later the khan invaded his territory but was defeated in a great battle on the Oka. The great "Golden Horde" was then broken up into three khanates, or Tatár princedoms, viz. :—the khanate of Kazán, the khanate of Astrakhan, and the khanate of the Crimea. During Ivan the Cruel's reign the khanates of Kazan and Astrakhan were conquered (respectively in 1552 and 1554). The third khanate, that of the Crimea however, remained very powerful and was destined once more to scourge the Muscovites.

Ivan III. issued a code of laws in 1497 which was re-affirmed by Ivan IV. in 1550. Some progress in civilisation and the arts was also made during the reigns under consideration. The building of the Kremlin at Moscow was begun under Ivan III. The Kremlin takes the place in the chief Russian cities that the Acropolis did in those of ancient Greece; but as Russia is a flat land the Kremlin could not be stationed as the Acropolis used to be, crowning a hill and overlooking the city.

Ivan IV. succeeded his father Basil whilst he was yet only in his third year. For five years he was under the tutelage of his mother and after her death for five years more under that of the great territorial nobles (the boyárs as they were called). He then attempted to throw off their tutelage and pursue an independent course of action, but a boy in his thirteenth year however ambitious was too young effectually to do this. Four years later however he was actually crowned, and he then married Anastasia Romanova, a Russian. She exercised much influence over him till'her death in 1560. This part of his reign was markedly superior to what followed. From the time of her death it is signalised by horrible cruelties and barbarities. It is indeed probable that he became partially mad. His domestic arrangements resemble those of our own Henry VIII., for he had no fewer than seven successive wives. He was very superstitious and spent much of his time in churches. Although his reign saw the continuance of the growth of empire which had taken place under his father and grandfather, he was said to be destitute of personal courage, and when the Crimean Tatárs invaded his territory in 1571 the story obtained that he purposely shunned a battle with them. On this occasion Moscow was burned. In one of the ungovernable fits of rage to which he was subject he killed his eldest son John (surnamed the young). At his death there remained only one other son by his wife Anastasia, viz., Feodor, then 27 years old, and the infant son of his seventh wife, who was called Dmitri, or Demetrius.

Feodor who succeeded reigned from 1584 to 1598.

He was a sickly, superstitious, imbecile prince who fell completely under the influence of his father-in-law a boyár of Tatár descent called Borís Godunóv. Borís was the real ruler of the country and he was anxious to succeed Feodor as Tsar. The young prince Dmitri died unaccountably in 1591 and Borís was supposed to have played the same part towards him that Richard III. did in relation to the princes in the tower; he was accredited with the murder. Later he suffered the penalty; for the false Demetrius, the Perkin Warbeck of Russian history, made his appearance on the scene before Borís had quitted the arena of his ambitions; (unlike the personator of Richard Duke of York, who did not trouble his "uncle").

In 1591 the Khan of the Crimea made another raid against the Muscovites, but was repulsed by Borís. Seven years later Feodor died and Borís was elected to succeed him. He reigned from 1598 to 1605. In 1601 the false Demetrius made his appearance in Lithuania. Sigismund III. King of Poland acknowledged him as Tsar. The pretender invaded the territory of Borís but was driven out again. Whilst his army and that of Borís's general were still confronting each other on the frontier, news arrived of the sudden death of the Tsar.

The years from 1605 to 1613 were a very confused time. The son of Borís, Feodor a youth of 16 was proclaimed Tsar at Moscow on his father's death. Borís's general Basmánov had been keeping the false Demetrius at bay but he now went over to the pretender. The united army marched on Moscow where Demetrius was proclaimed Tsar and Feodor was murdered in a popular tumult. The popularity of the new Tsar was however short-lived. He was altogether in the power of the Poles and did not fail to favour them; he even married a princess of that race. The Russians found their dearest prejudices both of race and religion outraged, and in 1606 both the new Tsar and Basmánov were murdered by the populace. During the next four years the tsarship was held by one Basil Shúishki a conspirator of the last reign who was elected to the supreme position by an assembly of the boyárs. He was harassed by the arising of a second false Demetrius who received the countenance of the widow of the first false Demetrius who fled to him. Basil suffered defeats both at the hands of this second pretender and of the Poles by whom he was finally taken prisoner in 1609. The King of Poland, Ladislaus, then caused himself to be made Tsar, but the patriotism of the Russians would not long tolerate a sovereign of alien race and of the Latin faith. The Poles were driven from the country and the boyárs were once more called together to elect a new Tsar.

Their choice fell upon the representative of a noble family who had already given to Ivan the Terrible his first wife Anastasia. The first of the Románovs (unless indeed we count as a Románov Feodor, the imbecile son of Ivan the Terrible), now (1613) ascended the throne in the person of Michael, a youth of 16.

> "The whole reign of Michael was a struggle to rid the country of the Poles and the Swedes, who were attacking it from without, and to put down the bands of robbers and marauders who were making disturbance within; for the troublous time had left a great legacy of difficulty to the new ruler." [1]

Michael reigned for thirty-two years, and was suc-

---

[1] Schuyler's "Peter the Great" (Introduction).

ceeded in 1645 by his son Alexis, in some respects the forerunner of his famous son Peter the Great, though more by virtue of possessing a yielding nature not indisposed to adopt new ideas, than as the wielder of an iron will determined to impose them. In his reign the military republics of the Cossacks of the Dnieper transferred their allegiance from Poland to Russia. Under Alexis too the Russians regained possession of Chernigov, Smolensk, and Kiev on the west.

A noted personage of the time is Nikon the Patriarch who, from the best authorities, revised the Bible and the church service books, into which many blunders had crept from the mistakes of copyists. The revision is an important fact to remember because of the great schism in the orthodox church to which it led.[1] Alexis died in 1676, and was succeeded by his son Feodor (1676-1682), whose reign was uneventful.

On the death of Feodor there were left of Alexis's children Feodor's brother Ivan, a prince of even less power than himself, his elder sister Sophia, a woman of great energy and ability, and his half-brother Peter, then ten years old. Some serious disturbances occurred before the order of succession was settled, a revolt taking place amongst the Streltsi, a body of household troops (1682). Finally Ivan and Peter were declared joint sovereigns, with Sophia as regent during their minority. Through her Basil Golitsin who had been minister during the preceding reign, became the person of most influence in the state. In 1687 he conducted an unsuccessful campaign against the Tatárs of the Crimea, and in 1689 a second expedition was not much more fortunate. After the latter event, when the period of power of Sophia and Golitsin had lasted seven years,

---

[1] See account of the "Old Believers," chap. vi.

a great deal of confusion occurred in the state, the boyárs and their followers on the one side, and the Streltsi on the other being greatly excited. It was then that Peter and his party struck the blow which decided the struggle for mastery between him and his half-sister Sophia. Peter with the aid of Gordon a Scotchman in command of part of the Russian army, after having accomplished the defection from Sophia of the Streltsi, gained the complete mastery. Sophia was shut up in a convent, Golitsin was banished, and Ivan who was practically an imbecile, made no difficulty about retiring from the field; (he died in 1696).

This is therefore the real beginning of the reign which may be regarded as the central point of Russian history, where mediævalism and Western Europeanism are subjected to an enforced introduction. Peter was but seventeen years old, and he had only just married. His reign was to last from this year 1689 to 1725, that is to say it covered the years during which William III., Anne, and George I. reigned in England, with the exception of the last two years of the reign of the last-named monarch.

Something like what the last quarter of a century has witnessed in Japan, was seen in Russia during the reign of Peter. Japan, from a condition of Chinese-like exclusiveness, has become the greedy imbiber of all the results of European and American civilisation and progress in manufactures and commerce, and in military, naval, and mercantile marine affairs. Those who have followed what has taken place in Japan since the revolution there of 1868 will the better be able to realise the extraordinary change that was wrought in Russia during the reign of Peter. At the present day in Japan there is a party, or at any rate there was such a party before the outbreak of the late war with China that regretted the old state of things now overthrown, and they would willingly have restored it. But in Russia it was not a comparatively small and impotent section of the people who opposed the reforms. Peter practically had to cut a path for western civilisation through the thick-set ranks of his opposing subjects. The mighty struggle was not decisively ended in his day. Even at the present time the force in Russian politics known as the Slavophil party represents the conservative retrospection of those who long for the Slavs that they shall have if not their own civilisation and their own culture, at all events their own manners and their own ways, which shall be distinct from, and uninfluenced by those of the Germans, the French, and the other nations of western Europe.

Peter's celebrated visit to the Netherlands and afterwards to England took place in 1697-1698, and was spent in a very practical way, principally in the dockyards of those countries, where he mixed freely with all conditions of men, especially those from whom he could learn anything concerning naval construction or navigation. He avoided as far as he was able all public functions and encounters with inquisitive crowds, having an intense dislike to being stared at.

Before this sojourn in foreign lands one or two public events of importance had occurred.

In 1695 and 1696 expeditions had been undertaken against the town of Azov, then in possession of the Turks. In the latter year it was taken. Peter himself and his general Gordon were present at both the sieges. It had been offered to a previous Tsar by the Don Cossacks who had taken it from the Crimean Tartars, but the Russians had not at that time felt themselves strong enough to occupy so distant a post.

But during the five or six years that intervened

between his accession to power and his visits to foreign lands, saving the initiation of his policy of naval construction by the building of warships on the Don, there are no other events which need detain us, as I shall content myself for the most part, with noticing the occurrences which bore directly on the main purposes of his policy.

From England he proceeded to Vienna where he heard news of another revolt of the Streltsi which was however subdued by Gordon. Nevertheless this caused Peter to return to Moscow. (Gordon died in the following year.)

On his return to Russia, Peter took up with vigour the threads of the reforms he had already initiated. Shipbuilding went on energetically on the Don; the calendar was reformed; amongst the higher classes social usages were entirely recast, European dress being introduced, and the oriental seclusion of women hitherto practised among them, broken through.

On the death of the Patriarch Adrian in 1700, the sacerdotal system was revolutionised. Peter postponed the election of a new Patriarch and entrusted the business of that office to the Metropolitan of Riazan, Stephen Navórski, as *locum tenens* of the patriarchal seat, and thus in fact the Tsar silently became political head of the orthodox church in Russia. The fact was that the power of the Patriarch had gradually been growing so formidable as to become a menace to the autocracy. At the election to the tsardom of Michael, son of Philaret, that highly esteemed and powerful boyár had secured for himself the election to the patriarchate, and during the whole of the reign the imperial ukazes had been signed jointly by the two potentates, son and father; virtually indeed it may almost be said that the father reigned concurrently with the son.

During the reign of Alexis the patriarchate of Nikon took place. He was extremely ambitious and aimed at making the patriarchate a sort of eastern popedom. The Tsar although inclined to treat the church with much piety, eventually broke with him and he fell from power but the danger which threatened when he was head of the Russian Church might at any time have come to the front again, if an equally able and ambitious man had secured the position. It was because Peter so clearly saw this danger that he acted in the decisive way he did. But it was not till 1721 that he avowedly entirely abolished the patriarchate, substituting for it a collegiate body which was called the Holiest Synod.

In an equally startling manner, but not till nearly the close of the reign, the hierarchy of the nobility was turned topsy-turvey. The old nobility of birth was not done away with, but titles of nobility became mere honorary distinctions of very little value and there was set up the Tchin or nobility based on military or civil governmental service. The officials in each of these were classified into fourteen corresponding grades.

> "Service henceforth took precedence of birth, and all distinction in the empire, even social, was to be obtained by service only. No one could be granted a high grade unless he had passed through the lower ones" (Schuyler).

Men of the lowest birth were now able through ability to rise to the highest positions. Thus Menshikóv who in his boyhood was of no rank attained almost the first position in the state. Foreigners too were entrusted with the most important posts. Gordon the Scotchman, and Le Fort the Genoese, are conspicuous instances.

The commercial classes too were organised, and the merchants were divided into guilds, and later in the reign separate departments of government, which might almost be called ministries, were established and an attempt was made at codification of the law.

As if to emphasize how little he was hindered by any conventionalities that may have been supposed to have restrained his predecessors, he married (after separation from his first wife Eudoxia) a Livonian peasant woman who had been discovered amongst the ruins of a plundered town. The marriage was at first (1707) privately celebrated, but at a later period of his reign (1712) it was solemnised again as a public function, and not very long before his death he caused the public coronation of his consort to take place. This was the remarkable Catherine who took no small share of the actual cares of state and activities of Peter's reign; at his death she succeeded him.

Whilst Peter was setting up factories of all kinds in Moscow, the object dearest to his heart was undoubtedly the making of Russia into a great sea power. He aimed at having a powerful navy and a great mercantile marine which would enable Russia to take her place in the commerce of Europe. But Russia at this time practically had no seaboard. Archangel (frozen six months of the year) was the only undisputed port. Azov to the South was won and again lost. It was to the Baltic and the great gulfs of Finland and Riga that Peter now looked. These as far south as Riga were surrounded on the east as well as on the west by Swedish territory, so that there now comes the long duel with Charles XII. of Sweden for possession of these coasts.

Only a very small nucleus of Peter's army was at first disciplined on European models; he seems at the beginning to have expected defeats and to have received them complacently so long as they were not too disastrous. War was declared by Russia, on a frivolous pretext in 1700, and she at first had the advantage of alliance with Denmark and Poland, who each had their grievances against Sweden, and hoped to attain territorial advantage. This did not prevent a serious defeat of the Russians at Narva (1700). Sir John Barrow says in his "Life of Peter the Great":—

"It has always been a subject for surprise that after the victory of Narva, when Charles might have carried everything before him in Russia, he should have directed his sole attention to Poland, treating the former as if unworthy of his notice; while Peter was left at full liberty not only to recruit and discipline a new army, but also to design and carry into execution many great and important improvements; such as introducing from Saxony flocks of sheep and shepherds to attend them, for the sake of their wool; erecting linen and paper manufactories; building hospitals; inviting from abroad braziers, blacksmiths, armourers, and other artisans of every description; and in fact, cultivating, in the midst of war all the arts of peace" (chap. vi. p. 149, in edition of 1883).

At the beginning of 1702 the Russians obtained an advantage over the Swedes near Dorpt. It was on this occasion that Peter observed:—

"Well, we have at last beaten the Swedes when we were two to one against them; we shall by and by be able to face them man to man" (*Ibid.*, p. 151).

In the same year they took the Swedish fort Noteborg which was renamed Schlüsselburg, and a few months later 1703) Peter began to carry out his idea of building a sort of Russian Amsterdam on the banks of the Neva.

"The whole surrounding country was a morass, in which not a stone of any description could be found; the people employed had little or no experience; according to Captain Perry, the labourers were not furnished with the necessary tools, such as pickaxes, spades, shovels, planks, and the like. 'Notwithstanding which,' the same author observes, 'the work went on with such expedition, that it was surprising to see the fortress raised within less than five months, though the earth, which is very scarce thereabouts, was, for the greater part, carried by the labourers in the skirts of their clothes, and in bags made of rags and old mats, the use of wheelbarrows being then unknown to them.' Under such untoward circumstances, in such a country, and amidst such difficulties, it is indeed surprising that a town should have arisen, in the course of a twelvemonth, said then to contain houses and huts, of one description or another, amounting to the number of thirty thousand. Peter, however, was not a man to be diverted from his purpose by difficulties; nor was he deterred from the attempt to make up, by sheer human labour, what might be wanting in skill and implements. For this purpose he collected together many thousands of persons from all parts of the empire —Russians, Cossacks, Tartars, Calmuks, Finlanders, and Ingrians" (*Ibid.*, pp. 171-2).

Charles XII.'s comment on all this was "Let him amuse himself as he thinks fit in building a city, I shall soon find time to take it from him, and to put his wooden houses into a blaze" (*Ibid.*, pp. 177-8).

In 1704 the Russians retook Narva. The war proceeded with varying fortunes till 1708, when Charles (like a much greater general than himself a century later) determined to invade Russia, march to Moscow, and dictate from the old Russian capital the terms of peace. The Russian armies pursued a policy of hovering about his van, wasting the country before him, harassing his troops, and without entering upon fixed engagements, drawing him on further and further towards the heart of the country. Two events decided Charles's enterprise in a sense unfavourable for him. The first was the successful manœuvre of preventing a junction of the two Swedish armies respectively commanded by the king and by his general Löwenhaupt. The latter separated from the main force, was disastrously defeated.

The second was the yielding of Charles to an invitation from Mazeppa the Hetman of the Cossacks, to march southwards into the Ukraine, where Mazeppa promised that a large army of Cossacks would welcome him as their deliverer. He was indeed joined there by Mazeppa himself, but the Hetman had succeeded in carrying over with him to the Swedish camp but a handful of his followers, instead of the powerful army promised. Charles now experienced, as Napoleon was to experience after him, the power of a Russian winter as a protection against an invading army of foreigners, and it happened that the severity of the winter of 1708-9 was most extraordinary. " Birds fell dead as they flew through the air and the snow in many places remained on the ground from October 1st to April 5th."[1] The spring was occupied by unavailing marches and counter-marches and his army terribly diminished in numbers was at length in July 1709 decisively beaten at the great battle of Poltáva. The power of Sweden was overthrown; Saxony, Prussia, Poland, and

---

[1] Schuyler's "Peter the Great."

Denmark were all willing to join Russia in a league, having as its object the recovery of the Swedish conquests of Gustavus Adolphus.

After Poltáva Charles XII. fled to Turkey where he represented to the Porte the enormous danger that threatened it through the growing power of Russia. His views were enforced by the evidence of the Khan of the Crimea, who gave an alarmist picture of the progress Peter was making towards establishing Russia as a formidable maritime power on the Euxine, in consequence of his works at harbours and arsenals at Azov and Taganróg, and the navies he was constructing at those ports and on the Don. The Turks took alarm, and raised a large army to fight Peter who himself invaded the northern Moldavian provinces where he was promised assistance from some of the Sultan's tributary princes. They however failed him as Mazeppa had failed Charles in the Ukraine, and he found himself as that monarch had done, in terrible straits, in a hostile country without supplies for his army. He was at length attacked by the Turks on the Pruth, and as his army was vastly outnumbered it might have been cut to pieces had the Turks been well generalled. The result however after three days and nights of very bloody fighting was not sufficiently disastrous for the Russians, to prevent their making a treaty on fairly advantageous terms, under the provisions of which they were allowed to make an honourable retreat (1711). The negotiation is said to have been facilitated by the activity of Catherine though the legend that she got together a very large present of jewels and money fo- the Grand Vizier is contradicted.[1] In spite of the conr

---

[1] See Note in Schuyler's "Peter the Great," Vol. II. p. 247, and the account of the whole matter in chapter xliii. to which it is appended.

ditions of peace being on the whole more favourable to the Russians than they could expect, it was agreed by them that Azov and Taganróg should be evacuated, so that the hold they had established on the Azov and Black Seas was lost. But this loss was more than made up to them by the ground they almost immediately gained on the coasts of the Gulfs of Finland and Riga, so that the main object of the warfare of the reign, establishing Russia's position as a maritime power, was accomplished. The Swedish navy was defeated in a great battle on the Baltic in 1714.

The war with Sweden was not actually concluded till 1721 when the Peace of Neustadt was signed " ceding for ever to the Tsar all his conquests; thus leaving him sovereign over Livonia, Esthonia, Ingria, Carelia, Wyburg, and the adjacent islands, and securing to him the dominion of the Sea of Finland, which, with the surrounding coasts, he had purchased with the toils and perils of twenty years" (Barrow's "Peter the Great," p. 340).

"The emperor had now leisure to look over those institutions and establishments which he had set on foot since the year 1718. In that year he entirely new-modelled a general police for the empire; he commenced several projects for uniting rivers by means of canals; he prohibited games of chance which might be called gambling; he instituted orphan houses and a foundling hospital; he established a uniformity of weights and measures; and he endeavoured to settle, contrary to every principle of political economy, the prices of provisions, and a maximum to the luxury of dress; he caused the streets of Petersburg and Moscow to be paved, and cleared of swarms of beggars, and made several regulations for safety, order and cleanliness. He took off the restriction of his subjects travelling abroad" (*Ibid.*).

Peter by his treaty with the Turks had been shut out from the Black Sea, and as soon as he had secured his position on the Baltic by his treaty with Sweden he turned his thoughts to the Caspian. In 1722 he undertook an expedition against Persia, but it had not been well considered, and the army retreated after having obtained but very slight advantages for the Empire. This was his last great military exploit before his death at the beginning of 1725.

It is necessary to refer briefly to a celebrated episode of this reign, viz. :—the death of Alexis, Peter's son by his first wife Eudoxia. The character of Alexis seems to have been as weak as that of Peter was strong. He appears to have been completely destitute both of energy and will. He was too much engaged in licentious living, alternating with religious or at any rate superstitious ceremonial observances, to have any care left for public affairs from which he withdrew himself.[1] Yet he seemed to have a sluggish indisposition to renounce his expectancy of the throne. One idea of public policy alone had been adopted by him; it was hatred of his father's reforming policy, and determination to reverse and undo it whenever opportunity might offer. His friends and advisers were of the reactionary school, and he became the somewhat passive centre around which gathered the malcontent party. Peter continually remonstrated with his son, hoping better things from him. In a notable letter addressed to him after the death of his ill-used consort in 1715 Peter says :—

---

[1] Schuyler in his "Peter the Great" depicts his character far more favourably. See Vol. II. chap. lxviii.

"I am a man, and consequently must die: to whom shall I leave the care of finishing what, by God's grace, I have begun, and of preserving what I have in part recovered? To a son who, like the slothful servant in the gospel, buries his talent in the earth, and neglects to improve what God has committed to his trust? . . . You loiter on in supine indolence: abandoning yourself to shameful pleasures, without extending your foresight to the dangerous consequences which such a conduct must produce both to yourself and the whole state: . . . I am determined, at last, to signify to you my final purpose; being willing, however, to defer the execution of it for a short time, to see if you will reform; if not, know that I am resolved to deprive you of the succession, as I would lop off a useless branch. . . . Since I spare not my own life for the sake of my country, and the welfare of my people, why should I allow an effeminate prince to ascend the throne after me, who would sacrifice the interests of the subject to his pleasures? . . . I will call in a mere stranger to the crown, if he be but worthy of that honour, sooner than my own son, if he is unworthy" (The letter of Peter to his son dated in October 1715).

The quarrel between father and son became more and more acute. In fact it would be difficult to imagine a character or a want of character more calculated to arouse the angry contempt and personal irritation and antagonism of Peter than that of Alexis. There was much talk of Alexis's renouncing the crown and becoming a monk, but on both sides it was felt to be somewhat unreal; it gave no security that Alexis would not on his father's death renounce his orders and claim the zardom. And so Peter continued to harp on his son's reforming, though a much stupider man might have known that in demanding an exertion of will and of moral power from Alexis he was asking for an impossibility. Originally of an exceptionally weak nature he had become completely demoralised by his surroundings and his vicious habits. He was morally, mentally, and in great part physically a wreck.

At last Alexis fled the country, but was induced to return by a promise from his father of pardon. He found however that his pardon was conditional. He had to pay the price for it of betraying all his friends and associates. He was of too mean a character to hesitate to do this, and there followed terrible torturings and executions in the style of horrible barbarity with which Peter was accustomed to treat those whom he conceived to be his enemies. But nothing availed to save the life of Alexis; he was brought to trial before the notables and sentenced to death. It was then publicly announced that he had died in his place of imprisonment by one of those fits of apoplexy which when they have come at opportunities so timely as the one in question have generally been accepted as an official euphemism for foul play. It is known that he was racked three or four times, and it is probable that he died from the results of his torture. The whole tragic story has been told by the Russian historian Kostomarov in a chapter as vivid and enthralling as any ever written by Macaulay. It is a pity that the sketch has not been seen in an English dress.

History one thinks must always be formed by a compromise between the impressions made on the story of the world by great personalities, and the general level to which the surrounding mass of humanity has attained. Carlyle of course believed almost exclusively in the former influence; he held that history was made by the great men, by his "heroes." Other historians have held a theory very much the reverse of this; so far from regarding history as being made by great men they have regarded great men merely as the embodiments of the spirit of the ages in which they have lived and have held that the advance of history takes place according to general laws, and that its course is inevitable. The truth appears to me to lie between these two extreme views; but if we were asked to give an example of the formation of history by means of a great personality one would at first sight suppose that no more striking example could possibly be adduced than the story of Peter the Great's reign in Russia. Peter's personality was of such extraordinary power that had he been born to such comparatively obscure positions as were Oliver Cromwell and Napoleon Buonaparte, he would in all probability have made as conspicuous a position for himself in the world as did either of them. Actually he was born to that stupendous position of autocratic power over millions of his fellow-men which renders a commonplace man, if once he be in possession of the tzardom, a creature of the utmost importance. Added to all this, he possessed a physique of exceptional strength and endurance. With such a man in such a position what might not be expected? The only circumstances which seemed likely to detract from his omnipotence were that (so far as ordinary schooling was concerned) he was an uneducated man (a circumstance he never ceased to regret), and that he presumed too far on his great constitutional strength, especially when he was a young man, giving himself up to occasional wild drinking-bouts and the like.

Yet even so abnormal a man as Peter, advantageously placed as we have seen him to be, does his work within limits that are laid down for him by the time in which he lives, and the people amongst whom he lives. The changes he introduced, great as they apparently were, were limited in two ways. Firstly it was only the upper, the governing classes that were much affected by them; the great mass of the people, the peasantry remained unmoved by the civilisation of St Petersburg; and secondly the changes wrought in the upper classes had unmistakably upon them the mark of superficiality. This has been pointed out in an interesting passage by Kostomárov. He says:—

"It was these measures" (*i.e.*, the measures of Peter) "that accustomed the Russians eagerly to grasp the outward signs of civilisation, very often to the disadvantage of, and with utter disregard to, its essence. . . . Between those who adopted the outward ways of Europeans and the rest of the people there opened an abyss. And even those who did adopt the outward polish of Europeanism long retained all their innate attributes of ignorance, roughness, and laziness. . . . The reformer of Russia introduced a great many new institutions and practices into Russian life, but he was not able to give to Russia a new soul" ("Russian History in Biographies of its Great Actors").

The following may be read in amplification of the contents of this chapter :—

    Some text-book of Russian history as far as the end of Peter the Great's reign (perhaps Morfill's "Russia" in "The Story of the Nations" Series is as good as any available in English).

    Leroy-Beaulieu, Vol. I. Bk. IV. chap. iii. and chap. iv., the latter as far as p. 268 in the French edition of 1890, or as far as p. 291 in the English edition of 1893.

    Eugene Schuyler: "Peter the Great," or (shorter though hardly so authoritative) Sir John Barrow : "Life of Peter the Great."

# CHAPTER III.

## HISTORICAL SKETCH FROM THE DEATH OF PETER THE GREAT TO THE CRIMEAN WAR.

## CHAPTER III.—*Contents.*

CATHERINE I.'s reign, 1725-27 — Peter II., 1727-30 — Anne, 1730-40 — Ivan VI. (under regency of his mother), 1740-41—Elizabeth, 1741-61—Peter III., 1761-62.

Catherine II. ("the Great"), 1762-96—Partitionings of Poland : first, 1772; second, 1793 (resistance of Kosciuszko) ; third, 1795.

Wars and territorial acquisitions — Other characteristics of Catherine's reign—Paul, 1796-1801—Suvórov in Switzerland—Paul and Napoleon—Alexander I., 1801-25—The Napoleonic invasion, 1812 — Battle of Borodino — Moscow occupied and burnt—The retreat—Ascendancy of Arakcheiev—Nicholas I. 1825-55—The Decembrist Revolt —Polish insurrection, 1830—The Crimean War breaks out, 1854.

The ideals discoverable in Russian policy : (*a*) The oldest is that she shall be great, solidified, and homogeneous ; (*b*) from *temp*. Peter the Great she has also aimed at being European ; (*c*) the nineteenth century has witnessed the birth of the ideal of political freedom.

Forecast of the reign of Alexander II.; it begins by the setting on foot of wide-reaching reforms ; but they are the reforms of an autocrat, and in the second part of the reign are in great part nullified by the autocratic will.

# CHAPTER III.

### HISTORICAL SKETCH FROM THE DEATH OF PETER THE GREAT TO THE END OF THE CRIMEAN WAR.

In my last chapter I drew the attention of the reader to the reigns of three strong monarchs who by their conquests, and annexations, laid the foundations of the territorial greatness of Muscovy. These three sovereigns (Ivan III., Basil, and Ivan the Cruel), it will be remembered were contemporary with the last part of the Wars of the Roses, and the greater part of the subsequent reigns of our Tudor monarchs. The period covered by these three reigns was from 1462 to 1584.

We must now observe the connection which exists between two other reigns, and to a lesser extent to another which precedes them. These also are marked by territorial expansion; but they are marked by something more. The trend of the policy of the sovereigns in question, probably we may even say their conscious object, was to rescue Russia from her state of semi-Asiatic isolation, and to establish her in an important position in the great European family. To some extent Alexis I.—but far more markedly Peter the Great, and Catherine II.—were progressive. They may be called the great Europeanising monarchs. Unlike the great territorial consolidators of the 15th and 16th centuries, their reigns did not succeed each other without interval;

had they done so they would have covered slightly more than a century; with the intervening periods they cover slightly more than a century and a half.

Alexis, the second of the Romanov line, came to the throne in 1645; Catherine II. died in 1796; so that the period we have under consideration is from the time when Charles I. of England's troubles were gathering thickly about him to the end of the years of the French Revolution.

This period divides itself naturally into five during which the course of European progress alternately makes visible headway, or remains in a somewhat passive condition.

First we have the reign of Alexis, 1645-76. Then from 1676 to 1682 we have the colourless reign of Feodor followed (till 1689) by the reign nominally of the children Ivan and Peter, but the real rule of Sophia and Golitsin. Then 1689-1725 follows the real reign of Peter with which so much of our last chapter was occupied. And now we have to enter upon a period of thirty-seven years before the next strong progressive sovereign Catherine II. mounts the throne, a period of weakness, internal disturbances, and in some respects actual reaction from the tendencies of Peter.

It is of course inherent in the nature of despotism that those who succeed to autocratic power should some times be incompetent and weak-minded. During reigns of this character ambitious relatives of the reigning house, court favourites, and successful generals struggle for mastery over the mind of the nominal monarch. We often see some personality rising to almost unbounded ascendancy in the State. Such ascendancies not unfrequently begin and end in popular disturbances. Sometimes the personage who has seized the position of power in the State seeks himself to found a new dynasty as did Borís Godunóv in the confused years which followed the reign of Ivan the Cruel; sometimes he is content with being actually the most important power in the realm.

On Peter's death his widow Catherine was chosen Tsarina, but the chief power fell into the hands of Menshikóv. Like that of the Empress, his origin had been of the humblest character, but he was the victor of Poltava, and had grown to be Peter's principal general and prime favourite.

The Empress Catherine who had during her husband's life conducted herself discreetly, now degenerated in character, and gave herself up to a life of excess. In two years she died (1727). Peter the Great's son by his first (his divorced) wife Eudoxia, the unfortunate Alexis, had left a son. He also was called Peter, and it was this Peter II. who now succeeded. By Catherine's will he was to be under the guardianship of Menshikóv during his minority, and to be betrothed to that minister's daughter. But he fell under the personal influence of another family who became the prime court favourites,—the Dolgorúkis. By a palace revolution the power of Menshikóv was overthrown, and he and his family were exiled to Siberia, whilst Peter was betrothed to a Dolgorúki. Under the influence of his wife's family, he practically gave up his entire life to hunting, and left the guidance of the State to them, and to the reactionary and clerical party. Moscow was re-erected the capital. The reign was a short one, Peter dying of small-pox in 1730.

After considerable debate the Supreme Council invited Peter the Great's niece Anne, Duchess of Courland (daughter of his brother Ivan), to fill the throne. On the proposal of the princes Dolgorúki and of Golitsin a sort of constitution was to be imposed upon her at her accession. The constitution would have given great powers to the oligarchical Supreme Council; this body had been created in the reign of Catherine I., and not only had it superseded the power of the Senate, but it had obtained a position which that body had never possessed. The limitations proposed on the power of the throne might further in time even have secured the beginnings of constitutional rights for various grades of Russian subjects, but though Anne signed an agreement accepting the conditions when the throne was offered to her, her actual accession brought opportunities to her of renouncing it. One of the most powerful figures in the State at the time was Ostermann; another of those who had risen from a position of lowly birth to one of the highest importance. He considered that the pathway of his ambition would lie smoother under an autocracy than under the rule of the Supreme Council. With his support, and with that of a section of the nobility, of the courtiers, of the clergy, and of the army whom she had won over to her views, Anne publicly tore the articles she had previously signed in pieces, and declared herself autocrat. The Dolgorúkis were banished and afterwards barbarously executed.

The chief personages of the ten years' reign of Anne are Ostermann, her general Münich, and her favourite, whom she had brought with her from Courland, Biren, who has left behind him a very evil reputation for cruelty, tyranny, and bloodthirstiness. Anne cannot be altogether regarded as carrying out a policy opposed to that of Peter I. She completed the great canal from Lake Ladoga to St Petersburg. She concluded a commercial treaty with Great Britain, and she favoured the settlement in the country of foreign skilled workmen and artisans to perfect the manufacture of silks and woollens.

On the death of the Empress Anne, Biren enjoyed the regency for only a short time before he was ousted by Field-Marshal Münich.

The genealogical diagram is the easiest way of showing the relationships which were declared to exist between the successive occupants of the throne from the middle of the eighteenth to the middle of the nineteenth century; but the sexual relations of the various Tsars and Tsarinas render other than the reputed paternities probable in several instances. Blots on the 'scutcheon resulting in irregularities in the succession can however add very little to the humiliation imposed on humanity at large by the existence of the Russian autocracy both in the past and in the present. So long as a man or a woman has at his or her disposal the lives, liberties, happiness, and prosperity, of millions of his or her fellow-creatures, however incompetent, cruel, foolish, or profligate, he or she may be, it really does not matter whether the person existing by so terrible an exercise of toleration has some of the blood of the Románovs still flowing in his veins, or whether he must trace his descent from the *liaison* of a Wurtemburg princess and an Alsatian grenadier.[1]

The monarch was now (1741) a great-nephew of the late Empress Anne,—Ivan, whose mother Anna Leopoldovna, wife of Anthony Ulrich, Prince of Brunswick, succeeded to the regency after the banishment of Biren.

Before the year was out however a *coup d'état* placed on the throne Elizabeth, daughter of Peter

---

[1] *Vide* Harold Frederic's "New Exodus," pp. 41, 42.

the Great. The new reign was opened as usual by the abasement of those who had previously held the highest positions in the State. The Prince and Princess of Brunswick, Ostermann and Münich, were banished to distant parts of the empire. The young Ivan was confined in the fortress of Schlüsselburg.

Elizabeth reigned for a score of years; one of the principal events of the period is the waging of a successful war against Frederick the Great of Prussia. During her reign population was said to have increased by one-fifth; literature and the arts made some progress, and through the munificence of Ivan Schuvalov the first Russian University was founded at Moscow. Some intermediate schools too were set up. But the reign exhibits some terrible features; personal tyranny could hardly be carried further than this woman carried it, and she is accused of horrible acts of cruelty, though her vanity caused "Elizabeth the Clement" to be inscribed on her medals. Like so many other of the Russian sovereigns from Ivan the Cruel to Alexander III. she was devoted to that woodenly formal pietism, which rigorously observes fastings and ceremonies, but is compatible with, if it does not actually enjoin, cold-blooded and deliberate cruelty on a very extended scale. Clerical influence was supreme, and the Raskolniks, the religious dissentients who had refused to accept the improved readings of the Scriptures introduced by Nikon the Patriarch, were severely persecuted. There was established too a political court of inquisition called the "Secret Chancellerie." This tribunal was composed of a few members chosen by the sovereign, and it had the lives and fortunes of everyone at its mercy. Its evidence was gained by espionage and it proved a terrible scourge. The maintenance of public order too does not seem to have been good. The Russian

## HISTORICAL SKETCH. 67

historian Soloviev mentions an enormous amount of brigandage as a feature of the reign.

Elizabeth named as her successor her nephew Peter, a dissolute, coarse-minded youth, and married him to the Princess Sophia of Anhalt-Zerbst when neither of the couple were much more than children. According to a barbarous custom which still obtains, a princess marrying the heir to the Russian throne undergoes "conversion" to the Greek communion, and is very often rechristened by another name. We accordingly know Princess Sophia as Catherine, afterwards Catherine II, the most remarkable figure of this period.

Peter III. who now ascended the throne was the son of Elizabeth's sister Anne, and of the Duke of Holstein-Gottorp, and grandson of Peter the Great. He reigned for six months only, viz., during the first half of 1762. He rendered himself unpopular by acts which kindled the indignation of all the powerful classes of his subjects. He entertained an ardent admiration for his cousin Frederick the Great, and because of his personal veneration for him, made peace with Prussia, relinquishing the conquests that had been made from that country in the previous reigns. To complete his unpopularity with the military, and with those who followed with interest the fortunes of their country in warfare, he followed up what appeared to be the wanton abandonment of Russia's conquests by embarking on a war against Denmark, to avenge the wrongs which his father's duchy of Holstein had sustained from that country. This war was regarded unfavourably by the whole nation.

The religious susceptibilities of his subjects were spared no more than were their military aspirations. Peter paid no particular pains to prove himself a good son of the orthodox church, and attempted to confiscate to the State the ecclesiastical lands. He had a severe struggle with the Archbishop of Novgorod whom he attempted to depose from his see. The position of the Archbishop however, was too strong for him to be able to effect this. The priests whom he ordered to cut their beards also successfully resisted his authority.

His wife Catherine was a fit person around whom might gather the discontent of his subjects. Her character was strong and unscrupulous, and many circumstances joined together to make her hate and despise the Tsar. He no longer lived with her, but with a mistress, and he was careful to inform the world that the Grand Duke Paul might be Catherine's son, but that he was not his father. The Empress was surrounded with spies, and in great danger of her life.

Under these circumstances it was not surprising that a contest should occur in which either the one or the other must be destroyed. Catherine by her superior force of character and greater discretion carried all before her in spite of the disadvantage of being merely a German Princess pitted against the grandson of Peter the Great. Her husband it is true had abolished the "Secret Chancellerie," and had recalled from exile some of the most notable of those who had been sent thither, such as Lestocq, Münich, Biren, and the Duke of Courland and his wife. But though these measures were popular, most of his actions were so extravagantly indiscreet, and he was so entirely wanting in the firmness of character necessary to carry through a policy of startling changes, that there is no wonder that the soldiery went over to Catherine at the solicitation of the knot of conspirators around her, and that she was placed on the throne by a bloodless revolution. Bloodless however it did not long remain, for a few days afterwards Peter was murdered by some of Catherine's adherents.

There now begins the reign of Peter's consort Catherine II., who soon earned for herself the title of Catherine the Great. She reigned for a third of a century, and the period is regarded as being as illustrious in the history of Russia as was the reign of the Tudor Queen Elizabeth in that of England. She appears to have inspired the great men of her reign with a somewhat analogous personal devotion, and in each case we observe anxiety to establish the country in a splendid and glorious position in relation to its neighbours, united with tireless energy in pursuit of its advancement in every direction in which civilisation, literature, and the arts might be fostered. But the reign of Catherine is incomparably more ferocious and bloody than that of Elizabeth, for her own subjects as well as for her enemies. In the catastrophe to the Spanish Armada, England's foe suffered one enormous disaster, but the history of Catherine's reign is a continued record of the savagest butcheries. The three partitionings of Poland, the wars with the Turks, the suppression of the revolt of Pugachev, the naval war with Sweden, and finally the ill-conceived expedition against Persia, squandered multitudes of lives.

On Catherine's accession the only conspicuous representative left alive of the old imperial family, unless we except her own son Paul, was Ivan, son of the Prince and Princess of Brunswick, who was still kept in captivity. His violent death two years afterwards (1764) relieved her of one source of anxiety, and her strong character and politic behaviour soon firmly established her on the throne.

The strength which she felt herself to possess was shown in this very year by her being able to carry into execution the ecclesiastical measure which Peter III. had conceived, but which he had not found himself in a position to carry through. The lands and serfs of the Church were confiscated to the State, the clergy and monks being compensated with fixed incomes.

As I have already intimated warfare is a chief characteristic of this reign, and to a power anxious to extend its territory, Poland seemed an easy prey. Poland was at a heavy disadvantage amongst the states of Europe by reason of its being saddled with a perfectly impracticable constitution. The "liberum veto," as it was called, enabled any single member of the assembly of nobles to veto any legislative proposal. Such an institution barred progress, and even rendered the conduct of the necessary affairs of a State almost impossible. The Kings of Poland at this time were not of the calibre required to combat such difficulties. Augustus III., who died in 1763, was a man of contemptible character. He was succeeded by Poniatowski, who had formerly been a lover of Catherine herself. It was in 1772 that the first spoliation of Poland took place. The conspiracy for its dismemberment was hatched between Catherine, Frederick the Great (who sent his brother Henry to confer with her on the subject), and Joseph II., Emperor of Germany.[1]

Austria was given a considerable slice of territory, viz., part of what was called Red Russia, and of Gallicia with its capital Lemberg. Russia obtained

---

[1] Joseph II. was Emperor of the "Holy Roman Empire of German Nations," or shortly, Emperor of Germany, having succeeded to that dignity on the death of his father, Francis I. (1765). His mother Maria Theresa, was monarch under various titles of all the States included in what was called "Austria." But to these Joseph was heir apparent, and in them he was chief minister of war. His influence was so great that virtually he was fellow-sovereign with his mother in her dominions.

the provinces of Vitebsk and Mohilev, part of Minsk, and whatever lay east of the Dnieper; also part of Livonia. The slice awarded to Prussia had a coast-line on the Baltic, and included the port of Dantzic.

The second partition of Poland did not take place till twenty-one years later (1793). The unhappy country had on 3rd May 1791 adopted a new constitution which made the throne hereditary, gave representatives to cities and towns, and partially emancipated the serfs. This afforded a sufficient excuse for a renewal of the attack by the wolves on the lamb, whose offence was drinking of the lower waters of the brook. But on this occasion the Poles gave a very good account of themselves, for a patriotic general of the very highest quality came to the front in Thadeus Kosciuszko. Everything that could be done for the salvation of his unhappy country the hero did. He won gallant victories against numbers much larger than those he commanded, and when he was defeated by overwhelming odds he played the losing game with equal valour and discretion. He inspired, as well he might, perfect confidence and unbounded enthusiasm in his countrymen, and was created by them dictator whilst the national crisis should last. The disparity of the numbers that could be brought into the field was however too great. Eventually the Russians sent into Poland their great general Suvórov at the head of his army of veterans who had never known defeat; he had established his reputation in the wars against the Turks, as being determined on victory at whatever cost of life. He stormed Praga, a fortified suburb of Warsaw, and took it after a most bloody resistance by the Poles, in the course of which more than half their army was slain. Suvórov then entered the capital, and the unhappy Poles had to submit to any conditions of peace that might be accorded to them. The territory taken on this occasion was much more extensive than at the first partition. Russia received the greater part of the provinces of Vilna and Minsk; also of the part of Russia known as Little Russia or the Ukraine; the greater part of the province of Volhynia; and parts of those of Podolia and Kiev. Thus a large number of the Ukrainians or Little Russians ceased to be Polish subjects only a century ago. The claim often advanced by the Poles however, that they should be regarded as their fellow-countrymen in the complete sense of the words, is not recognised by the Ukrainians themselves, for though they were territorially united with them they did not feel much more closely akin to them than they do to-day to the great Russians.

Prussia sliced off a large portion on the western side of the country. Austria acquired nothing on this occasion.

Two years later, however (1795) at the third and final partitioning of the unfortunate country, Austria received a large additional slice, including Cracow: the portion that Russia then acquired bounded on the west by the Niemen and the (northern) Boug, included most of the province of Grodno and part of the territory lying to the north of that province, etc. Prussia received the rest, including Warsaw, a city she retained till the fresh treaty arrangements that followed the fall of Napoleon.

The period between the first and second partitions of Poland witnessed an abundance of fighting. The territory of the Crimean Khanate was annexed, and the sanguinary warfare with the Turks resulted in some accession of territory. In 1773 a sort of peasants' jacquerie broke out amongst the Cossacks of the Don, headed by one Pugachev, who followed the usual course of personating one of the imperial family who had pre-

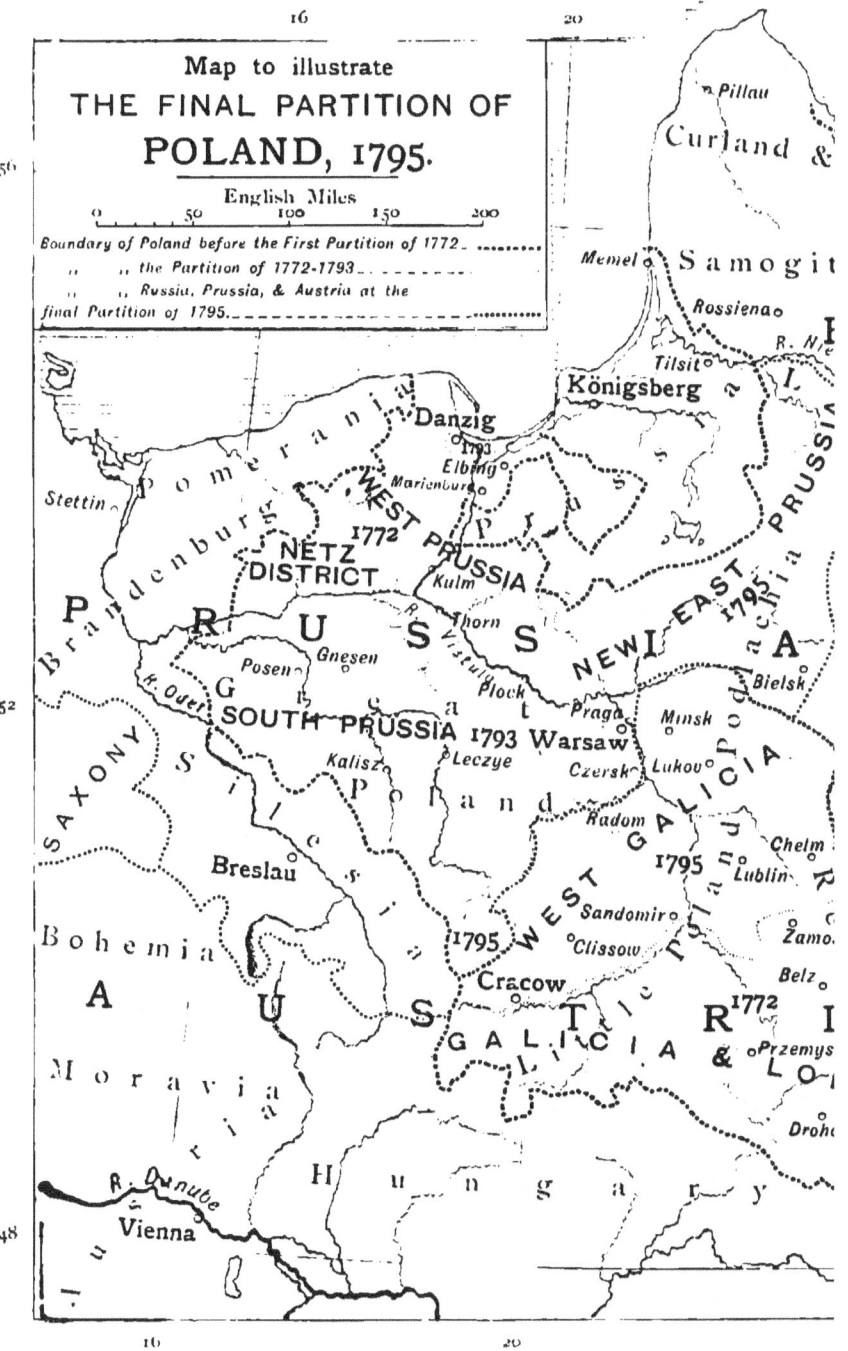

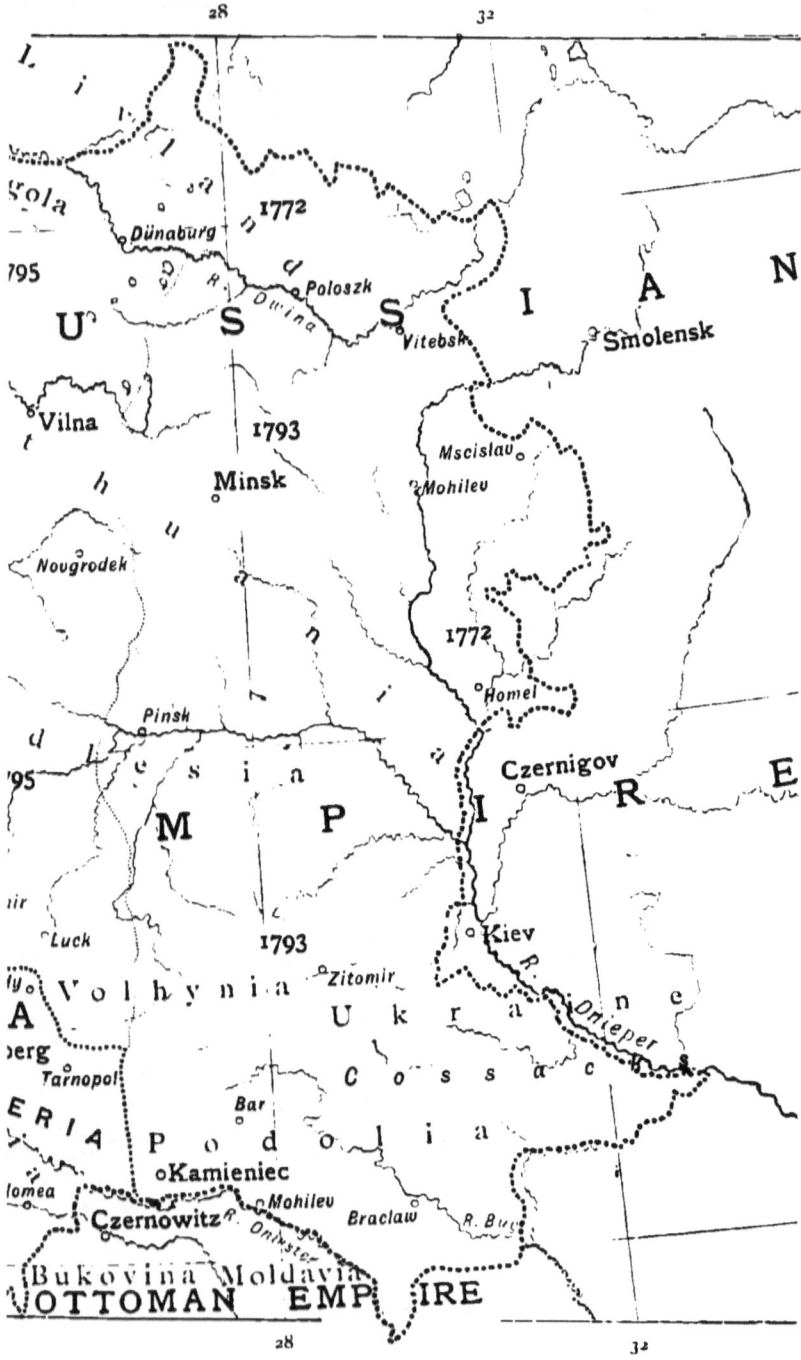

viously met with a violent and mysterious death. He gave himself out to be the Emperor Peter III. He finally surrendered and was executed. The Russians also came victoriously out of a naval war with Sweden.

Further annexations of territory were effected by diplomacy, the most important of which was the Duchy of Courland. The whole of what are called the Baltic Provinces were thus united with Russia.

With so much fighting it is not surprising that the most notable men of the reign should have been great generals. Of these the most remarkable are Suvórov, Rumantzev, Gregory, Orlov, and Potemkin. The last was for many years, as Orlov was at an early period, first favourite at the Court, and swayed almost unbounded power in every department of the State. Catherine tired of his personality and sent him to the wars; there he distinguished himself as markedly as he had previously done at the Court, and his authority remained unimpaired.

Catherine undoubtedly completed Peter the Great's design of establishing Russia as a great European power. She immensely enlarged her territory, and established herself on the Black Sea where many thriving ports, amongst others Odessa, were founded.

She projected a codification of the laws, which however was not completed. To assist in this work she summoned a representative commission, but as on so many other occasions in Russian history when one fancies the germ of constitutionalism may be planted, the commission may almost be said to have ended in smoke. It was but a consultative body, and after the authorities had heard the opinions of the delegates they were dismissed and the actual work of codification was proceeded with without their assistance.

Catherine is also remembered for the extraordinary

magnificence of her Court, for the imposing character of her great progresses through the country, for her munificence to the arts and sciences, for her successful attempts to people some of the rich but uninhabited tracts of country in South Russia by emigrants from other lands, and for her division of the country into provinces. During her reign too banks were first established.

Though Catherine enjoyed a reputation for liberality of thought she was greatly alarmed at the prospect of a possibility of the spread of the principles of the French Revolution to Russia. "After the occurrence of that event, she issued an edict ordering all the French of both sexes, without any exception, to quit the empire. All intercourse with France was suspended." French vessels were prohibited from entering any of the ports of Russia, and the introduction of any French books or periodicals was forbidden. No Russian subjects were allowed to travel in France or hold intercourse with that country (Fowler's "Lives of the Sovereigns of Russia," Vol. II. pp. 298-99).

She was succeeded (1796) by her son[1] Paul who during her reign had been studiously kept in the background. He appeared bent upon reversing her policy in many important particulars, if not on dishonouring her memory. He immediately had the body of Peter III. disinterred from its rather obscure place of burial, and whilst Catherine II.'s body lay in state the coffin of her murdered husband rested by its side. They were then buried together in the church of St Peter and St Paul, Count Alexis Orlov and Count Bariatinski, who were the supposed regicides, being obliged to follow in the funeral next to the coffins, after having been pre-

---

[1] See note to genealogical diagram.

viously set each night to watch the remains of the late Emperor. Immediately afterwards they were banished. The incident was a typical one. Paul was for five years to govern Russia on the same principles that an active boy might follow in managing a nursery menagerie of domestic animals. We have the humiliating spectacle of millions of human beings tremblingly waiting on the fantastic whims of a crazy lout. On Paul's approach in the public street everyone was to kneel in the mud. One lady, hastening for the doctor to attend her dying husband, perhaps inadvertently neglected the rite, and was immediately imprisoned. The husband died and the lady became insane. It became a crime to wear a round hat. To the disgust of a practical general like Suvórov the serviceable costume of the soldiery was to be replaced by stiff and elaborate uniforms such as the Germans wore, and the peasant soldiers were compelled to fasten artificial curls to their heads.

One of the innumerable ukazes issued by Paul seems to have had some practical value at least from the point of view of the monarchy, and it is probably for this reason that it has been subsequently observed. Peter the Great had ordained that the Tsar of Russia should have the right of settling the succession to his throne by will. Paul himself had very nearly suffered under this ordinance, for it is supposed that Catherine II. had in her will excluded him from the succession in favour of his own son Alexander, but that one of his partisans had obtained access to the will and destroyed it. The new ukaze settled the succession on the eldest son.

The latter half of this short reign is occupied by war, first against Napoleon, who was then First Consul of France, and afterwards in alliance with him. Paul being aroused to a sense of the danger his own empire might run from the rapid advances of Napoleon, resolved to participate in the war against his encroaching power, and Russian armies were sent westwards. They were however badly generalled, and the commanders who had in the first place been appointed had to be recalled. They were replaced by the great Suvórov who defeated Napoleon's generals in Italy, but was finally obliged to retreat before the French armies in Switzerland. He crossed the St Gothard Pass with great difficulty and serious loss of life, but the second Russian army in Switzerland by which he expected to be supported, had sustained a disastrous defeat from the French. Suvórov the slayer of thousands of his fellow-men, in spite of indefatigable energy, and efforts that could not be surpassed, failed in his latest effort to obey the commands of the crown of Russia. The incompetent booby, in whose service he had spent his strength and even shattered and wrecked his own exceptional vigour of body, now publicly disgraced him, and sent him to die in the obscurity that reigned outside the circle lightened by the smile of his insane master.

The end of the reign witnessed one of those sudden total reversals of policy to which Russia under Paul's rule was subject, the matter of policy being in this instance of much more moment to the European world than on any other occasion. Paul suddenly conceived a personal admiration for Napoleon similar to that which Peter III. had felt for Frederick the Great, and entered into close alliance with him. He declared war on Great Britain, and laid an embargo on all British shipping found in Russian ports. Three hundred vessels with their cargoes were thus confiscated. England retaliated by issuing letters of *marque* against the northern powers now leagued against her, who were making themselves the cats-paw of Napoleon.

But the Franco-Russian Alliance was of short duration. A palace plot was formed to assassinate Paul and place his son Alexander on the throne. This was successfully carried out, and an alliance with Great Britain was once more entered upon.

Paul was succeeded by his eldest son, Alexander (1801-25). During his reign Russian territory was enlarged by the incorporation of Georgia to the south (1801), and of Finland to the north-west (1809). Georgia had been so harassed by Persia that it threw itself into the arms of Russia for protection. Finland was surrendered by Sweden; on being accepted into the Russian empire the constitution of the country was guaranteed. The inroads that were made on the integrity of this constitution during the reign of Alexander III. form one of the chapters of contemporary Russian politics.

Almost everything else in Alexander's reign is overshadowed by the invasion of Russia by Napoleon. Russian troops had been defeated at the Napoleonic victory of Austerlitz (1805), but in 1807 the two emperors made peace (Peace of Tilsit), and it appeared that they had come to a sort of agreement to divide Europe between them. There were however forces at work to bring about a rupture. Russian trade suffered, especially from the outrageous claim which Napoleon tried to enforce that all English shipping should be excluded from the ports of France, and from those of all the allies of France, and later (Berlin Decree 1806), that the British Islands were under blockade, and that English manufactures were lawful prize. There followed decrees both on the British side (Orders in Council 1807) and on that of Napoleon (Milan Decree of the same year) which rendered the position of neutral trade almost unbearable. An Act passed by the Government of the United States in 1809 illustrates how much this was felt. It enacted that there should be no intercourse with Britain and France till those countries should respectively revoke their obnoxious decrees. The alliance between the emperors could not bear the strain to which it was subjected.

1812 was the year of the Napoleonic invasion of Russia,—three years before Waterloo. Napoleon raised an army of more than 500,000 men, and entered Russia through Poland by Kovno. The Poles, who had some ill-grounded hopes that he might re-establish their kingdom, joined his army to the number of 60,000. It was not till he was within fifty miles of Moscow that a battle of the first magnitude was fought. But at Borodino there was a stubborn contest lasting all one day (September 7th), in which the Russians lost 40,000 and the French 30,000 men. After this the French were able to advance to Moscow, but they found the city deserted, and almost immediately after its occupation a fire broke out, doubtless kindled by the Russians, which destroyed nine-tenths of the capital. Nevertheless Napoleon lingered five weeks there, waiting in vain for Alexander's submission, so that it was the 19th of October before a retreat, which Napoleon had at length resolved upon, was begun. We know how in Russia there is hardly any interval between summer and winter, and now the Arctic winter had arrived. In the midst of its snows and terrible winds the French army was to retreat along a track which they had themselves desolated on their invading march. The narrative of this six weeks' march is one of the most terrible chapters in the history of war. Of the invading army of upwards of 500,000 not more than 80,000 reached the frontier on their retreat.

Two and a half years later, after the battle of Waterloo, a readjustment of European territories was arranged at the Congress of Vienna. Most of the Duchy of Warsaw was made over to Russia, and Alexander was crowned King of Poland, at the same time granting to that country a constitution.

The last part of Alexander's reign was under the ascendancy of Arakcheiev, who had had much influence in the reign of Paul, and was now installed almost as principal adviser to the throne. He was a specimen of the thoroughly brutal type of Russian official. He devised the plan of military colonies in the south of Russia which caused great dissatisfaction, and indeed led to revolts which were suppressed with bloodshed. The plan was to settle regiments of the line amongst the farms of the serfs on the crown domains. He fell from power in consequence of some horrible brutalities practised on the serfs of his own estate just before the death of Alexander in 1825.

Alexander, who had left no children, was not succeeded by his next brother Constantine (who had renounced his right to the succession), but by the younger brother Nicholas who reigned from 1825 to 1855.

His advent to the throne was greeted by a dangerous military revolt called the Revolt of the Decembrists (because it took place in December 1825). Its leaders were men of the noble classes and almost all of them were officers in the army. The object was to obtain a constitution, and it is an exceedingly interesting episode quite distinct in character from the ordinary palace revolutions so many of the narratives of which we have read, the object of which was usually merely to replace one by another absolute monarch. During the reign of Alexander two predisposing causes had been at work, which naturally lead up to such a movement.

The liberalism rather markedly displayed at the beginning of his reign had been reversed at its close; and the army which had been so constantly in foreign parts had, especially during its occupation of Paris, imbibed the more liberal political views which were found outside of Russia. Many of the Decembrist leaders no doubt, had nothing more in view than an advancement of their class, or of their own personal interests, but the initiative in the movement was taken by a group of men with purely patriotic aims, and they succeeded in leavening the heterogeneous mass of malcontents that were banded together to the extent of imbuing the combination with the most liberal ideas of the time as to Russian political reform. Alexander's death occurred unexpectedly, so that the moment for action came upon the conspirators suddenly. Unfortunately at the critical time courage was displayed by the few alone who had engaged in the combination from patriotic motives, and the cause was wrecked in great measure by the treachery and cowardice of their companions. The leaders of the revolt were mercilessly dealt with by execution[1] or by exile to Siberia.

At the end of 1830 the Polish insurrection broke out. It was however crushed after brave and stubborn fighting, and early in 1832 the Polish constitution which Alexander had accepted, was declared cancelled, and the country was afterwards assimilated to Russia and divided into Russian provinces.

The suppression of the Polish insurrection was followed by an evil time for the Roman Catholic Church in that country and for the Uniats as they were called there and in Lithuania and other neighbour-

---

[1] The leaders who were hanged were Pestel, Bestuzhev, Kakhovski, Rileyev, and Maraviov-Apostol, all of them remarkable men.

ing countries subject to the Tsar. The religious body called Uniats arose after the conquest by Catholic Poland of provinces peopled by a Greek orthodox population in 1595. They retained the Greek forms of worship but acknowledged the Pope as the supreme head of the Church. Centuries of a separate religious communion had created many differences between them and the Greek Orthodox Church, but now after a petition for reunion to the Orthodox Church had been presented by a small minority of their clergy, a ukaze was issued boldly proclaiming the accession of three or four millions of Uniats to the Church of their conquerors.

The reign of Nicholas was reactionary thoughout. He was the sworn foe and merciless represser of liberal tendencies in politics. Nor were his services to the cause of despotism confined to his own territories. In 1849 he helped the Austrians to subjugate the Hungarians who had set up a republic under the famous Kossuth. They were dealt with in barbarous fashion. In 1854 the Crimean War broke out, and in the midst of it Nicholas died (1855) and was succeeded by his son Alexander II. The war ended in the defeat of the Russians.

At Alexander's accession we may well pause a moment to ask whether Russian history is a mere congeries of anarchic events, a succession of wars, of murders and assassinations, of palace plots, and of fantastic remodellings of the lives of an enormous people according to the caprices of the autocrat of the moment, or whether some sort of ordered march of events can in the long run be recognised. Is Russian history an endless and bloody series of extracts from the annals which recount the lives of a nation of marauders and assassins, or is it an Epic?

Two great facts have, I think we shall see, been established. The course of Russian history for six and a half centuries has steadily set first to the creation, then to the solidification, unification, and extension of a mighty state. The Muscovite power has grown first of all by the subjugation of its brother Slavonic states, then by driving out or conquering the Tatárs, and occupying the vast plains of South Russia previously held by them, and by an enormous extension of territory across Northern Asia, and a considerable extension by the absorption on its other borders of states of such various races as Finland, Lithuania, Poland, and the countries of Transcaucasia.

Meanwhile the central part of the empire has continually been subjected to a unifying process. The Muscovite millstone has ground the ethnological meal practically to one sample where it comes most directly under its pressure; but the further one travels from the central vortex the less homogeneity is discernible and at the edges the different racial "feeds" (if, to carry on the analogy, we may so call them) are as yet hardly commingled at all.

The other dominating feature of the development of Russian history has been in force for a period not half as long and has been followed neither so consistently nor so energetically. Yet on the whole it has triumphed and established its position. Although the beginnings of the coming importance of the idea are revealed in the time of Alexis, speaking broadly it dates from the time not quite three centuries ago when St Petersburg was built. The great Tsar after whom that city was named may be said to be the apostle of the idea that Russia was not only to be great, solidified, and homogeneous, but that she was to be *European*. From that time it may be taken to be a settled thing in the history of the world that Russia is not to be a second enormous China, closing herself to all influences, to all ideas, and as far as may be to all material communication with the outside world; but that she is to be a member (and at times she has aspired to be the leading member) of the European family of nations.

This second great ideal of the Russian race in no way arrested the march of the first. The reigns of Peter I. and Catherine II. are as remarkable for their continued territorial conquests as for their insistence on a policy of European civilisation in opposition to Asiatic isolation.

With the accession of Alexander II. to the throne, a third idea certainly as majestic as those which in Russia had preceded it by centuries, for the first time makes its effective entrance on the political stage. Of this there had indeed been premonitions. The very fact of admitting European ideas, and European thoughts into Russia carried the necessity with it of some knowledge of, and some influence from, the political institutions of the more advanced states of the west. In the time of Peter I., in the time of Catherine II., in the time of Alexander I.,[1] and even in that of Nicholas some facts may be pointed out which show that the Tsars occasionally regarded their subjects not merely as so many millions of body-servants. But it was reserved for Alexander II. and the able group of liberals (Miliutin and others) who worked with him in the early part of his reign, to introduce solid liberties and privileges for great masses of his people fundamentally altering the material conditions and the security of their lives. At the entrance then to this chapter of

---

[1] Alexander I. abolished serfdom in the Baltic provinces. He did not however dower the enfranchised serfs with lands.

Russian history the English student feels that at length he is coming into contact with problems and political phenomena more familiar to him. He has henceforth to watch, as for centuries he has watched in England, the gradual growth of the liberties and privileges of the people.

For a dozen or so years it seems that his anticipations are justified. Serfdom is abolished, local government, in which the principle of representation plays a not unimportant part, is established, judicial process is reformed, and the courts themselves cleansed of corruption; considerable liberty is granted to the press, active religious persecution ceases, and religious disabilities are relaxed.

But over this smiling landscape there sweeps a thunderstorm; all the heavens are obscured, the whole picture is changed. Alexander employs the second half of his reign in diligently and systematically minimising, counteracting, and as far as the march of accomplished events will allow, actually in undoing the reforms which he has with so much care built up.

The historical student then for the first time remembers the enormous difference between the march of liberty in England and in Russia. How in England our liberties have been wrested from those above, first by the nobles, then by the trading classes, and finally by the great democracy; how it has thus from the first had a firm foundation, and how it has ended in having a broad one. He is reminded that in Russia on the contrary the mainspring of reform has been the will of an autocrat, an autocrat whose personality is confused with that of the Almighty by many of his subjects so that the Russian peasant if he recognised the significance of the change of view of his Cæsar

Emperor, might meekly murmur:—"The Lord gave and the Lord hath taken away; blessed be the name of the Lord."

Miliutin and the rest look sadly on at the overthrow of their work. They sigh for the day when the great Epic may be completed, when the liberties of the people may be founded broadly and deeply in the people's own will; but for the most part they take the view that the time has not yet come, and dejectedly fold their hands. One small section however more hopeful, perhaps more energetic than the rest, refuse to acquiesce in the giving up of what was thought to have been gained, and persistently assert their rights. A conflict ensues with the authority of the Tsar which becomes more and more intense and more and more deadly, till it resolves itself into a duel, the Government on its side suspending the ordinary law, trying the so-called "Nihilists" by court-martial and hanging them; the "Nihilists" after due warning and formal sentence "executing" by assassination first of all the head of the secret police, and finally after previous unsuccessful attempts by a pistol shot, by trying to blow up a palace, and by attempting to wreck a train the Tsar Alexander II. himself, once called "the Liberator," is on March 13th (1st) 1881 blown to pieces by a bomb.

The following may be read in amplification of the contents of this chapter:—

    Morfill's "Russia" or some other text-book of Russian history from the end of Peter the Great's to the end of Nicholas's reign.

    Leroy Beaulieu, from p. 268 in the French edition of 1890, or from p. 291 in the English edition of 1893, to the end of chapter iv.

E. A. Freeman, "General Sketch of European History," chapter xv. sec. 8 (pp. 313-6), sec. 11 (pp. 317-9), sec. 14 (pp. 321-4); chapter xvi. secs. 12 and 13 (pp. 341-3); and chapter xvii. secs. 9 and 10 (pp. 357-8).

*For biographical sketch of Kosciuszko :—*

George Fowler, "Lives of the Sovereigns of Russia from Catherine to Paul," chapter iv. pp. 205 *et seq.*, also pp. 366-7.

*For history of the Decembrist Revolt :—*

"Russian Conspirators in Siberia. A personal narrative by Baron R———, a Russian Dekabrist."

"Revelations of Russia ; or the Emperor Nicholas and his Empire, in 1844: by one who has seen and describes." **Vol. I.** chapters ix. and **x.**

# CHAPTER IV.

## THE PEASANTRY: THEIR EMANCIPATION FROM SERFDOM, AND SUBSEQUENT TREATMENT AND CONDITIONS OF LIFE.

## Chapter IV.—*Contents.*

How Serfage arose—The *obrok* and the *corvée;* the former always obtained on crown domains—The emancipation, personal freedom only, or that united with the possession of land?—Personal freedom granted on the lands of private proprietors to whom rent was to be paid (1861); permissive regulations introduced for the purchase of lands by the peasants (1863); above regulations extended to crown domains (1866); permissive regulations made obligatory with view of establishing a peasant proprietory (1883)—The peasant unit of administration is the *Mir* or Village Community—Division of land amongst the peasantry within the Mir.

The forces which brought about the liberation: Literary (Belinski, Tourguénev, Herzen); public opinion at the close of the Crimean War; the character of Alexander II.

The reaction: Alexander II.'s fear of democracy after Polish Rebellion of '63—All-importance of the autocracy; the bureaucracy charged to preserve it at all costs; in its insistence that it must have a free hand for this purpose, it finds a shield for its own corruption; departmental and local tyranny become rife, and physical conditions forbid that one man should be able to keep them in check.

The village communes: the *Mir*, the *Volost*—Subjugation of the headsman (*starshinas*) to local officialdom—The communal clerk (*pissar*) also becomes its tool—The rural classes subjected to representatives of the nobility (*natchalniks*) — The present material condition of the peasantry compared to what it was before the emancipation—Crushing weight of taxation—Evidence of the present comparative poverty of the peasantry.

# CHAPTER IV.

**THE PEASANTRY: THEIR EMANCIPATION FROM SERFDOM, AND SUBSEQUENT TREATMENT AND CONDITIONS OF LIFE.**

THE history of the reign of Alexander II. resolves itself in great measure into an examination of the reforms instituted during its earlier period, and of their subsequent fate during its latter period. The most striking of these is the enfranchisement of the serfs.

The essence of serfage was being *bound to the land*, and the institution thus understood only came into existence at the end of the sixteenth century. True in ancient Russia there were *slaves;* they were generally prisoners of war, insolvent debtors, or people who had been compelled by abject penury to sell away their liberty. But the slaves were not numerous and the mass of the peasantry was considered to be free. In early times however a distinction made itself felt between the warriors and the workers in the fields. It became the function of the latter to support the former, and their status became a distinctly inferior one. They became attached to masters, but still they could choose their own masters quite freely. Usually they hired themselves out for a whole year something in the same way as labourers used to engage themselves in rural England at what were called "mops" or "hiring-fairs." It became customary to make new engagements only once a year, viz. at the feast of St George in November when the work of the cereal year was at an end; they were then free to leave the lands on which they had been working and settle elsewhere. But during the last part of the sixteenth and the beginning of the seventeenth centuries opportunities and temptations to wholesale self-transportation presented themselves to the peasantry, which appeared a menace to the Empire, both as sapping its taxable strength, and the sources from which its army could be drawn. The lands of the south, wrested from the Tatárs, some of which were very fertile, invited colonisation, and the free life of the Cossacks of the steppes offered a bright prospect to the more adventurous spirits who were received as welcome recruits to their wandering communities. To the east Permia, and Siberia opened up other tempting fields of colonisation. In addition the conditions of the peasants' lives through direct and indirect taxation, and the abuses in the administration (especially of justice), were becoming more and more onerous. The body of regular troops was being largely increased which caused the Government to endeavour to raise larger sums by taxation. At the same time whole classes of the population, such as the clergy, and some of the fighting castes (for example the streltsi), were privileged to exemption from taxation. This of course made it all the harder for the taxpayers who remained. All these causes were so many goads to the people impelling them to seek better conditions of life in new settlements.

There was then a real danger of depletion of population, and under the Tsars Feodor (son of John the Cruel) and Boris Godúnov and their successors, the peasant was attached to the soil by edicts forbidding him to change his domicile at the feast of St George, and he became a serf. The measures announced by these edicts, which began by being temporary, became permanent.

The loss of the right to change their domicile and their lords, put the peasantry completely within the power of the proprietors to whom the Government practically handed over the internal administration of their domains.

Serfage and dependence on the will of the landowners was not equally prevalent in all parts of the Empire. It was most firmly established and most rigorously administered in the central parts, and became more lax in the outlying regions where Russification was less complete.

The rights of the proprietors over their serfs were usually embodied in the system either of commanding a certain proportion of their time for labour on their estates (the corvée), or in default money compensation (the obrok). The conditions of the corvée were generally understood as claiming about half of the work of the serfs for the proprietors, the other half being devoted to the lands which had been assigned for the peasants' support. Where however the obrok was customary the conditions for the serf were greatly improved, for he then (subject to the payment of a sum of money usually equal to £1 or £2 sterling per annum), regained his personal liberty. He was thus for instance frequently enabled to take up his residence in a town, and exchange his agricultural for industrial work.

The crown peasants enjoyed a good many advantages over those on the estates of private proprietors, amongst others that with them the institution of the obrok or money commutation always obtained.

A great part of the estates in Russia belonged to the Crown, that is to say they had no proprietor save the State. The peasants on these lands (men and women together), numbered some twenty-two millions. There were about an equal number of peasant serfs on the lands of the territorial nobles. It was with these latter, who as we have seen were the greater sufferers, that the new measures of Alexander II. dealt with in the first instance; their emancipation dates from 1861, whilst that of the crown serfs did not take place till five years later (1866).

The idea of the Liberation came to the serfs as the realisation of a cherished dream; for tradition had never allowed the memory of the ancient right of personal freedom to die out from amongst them. But when details of how the Liberation was to be brought about began to be discussed, a discrepancy at once exhibited itself between the ideas of the landowners and those of the peasantry on the subject. On the domains of the landowners, whilst certain parts of the estates were retained for the proprietors' own use, and cultivated by means of the corvée, other parts were handed over to the serfs to be cultivated by them for their own support. The serfs now regarded these latter as their own lands. To the landowners they said:—"Our labour (or part of our labour) has been yours; but the lands which we occupy are ours." When then the announcement came of personal freedom for the serfs, they pictured to themselves that they would possess the same lands that they had occupied heretofore, but that they would have the whole instead of half their time to spend upon it; or if three days a week sufficed, that they could hire themselves out for the remainder of their time and so improve their position. The landowners on the other hand said:—"No: if the corvée and the obrok are to be given up we suppose there is no help for it (though we do not altogether acknowledge the justice of depriving us of our labour-power without compensation), but in that case we are at any rate entitled to re-enter into possession of our lands which you have hitherto enjoyed rent-free in return for your services. If you are to continue on these lands now you are free men, you must either buy or rent them from us." The Government thus found themselves face to face with an agrarian difficulty resulting from the difference of view of the two classes concerned. The situation had some points of resemblance to the difficult agrarian questions which have arisen in Ireland.

The course actually decided upon was that the peasantry should indeed retain something like the lands they had been accustomed to occupy, but that they should pay rent for them either in money or by personal service.

The advantages accruing to the peasantry were by no means uniform. Whilst in some instances they soon acquired the privileges of almost fully freed men, in others, the substitution of a stipulated labour-rent for the old corvêe created a change of little practical effect.

During the first two years then after the Emancipation ukaze, the new arrangements were carried out on the basis of settled rent payments or services by the peasants. These were fixed by mutual agreement if possible, but failing this by official arbitrators. The men first appointed as arbitrators, although drawn from the ranks of the nobles, acted fairly and even generously towards the peasantry; but they were succeeded by others who were less scrupulous.

The fixing of these rents and personal services could only be considered a half-way house on the road to emancipation. The peasantry it was true were delivered to some extent from the capricious and arbitrary personal control of the landowners, but their economic position generally remained much the same; for the new rents and obligatory services corresponded in the majority of cases pretty closely in amount to the old obrok and corvée on which indeed they were for the most part based.

We now therefore enter upon the second stage in the process of Liberation. Measures were set on foot of a more far-reaching character, aiming at the creation of a peasant proprietary, and the arrangement of rent payments was replaced by one of annual redemption payments for the eventual purchase of the land.

With regard however both to the original fixing of the area of the land to be allocated to the peasants, and the fixing of rent, or subsequently of redemption price, to be paid for them, the problems that arose were sufficiently complex. Not only were there particular local customs which had to be taken into account in various parts of the country such as Little Russia, Lithuania, and the ancient Polish provinces; but even in Great Russia, where a certain amount of uniformity reigned in these particulars, the conditions of the forest zone were quite different to those of the steppes, and the fertility of both was very much surpassed by that of the black earth zone, so that what would be an adequate assignment of land for the support of a family in the last, would be an altogether inadequate acreage amongst the forests.

The assemblies of the nobles were called together in

the various provinces, but it was merely that they might have an opportunity of presenting their views. The detailed work of deciding what acreage of land was to be assigned in each case, and later on what the scale of its redemption price should be, was left to a special commission. Fortunately some very able men, liberal in their ideas and animated by the enthusiasm of the reforming years of the 'sixties were found to take the chief part in the direction of this work. Conspicuous among them were George Samarin, Nicholas Miliutin, and Prince Tcherkaski. Yet as we shall hereafter see they did not carry out their work without committing errors of a very serious character.

Before pursuing the story of the establishment of a landed peasantry we ought to note by the way that one large class of serfs (numbering about a million and a half) received their personal liberty alone without any dower of land. These were the ones who had been employed as domestic servants in the establishments of the land-proprietors. After two years they were no longer to be under the obligation to serve their old masters, though they might continue to do so if they chose for wages. Many of these drifted into the towns, and added largely to the class to be found there living from hand to mouth without any constant or regular employment.

Returning to the other classes of the peasantry, the first regulations issued by the Government for the creation of a peasant proprietary by substitution of redemption payments for rents were purely permissive in their character. After the Polish insurrection in 1863 the Government made it compulsory in the ancient

Lithuano-Polish[1] and in some other of the western provinces[1] as well as in Poland[1] proper, but in Great Russia it did not become obligatory till after the accession of Alexander III.

But although the purchase of the land by the peasantry was not at first made compulsory, the State endeavoured to facilitate the purchase by offering to advance to the peasants as a loan four-fifths[2] of the capitalised purchase price. (The usual basis on which the purchase price was arrived at was $16\frac{2}{3}$ years' purchase, *i.e.* by multiplying the obrok or the value of the corvée by $16\frac{2}{3}$; that is to say the obrok or corvée bore the proportion to the redemption price of 6 to 100.) The annual repayments to the State to cover interest and redemption payment were to be at the rate of 6 per cent. per annum for 49 years, at the end of which time the land would be the peasants' absolute property.

Perhaps we shall the better understand these arrangements if we work out an actual case. Supposing the peasant has assigned to him for the support of his family three dessiatines of land, *i.e.* about 8 acres, and

---

[1] The landowners in these parts were Poles, and the policy pursued in these provinces was an attempt to attach the peasantry to the Russian Government, and to dissociate their interests from those of the Poles of the landowning class.

[2] It is however to be noted that the proprietor had the right of initiating the redemption even when the peasant was unwilling. In this case however he received the four-fifths of the capitalised value advanced by the State only. As the peasant paid less by 20 per cent. when the land was redeemed on the demand of the proprietor than when it was done by mutual consent, he hung back from such mutual consent whenever he thought he could safely do so. Thus it happened that not more than two out of five of the redemption arrangements were entered upon by mutual consent, whilst three out of five were entered upon on the demand of the landowner.

that the annual rent payable is 9 roubles,[1] *i.e.*, 3 roubles per dessiatine, the capitalised value would be $9 \times 16\frac{2}{3} = 150$ roubles. Of this sum he would have to pay one-fifth [2] (say 30 roubles) down, whilst the State would advance him the remaining four-fifths (say 120 roubles). For 49 years he would have to pay the State 6 per cent. on this sum equalling 7·2 roubles. The total result so far as the peasant is concerned, is that he has at once to pay down a lump sum of more than 3 years' rent,[2] but his rent is then reduced from 9 to $7\frac{1}{5}$ roubles, and in 49 years ceases altogether.

The proprietors were reimbursed by being given government scrip, on which interest was payable together with redemption money which would in a similar manner pay off the obligation in a series of years. The advantage to them was that a government bond was substituted for the difficulties of rent collection.

The peasants largely availed themselves of the conditions of redemption held out to them, but it must be remembered that the arrangements for carrying it out could so far be entered upon only with the consent of the proprietor. In some provinces its accomplishment had been almost universal, but in others a quarter or a third of the peasants still remained in the first stage of emancipation which was very often really hardly distinguishable from the old serfage, for the landowners were under these circumstances invested with large police powers over the village-communities of the peasantry. At the accession of Alexander III. twenty

---

[1] The value (by weight) of the silver rouble is a little over that of the German thaler or of 3s. English. The fall of silver has caused its (international) value to be much depreciated. For purposes of internal trade, rent, taxes, etc., the *paper* rouble is principally used, and this suffers a further considerable depreciation of value compared with the silver rouble.

[2] See note [2], preceding page.

years after the first measures of Emancipation, there were still some millions of peasants in this condition. Many proprietors especially in the fertile districts, found the old state of things more profitable to them than the new promised to be, and refused their assent to redemption. In 1883 Alexander III. issued a ukaze making the redemption obligatory everywhere.

As the redemption price was based not on the market value of the land, but on the old obrok and corvée, great inequalities manifested themselves, for the obrok and corvée did not take much account of such considerations as fertility, accessibility, and the general value of the land. So it came about that in the fertile regions of the black earth the proprietors put off the redemption as long as possible, only putting it into operation when they were compelled to do so by the ukaze of Alexander III., whilst the proprietors of the forest zone forced the redemption on the peasants though by so doing they were obliged to allow a fifth off the scale of the redemption price. Even so it is calculated that the peasants in these regions paid from 10 up to 100 per cent. above the market value for their lands, whilst on the contrary those in the black earth zone paid from 10 to 100 per cent. too little for theirs on that computation, when at last they were enabled to buy. Naturally under these circumstances, those in the forest zone took up the minimum of land that they were legally allowed to do.

The peasantry on the other hand in the fertile regions often missed the opportunity of receiving the full advantages which they might have claimed under the redemption regulations. For example within certain limits, when the initiative had been taken by the landowners, it was at the option of the peasantry to determine how much land they would take up under the conditions of redemption. Thus the maximum which they might legally claim often exceeded by 100 per cent. the legal minimum which they were obliged to accept. In the fertile regions where the terms were so favourable to them, it was obviously their interest to take up the maximum. Nevertheless it was much more frequently the case that only the minimum was claimed. They viewed the arrangements with suspicion —and besides they regarded the land as being rightfully theirs rent free. As according to their view the redemption-rent was an imposition, the less land on which they paid it the better they were pleased. Eventually it often came about that they leased the additional lands that they might have had from the proprietors, at a rent very little below the redemption-rent, which in half a century would have given them the freehold. Another instance of the peasants' acting against their own interest was exhibited by the operation of a permissive clause the insertion of which was contrary to the wishes of Miliutin, Samarin, Tcherkaski, and those who thought with them. By mutual agreement between proprietor and peasant, a free gift of a quarter of the acreage might be substituted for the sale of the legally stipulated amount of land under the redemption conditions. This was extensively done in the black earth regions, though it was a very bad bargain for the peasantry. The fact that it was so, was after a year or two realised, and those who had closed with the landlords on these terms bitterly repented their want of foresight.

It will be remembered that in speaking of the initiation of the reforms it was mentioned that they were at first applicable to the lands of private proprietors only, and that the crown lands were not affected. The peasantry on the latter numbered nearly half the total of the serfs. Their condition in 1861 was more advanced than that of the serfs on the private domains, for they no longer gave the corvée, and were subject to the obrok only. But the land purchase law applicable to the others left them in the lurch. In 1866 however, by a ukaze of Alexander II., the redemption regulations were extended to them.

The following dates then form the landmarks of the Emancipation:—

- 1861 (Feb. 19/March 1 — Substitution of rent charges in money or personal service for the obrok and the corvée.
- 1863—Permissive regulations for the purchase of land by the peasant.
- 1866—The above regulations, applicable hitherto to the lands of private proprietors only, extended to the crown domains (on which nearly half the serfs lived).
- 1883—Permissive regulations made obligatory.

In discussions on the agrarian questions in Ireland it has sometimes been pointed out how contradictory are the ideals as to land tenure, of different accredited representatives of the Irish people. The late C. S. Parnell for example seemed to aim at the establishment of a peasant proprietary, whilst Mr Michael Davitt is a known advocate of land nationalisation. "What," it has been asked, " can be more opposed to each other than two such land systems as these? They differ as widely as does individualism from state socialism." Doubtless the criticism, so far as Ireland is concerned, is well founded. I have heard of no proposal applicable to that country which would unite the characteristics of both policies. But it is not a little curious to remark that the Russian system of land tenure does appear in great measure to combine the characteristics of a peasant proprietorship, with those of the common holding of the land by the community for the community.

We have remarked that in the times of serfage a certain proportion of the estates of the landowners were given over for the use of the peasantry, and that after the emancipation similar portions of the land were made over to the peasants on certain conditions. We have now to observe that the agrarian agreements of the Government are not with individual peasants. The unit so far as the peasantry is concerned is the *village community*, the "mir" as it is called. It is the mir collectively that is to-day responsible for so much of the imperial taxation; and it is the mir collectively that must raise and pay over to Government the necessary amount of redemption-money for the lands that have been assigned to it.

The lands of the mir are divided into pasture land and land for tillage.[1] The former is usually enjoyed in common by all the members of the village community; the latter is divided up periodically amongst the villagers to be cultivated by them, the fruits of their labours going to the individual families of peasants, but the lands themselves being always subject to redivision when the mir in its corporate capacity shall so ordain. The division is sometimes made equally amongst the adult males; sometimes amongst the households, but taking into account the circumstances as to children of working age in each.

In Russia the family group will often include a large number of couples and their descendants, all living under one roof or at any rate round one court, and governed on absolute and patriarchal principles by the head of the family. In Little Russia, however, the families have not clung together in this way.

---

[1] Compare the old English and the old German "Mark."

New divisions become necessary through the changes brought about by births, marriages, and deaths. Their frequency differs very much in the different communes. In some the division is triennial, in others as seldom as every six, nine, twelve, or even thirty years, whilst in some it is said not to have taken place since the emancipation. The average time is perhaps between ten and fifteen years. There are grave objections to frequent re-divisions, and the tendency amongst the peasantry is to have recourse to them less often than they used to do.

The peasant does not attempt to build his cottage on or close by the land he happens to have in his occupancy at any given time, for he may be ousted from it by a re-distribution, but all the houses are built together in a village in some central position on the communal estate. In any case the Russians might incline to this arrangement, for their social instincts are strong, and the distances in their country are great. The cottages themselves, and the enclosures of garden land attached to them, are not subject to communal re-distribution, so that they are private, or more generally family property.

The view I shall be presenting of the reigns of the two last Alexanders is that a series of reforms covered the early part of the first monarch's reign, viz. from 1856 to the year of the Polish rebellion (1863), and less energetically from then to about 1870, and that there followed a period of reaction which set in about 1870, and has continued to the present time, so that in the last quarter of a century the progress made in the preceding dozen years has to a large extent been nullified.

In some particulars and to some extent the retrogressive action of the monarchs has I think consciously been aimed at making of no effect or at minimising the concessions granted by the autocracy in the earlier period, but neither the reforms themselves (and especially not the emancipation), nor the subsequent curtailment of the reforms, can be considered exclusively as the result of the will of the autocrats. Other and still more important influences have been at work.

Thus the matter of the liberation of the serfs had, so to speak, been "in the air" during the whole century, and even during the reigns at the end of last century. It had become the dominant idea of any liberalism that was to be found in the Empire, and at any times at which the suppression of thought was relaxed, the voice of the best part of the patriots of the country became audible in its favour. Several of the Tsars had themselves dallied with the question. Even Nicholas had the reputation of indulging in a dream of general liberation, though in his more practical moments no actual measures in that direction commended themselves to him. Yet the cause gained immensely during his reign by the advocacy of literature. The writings of Bilinski the critic were continually enforcing the idea, though in so veiled a way that they were enabled to pass through the hands of the censors without mutilation. More important still and more direct was Tourguénev's "Notes of a Sportsman," which did an immense deal to awaken the national conscience on the question. It was one of the earliest of those novels with a political purpose which have since become such a feature of Russian literature, and in its importance in relation to this particular question was comparable to Mrs Beecher Stowe's "Uncle Tom's Cabin" in regard to the abolition of slavery in America. Nor must we leave unmentioned the extraordinary influence exercised by Alexander Herzen, a political refugee in England. He was a man of noble birth and he had a circle of influential friends in Russia. When he fled to England the Russian Government desired to seize his fortune but he made over his interest in his property to one of the Rothschilds and the Ministers of the Tsar were unwilling to risk offending so influential a person by refusing to recognise the validity of the transaction. Herzen had a sufficiently powerful personality and literary aptitude soon to be recognised as the leading spirit amongst the Russian friends of liberty. He published in London a Russian periodical called the "Kolokól" ("The Bell"), as well as an "almanack," and many other fugitive writings, and several books. These although they were of course stopped at the Russian frontier so far as the public were concerned, had a very large clandestine circulation amongst those who were inclined towards liberalism. The utterances of the "Kolokól" were so important that it was regularly read by the high functionaries surrounding the Tsar, and by the Tsar himself. It ruthlessly exposed the scandals and corruptions amongst the officials which would otherwise have been successfully hushed up, and no more dreaded threat could be extended towards a peccant official than that Herzen should be informed of his misdoings. There was no subject upon which the "Kolokól" was more insistent and more urgent than the freeing of the serfs, and it did not stint its praise of Alexander II. when he took the first steps in that direction. But in Nicholas's time the whole real trend of the governmental policy was in quite an opposite direction. The whole energy of his reign was devoted to impressing the nation with a deep mark from the iron-shod heel of his despotism. At its close came the Crimean War.

The system of cast-iron despotism which had been so laboriously perfected throughout his reign, entirely broke down at this national crisis, and the mind of the nation revolted against the continuance in its entirety of a system which had worked such disastrous results. There is much ground then for the view which M. Leroy-Beaulieu puts forward that the movement for the liberation of the serfs was the first great assertion of public opinion in Russian state affairs:—

"The work of Alexander II. is entirely different from that of Peter the Great, and exhibits all the progress that Russian society had made in the interval: the first was the work of one man, but the second may be said to be the work of a people. At the time of the emancipation of the serfs, we no longer behold Russia as a sort of passive subject meet only for administrative experiments, or (as a Russian who has adopted France as his country has expressed it), a sort of sociological laboratory; it is a nation which has left childhood behind, and instead of blindly giving itself up to the guidance of a father or teacher is working out its own development." [1]

Indeed everything now favoured the coming to the front of the liberal element in the ranks of the politicians and that element was now stronger than it had ever been before. It remained only that the enormous power of the Tsar should not be actually opposed to this new force. The new Tsar Alexander II. certainly had the power in his hands of frustrating or of making much more difficult the liberal movement. He was something of a sentimentalist and may sometimes have cared more for the semblance than the

---

[1] Vol. I., English edition, p. 420; French edition, p. 414.

reality of humanitarian endeavour. Yet there is no reason to suppose that he was not genuinely a well-intentioned man. At any rate there belongs to him the credit of having opened at once and decisively the gates through which rushed this new liberal flood of action. So far as he was responsible (and I think he was responsible in a large degree) for the emancipation of the serfs, it can hardly be denied that he was actuated by benevolent and humane motives. Nor can one suppose that between 1863 and 1870 his disposition towards his people underwent a radical and entire change, and that from that time he was governed by inhumane impulses. Such a view it seems to me would have little to support it. On the other hand it would be easy to adduce instances where important emendations and additions to the Emancipation Acts have been made in the later years of Alexander II. and also during the reign of his successor aiming at carrying out more easily and more perfectly the scheme of emancipation and the land settlements for the peasantry.

But though, at any rate so far as the great bulk of the peasantry are concerned, the late Emperor no more than his predecessor can be charged with actual cruelty or malevolence in intention; even though it may be admitted on the contrary that they have both had the material interests of the emancipated serfs at heart; there have been another set of considerations which have overshadowed these, and where the two have clashed it has not been the latter that has been obliged to give way. Alexander II. perhaps actively strove, Alexander III. passively acquiesced in being benevolent in his autocracy, but the earlier monarch almost as much as the later one, refused to give way an inch if the autocracy itself were called in question. It is probable that though his humane disposition did not change during his reign, his mental point of view did. To a certain extent he became frightened at his own actions. In the measures he had taken for the welfare of his people, he became aware he had given a strong impulse to democratic tendencies, and towards these he was more than ever antagonistic after the events of the Polish rebellion of 1863, and so it came about that though his benevolent interest in the emancipation of the peasantry and their settlement on the land hardly diminished, it was not in any way allowed to stand in the way of preserving perfect and unchecked the autocratic power, and a gigantic department of the State had as its sole function the protection of the majesty, the inviolability, and the safety of his office and person.

That a monarch's own safety should be his dominating care may appear to be a little contemptible, but one could hardly look for it to be otherwise. Even if brave and self-sacrificing men alone were born to the throne, is it possible that they could withstand the subtle temptation of identifying themselves with their office, of believing what they are continually being told by all around them, that their office is the personification of the welfare of their country, that any blow struck against the Tsar is struck against the Tsardom, and that a blow aimed at the Tsardom is a blow at Russia itself?

Thus inflated with the well-being supposed to be inherent in himself of 120,000,000 of other human beings, the Tsar, if he is a well-meaning and conscientious man, endeavours to carry out a benevolent policy through the agency of the Tchin. The Tchin was created by Peter the Great, and consists of a huge hierarchy of officials, departmentalised and centralised. Every department finds its head centre in the Tsar himself.

And now we see two sets of influences set to work which may easily account for the ruin of even such a beneficent work as the emancipation of the serfs however unchanged may remain the benevolent intentions of the autocrat. The Tchin is charged as its first duty to preserve the autocracy. Whatever else has to be sacrificed, that at least must remain safe. Whatever it is necessary to do for the preservation of the monarch's office from risks however minute must be done, and no distinction is recognised between the monarch's office and the monarch's person.

But this huge engine of government the Tchin is like the monster in Mary Shelley's romance "Frankenstein." It has got altogether out of the control of its supposed guider the Tsar. Even with the most perfect hierarchical arrangement, the limits of one man's time and strength and intelligence (especially when the last, as was the case in the late reign, was somewhat below the average), are not equal to governing so enormous a system. Corruption and departmental or local tyranny become not only prevalent but dominant. The Bureaucracy (the "Tchin") finds one of its readiest defences in the very fact that it is entrusted first and foremost with the protection of the Tsardom. For example, the Tsar could have no more valuable ally in checking the venality and corruption of his subordinates than a free press. But the Tchinovniks are masters of the situation; their reply is:—"If you allow a free press, tendencies inimical to the Tsardom may be fostered; we could then no longer answer for your safety." So there is no free press, and the Bureaucracy are saved the annoyance of awkward exposures of their abuses.

As Mr Stepniak wrote in an early number of "Free

Russia" (November 1890: article entitled "What can the Tsar do?"):—

"'Russia is governed by ten thousand *stolonachalniks*' (head clerks), was the cry of despair of Nicholas I., very characteristic from a man of his exceptional energy and activity. But since his time the population of the Empire has doubled, whilst the amount of administrative work devolving upon the central authorities has increased at least tenfold, telegraphs and railroads having made communication with the capital so much quicker and easier.

"Autocracy as a personal government has long ago ceased to exist in Russia. However unsatisfactory such a government might be, it has been practically supplanted by something still worse—the collective automatic despotism of a bureaucracy which has no heart to be appealed to, no brain, no lofty aims. Like a parasitic plant, it grows upon the body politic, sucking its vital strength and causing all its diseases.

"No change in the *personnel* can be of any avail. It is the system that must be changed. The Tsar may hit upon a gifted and honest Minister. But the amount of administrative work is so enormous in a country of the size of Russia, that even one single department cannot be carried on upon the centralised bureaucratic principle. The history of Russian administration offers us many instructive examples of well-intentioned, highly-talented Ministers, governors of regions and provinces, like Mouravieff of the Amour, whose best intentions were spoiled and whose energy proved powerless against the indifference, sluggishness, incapacity, and utter corruption of the hosts of subordinate officials they had to employ. On a smaller scale the experiment is reproduced and its shortcomings frankly avowed in private conversation by every high official of liberal views."

If this view is correct, to contend that Alexander III. and his father Alexander II. have been personally just and humane Tsars rather strengthens than weakens the case against the autocracy. If under them the defence of the institution implies the absence of good government,—if they, who to some extent have had the will, have not had the power to control the abuses of the tchinovniks,—what could be expected should they be succeeded by monarchs such as Peter II., who neglected the business of government that he might hunt all day; as Elizabeth, who immortalised her own cruelty by styling herself "the Clement"; or as Paul, the insane?

Having tried to realise the nature of the Russian autocracy we shall find it instructive to follow the fate, under its sway, of the serfs after their emancipation.

As we have seen the direct economic measures taken for their establishment as a free peasantry were not reversed; on the contrary, the policy seems persistently to have been followed up, and even afforded larger scope. It was not in their direct economic provisions that the arrangements for the emancipation of the serfs came into contact with the tchinovniks. The land division and the settlement of all the questions connected with it, were carried out by specially appointed commissions, apart from the regular bureaucracy. It is when we examine the sphere of *government* that centralised officialdom makes its first important entrance on the scene.

The "mir," or village commune, had a form of

government which had been handed down from the
Middle Ages through each intervening generation. It
was entirely independent of the official bureaucracy,
and would, we may suppose, fain have remained so.

The village assembly of heads of families had
supreme power; certain of the administrative functions
were entrusted to the head man or "starosta" who
was elected by it. No conception of government could
well be simpler, and the powers exercised were considerable. Practically the disposal and regulation of
all the communal property was in the hands of the
village assembly, and it also had police powers for
minor offences. It was very exceptional for any event
to arise in a peasant's life which required the assistance
of any other authority but that of the mir. Mr Stepniak,
in his "Russian Peasantry" (Vol. I., pp. 128, 134),
gives some interesting examples of communal judicial
decisions, founded on peasant custom apart from, and
sometimes in contradiction to the common law of the
land. If this primitive state of things could have
continued the peasantry would have remained, so
far as their everyday life went, tolerably free from
contact with the tchinovniks. But the governmental
organisation of the country has insisted upon the construction of connecting-links which have to a great
extent undermined the independence of the rural democratic communities.

The mirs or village communities are of very various
sizes. After the emancipation, the Government determined to introduce generally,—what had already under
Nicholas been established on the crown lands,—a unit
of area and government of more approximately equal
size, which should usually correspond with the ecclesiastical parish. Usually the *volost*, as this new governmental unit was called, includes a group of several

mirs, though how many go to compose it depends on their size. There are instances of very large mirs constituting volosts singly. Yet even the volosts show considerable disparity of size and population, the latter differing from a minimum of about 600, to a maximum of about 4000. The head man of the volost (the *starshina*), is, like the head man of the mir (the *starosta*) elected, but his authority is on a larger scale, and he exercises it more widely. It is in the starshina that the Government finds one of its principal instruments for garnering the peasantry to the bureaucratic mill, and it is through the starshina that the demoralising influence on the peasantry of official corruption exhibits itself. M. Leroy-Beaulieu speaks as follows on this subject:—

"One of the reasons of the tendency of the Starshinas to abuse the authority which is entrusted to them is that (contrary to the spirit of the Act of Emancipation) the *Ispravniks*, or officers of police, have gradually subdued these headmen chosen from amongst the agricultural class, to their direct influence, to such an extent that they are but too often reduced to the condition of being simply police agents or administrators. Some of the laws promulgated in the latter years of Alexander II. have contributed to this regrettable metamorphosis. Thus, in 1874, in opposition to the Act of Emancipation (on the provisions of which the administration has continually encroached little by little), a law conferred on the Ispravnik the right of fining or arresting the headmen of the village, or even of requesting the Provincial Governors to dismiss them. Such a measure cannot be calculated to make the humble functions of the headmen more honourable, or to attract the most capable of the peasantry to undertake them. The headmen of the volost subjected to the yoke of the lower representatives of official power have 'played up' to the weaknesses, the arrogance, and the cupidity of the tchinovniks on whom they find themselves dependent. Another reason of the abuses noticeable in the management of their own affairs by the peasantry, is that the volosts, which are in reality the administrative rural units, are of unwieldy extent. With such extended boundaries the headman can scarcely be personally known by those who elect him; it is more easy for him to elude their supervision; sometimes the only reason for his election has been pressure, or direction from the police. His functions, too, are becoming more complex and more absorbing; instead of devoting to them his spare time, the starshina tends to become a bureaucratic functionary, as venal and as tyrannical as the tchinovniks, who are not elected at all" (Leroy-Beaulieu, Vol. II., French edition, pp. 19, 20; English edition, p. 18).

Another source of corruption and demoralisation introduced still more intimately into the affairs of the peasantry is the *pissar*, or official clerk of the village community or of the volost. Mr Stepniak says ("Russian Peasantry," Vol. I. p. 157):—

"Now, in modifying the system of rural self-government the St Petersburg tchinovniks were inspired to transform this very modest and humble village elder into a diminutive tchinovnik, created in their own image and likeness. The task was not without its difficulties. The elder was as a rule deficient in the most essential qualification for his profession—he could not write! It was therefore necessary that he should be provided with a secretary, who could inscribe the paper to which he should affix his seal or his cross. This important person, the clerk, was generally a perfect stranger to the village, a man picked up from the streets. As the law must needs give him extensive powers, it was all the more desirable that he should be easily controlled.

"Our legislators proved equal to the task; for they blessed our villagers with a system of law-court proceedings which would do honour to much bigger places. To give some idea of their method, suffice it to say that the clerk of the volost is bound to supply his office with no less than sixty-five different registers, wherein to keep a record of the sixty-five various papers he has to issue daily, monthly, or quarterly. This was pushing their solicitude for the welfare of the countrymen rather too far, and taxing the clerk's powers rather too highly. In some of the larger volosts one man does not suffice for the task, and the peasants are compelled to maintain two, nay, even three clerks. It is needless to add that such a complication of legal business can in no way keep an adroit clerk in check nor prevent the abuse of his power. The opposite is rather the case. The figure cut by the pissar or clerk in the annals of our new rural local government is a most unseemly one indeed. In its earlier period it was decidedly its blackest point.

"The Government has undoubtedly had a hand in making the pissar such a disreputable character, by expressly prohibiting the engagement for this office of men of good education,—for fear of a revolution. All who have completed their studies at a gymnasium (college), much more those who have attended a high school, are precluded from filling this post. Only the more ignorant, those who have been expelled from college, or who have never passed further than through a primary school, have been trusted to approach the peasantry at such close quarters. Being generally self-seekers, and not particularly high-minded, they easily turned the peculiar position in which they were placed to their own advantage. The pissar, the interpreter of the law, and, more often than not, the only literate man in the district, could practically do whatever he chose. The elder, his nominal chief, in whom the word law inspired the same panic that it did in the breast of every other peasant, and who was quite bewildered by the bureaucratic complication of his new administrative duties, was absolutely helpless in the pissar's hands."

When we understand how completely the peasantry are in the hands of officers, who are themselves but tools of the police, we have the explanation of the frequent stories of tyranny by petty officialdom over the peasantry. One example from Mr Stepniak ("Russian Peasantry," Vol. I. p. 166) will illustrate my meaning:—

"The village communes have become for the country police a permanent source of income, often levied in a way which reminds one forcibly of the good old days of serfdom. Thus, in the Circular issued by the Minister of the Interior on March 29th, 1880, we find the significant confession that, 'according to the reports accumulated in the offices of the Ministry,' the country police-officers, profiting by their right to have one orderly to run their errands, were in the habit of taking from forty to fifty orderlies from the communes under their command, whom they used as their house and field labourers. In some cases the communes, instead of this tribute of gratuitous labour, paid a regular tribute of money (called obrok by former serfs), amounting in some provinces, according to the same authority, to from forty thousand to sixty thousand roubles a year per province."

The right-about-face of the governmental policy in relation to the communal liberties has neither been so decisive nor so well defined in point of time, as it has been in relation to some of the other reforms about which I shall speak later, but it has hardly been less efficaciously subversive. We have seen for example that the development of the policy of land redemption has been continued even during the past reign. Yet side by side with the second of the steps taken to make emancipation more wide-reaching, and more efficacious, we have another record of the gradual eating away of their communal rights. In this process we observe three marked steps. It will be remembered that about 1862-3 arbitrators were appointed called "mediators of peace" whose business it was to carry out the allotment of land to the peasantry, and to settle any questions that might arise between them and their old lords. At the outset the very best part of the nobility allowed themselves to be nominated to these positions. But about the year 1868, the first step in the downfall took place. M. Leroy-Beaulieu thus describes it:—

"When the great battle of Emancipation seemed to them ended and won, when the great

# THE BUREAUCRACY AND THE PEASANTS. 117

questions of the partitioning and redemption of the lands had for the most part been settled, the most disinterested and enthusiastic of these arbitrators of peace sent in their resignations in order to return to their old occupations. The moral and intellectual standard of these improvised magistrates, which during the first two or three years had been an unusually high one, rapidly degenerated, and they became as incapable, as venal, and as prone to illegalities as ordinary tchinovniks" (Leroy-Beaulieu, Vol. II. Book I. chap. iv. p. 49, French edition. This passage appears to be omitted in the English edition).

The second step was accomplished in 1874 when the Arbitrators of Peace were suppressed altogether, and their functions were entrusted to the police officials—the Ispravniks.

A ukaze of Alexander III. in 1889 marks the third step. By it were created a new class of officials entitled, "Chiefs of the Rural Cantons" or *Natchalniks*, who must be members of the local nobility and are at the same time made salaried functionaries of the State. They are nominated by the provincial governors, but the assemblies of the nobles have a consultative voice in the appointment.

"Everything that has to do with the administration, with the police, even with the finances of the village communities is thus referred to the new cantonal chiefs. So that the rural class finds itself subject to representatives of the nobility. The peasants retain their two-storied commune (obshchestvo and volost), they continue to elect their headmen of the village or volost (starosta and starshina); but before entering on their duties, those who have been elected by the communes must be confirmed in their office by the chief of the canton, and they may be dismissed from office by him. Further the *Zemskii Natchalnik* has the right of punishing the headmen (these mayors) without trial. By article 62 of the law of 1889 he can on his own authority, inflict the following punishments on them: surveillance, reprimand, fines not exceeding five roubles, arrest for not more than seven days. . . . . . The authority of the Zemskii Natchalnik extends over the mir, and over the communal assemblies, as well as over the communal authorities. Article 44 of the law for example provides that the rural chief shall preside on the occasion of the nomination of representatives from the peasant class to the provincial assemblies (the zemstvo assemblies); the presiding officers in the election offices are subject to his confirmation; in the course of the election any difficulties that arise are decided by him. The only thing the law forbids him to do is to cause himself to be elected by the peasants of his division. Neither the village assemblies nor the volosts can come to any decision without the concurrence of the natchalnik. In him the law reposes a right of veto on all their deliberations" (Leroy-Beaulieu, Vol. II. Book I. chapter iv., French edition, pp. 54, 55; English edition, pp. 52-3,—but the passage is curtailed).

Finally the natchalnik is empowered to punish by fine and imprisonment any disobedience to his legal commands. As it is left to him alone to pronounce on the legality of his own commands, this last law practically gives him unlimited power, at all events in all the smaller matters of everyday life. If such has been the undermining of the local liberties and privileges of the peasants from the political side have we any means of gauging the general result on the material well-being of the peasantry, of the Act of Emancipation, and the regulations for the redemption of their lands?

There is a concurrence of testimony that amongst the peasantry of to-day there does exist much misery; that for very many of them the material conditions are worse than before the Emancipation, for a very considerable proportion have got head over ears into debt to usurious money-lenders, and have pledged away the use of their lands and even of their personal labour for years to come.

This deplorable state of things is attributed by some to the improvidence, the laziness, and the drunkenness of the Russian peasant; by others the operation of these causes to any large extent is denied, and the poverty of the peasant is said to be caused by the inadequacy of the provision made for him in land, and the extortion and trickery of the officials of which he is the victim; a third view is that the conditions which contribute to his prosperity or the reverse, differ widely in the different regions; that whilst the peasant in the black earth zone has a large enough assignment of that fertile land to have a very good chance of making a living, the peasant of the north, though he is the possessor of a larger acreage, cannot make it suffice for his wants. There can I think be little doubt that inequalities of this kind exist, nor is there much question that the peasantry, connected as it is with rapacious officialdom by the links of the police-ridden starshina and pissar. suffers greatly from the rascality and tyranny of the tchinovniks. It is possible enough too that the peasant himself aggravates the hardness of his lot in many cases, by drunkenness; for, without taking the dark view of his character presented in Lanin's "Russian Characteristics," the general testimony is that, at all events at certain times, the peasant is greatly addicted to intemperance. It may be remarked however in connection with this point, that the average consumption of alcohol in Russia is less per head than in Western European countries, which seems to dispose of the idea that the Russian peasant spends his substance in riotous living, and ruins himself by excessive drinking. He seems however to be less prone to take his glass regularly day by day, and to prefer to concentrate his drinking, so that his festivals (which are numerous) become orgies. Thus whilst he drinks less, he becomes drunk more often than the working-man of other countries.

But are we able to form any broad and general idea of how the peasant's chances for material well-being (taking the Empire as a whole) compare before and after the Emancipation? I think we have data which may serve roughly to lead us to conclusions on this point.

We know that under the old serf corvée the usual arrangement was for the serf to work half his time for his lord, and half his time for himself. If then the total produce of an estate equalled a certain amount, half went to the lord and half to the peasantry. The object of the arbitrators in the settlement they made in 1863 and the following years, was as far as possible to leave this division of the produce unchanged. So far as their objects were carried out, half the produce generally speaking was handed by the peasants to the landlord in the form of rent, whilst half remained in their own hands to serve as their livelihood. There then followed the land redemption laws, which made the State instead of the landlords the recipient of rent payment. This probably made the actual payment to be made by the peasant less onerous, for though he had to pay equal to three years' rent down, the actual rent was reduced by one quarter. In some cases as we have seen, this reduction in the annual payment to be made was unaccompanied by the necessity for the initial payment of equal to three years' rent. But though we must I think conclude from this that so far as the direct demand for rent or for land-tax is concerned the peasant's position has improved rather than deteriorated, there is always going on an increase of the burdens they are called upon to bear for imperial and local taxation. According to M. Leroy-Beaulieu taxation proper now amounts to actually two-thirds as much as the redemption payments for the land. "The redemption tax," he says, "makes up about 60 per cent. of the burdens which press on the quondam serfs; the remainder goes to pay the impositions of the State and of local taxation" (Note, Vol. I., French edition, p. 565. This note is not given in the English edition).

The chief factor in the case as thus exhibited is the crushing weight of taxation, and if this view is correct, one hears without surprise of the gradual impoverishment of the peasantry, of their becoming the virtual serfs, almost the slaves indeed, of the money-lenders, and of many of them becoming landless men.

It would doubtless be a mistake to assume that the understanding about the corvée's only occupying half the time of the serfs under the old arrangements was rigidly adhered to. Though it may have been illegal for the lords to extort more from their serfs there was no one to keep their illegalities in check. Practically their actions had to be accepted without appeal. All that can be said therefore is, that enough was left to the serfs to furnish them with a bare "living wage," and when I use this expression I mean it to be interpreted pretty literally. Still it was then the lord's immediate interest to keep his serfs, as he would keep his cattle, not only alive, but as far as might be strong and healthy, and in good working condition, and these considerations may have acted more powerfully to preserve to the peasants their nominal rights than any legal status that they may have been supposed to possess. But this safeguard is no longer in operation. If the landlord finds that one set of peasants are worn out and in consequence of poverty and insufficient food unable to do a good day's work, he can cease to employ them, and take into his service others who have not been so unfortunate as their neighbours. There is therefore little probability of their being inclined to "temper the wind to the shorn lamb." If then under the old state of things, the peasantry could just scrape along, and if under the new state of things the financial burdens they have to bear for the benefit of the landlords are pretty much the same as they were then, how is it possible that taxation shall be immensely increased without reducing them, or a very large number of them to a state of ruin?

As to the general conclusion evidence which is pitilessly strong is furnished in the Blue-Book giving the results of the recent Royal Commission on labour so far as Russia is concerned (Foreign Reports, Vol. X., presented to Parliament, 1893; published 1894). We read there, for instance, that the extent of the holdings of the peasantry in land seems to have declined since 1861-6 by some 25 per cent. (Div. i., 4 d). In another part of the same Report we read: "Whilst the expenditure of the lower classes in Western Europe and the United States has universally increased during the last fifteen years, that of the Russian people has actually decreased. The consumption of both corn and textile fabrics has considerably diminished within this period." And again : "The increased exportation of grain from Russia is the result, not of increased production, but of diminished consumption, and of a diminished number of cattle " (Div. i., 1 d).

Meanwhile some gain has to be counted in having got free from the tyranny and caprice exercised in many instances by the old lords. It is something that it is no longer possible to write as Herzen wrote in the reign of Nicholas I.:—

> "Unfortunately the attributes of cruelty, corruption, and rage against the serfs and peasants are more unfailing with our nobility than honesty and honour. Of course, there is a minority of civilised landed proprietors who do not quarrel from early to late with their servants, who do not whip their peasants every day, but still also among them are some who are not too far from Soltikow and the American planters.
>
> "Entire martyrologies of the most frightful crimes are buried in the ante-rooms, the maid-servants' chambers, the villages, and the chambers of torture of the police; recollections of them ferment in many hearts, ripening through many generations for a bloody, hopeless revenge " ("My Exile," Vol. II. pp. 203-204).

The following may be read in amplification of the contents of this chapter :—

Leroy - Beaulieu, Vol. I. Book VII., and Vol. II. Book I. chaps. i., ii., and iv.

Mackenzie Wallace's " Russia," chaps. viii., xxix., xxx., xxxi., and xxxii. This book is referred to in future pages as Wallace.

Stepniak, "Russian Peasantry," Vol. I., page 114 to end of vol. ; " Royal Commission on Labour Foreign Reports, Vol. X. (Russia)."

# CHAPTER V.

PENELOPE'S WEB: AN ACCOUNT OF OTHER REFORMS UNDERTAKEN IN THE 'SIXTIES, AND THEIR SUBSEQUENT PARTIAL UNDOING.

## Chapter V.—*Contents.*

LOCAL Government: The *Zemstvo*-Assemblies for country districts established 1863; the *doumas* or municipal assemblies of large cities, 1870; curtailment of privileges granted to both these.

Legal reforms of 1863-4: privileges then granted gradually whittled away: privilege of electing justices of the peace withdrawn; the *cause célèbre* of *Véra Zasúlitch*.

Army Reform: short service, and education for the soldiers.

The press and its censorship: relaxations in the early years of Alexander II., followed by renewed rigour; the " Golos," the " Moscow Telegraph," the " Annals of the Country "; position of the provincial press.

# CHAPTER V.

PENELOPE'S WEB: AN ACCOUNT OF OTHER REFORMS UNDERTAKEN IN THE 'SIXTIES, AND THEIR SUBSEQUENT PARTIAL UNDOING.

### Local Government.

The Act of Emancipation for the serfs in 1863 was followed in the succeeding year by the establishment of local governing bodies called *Zemstvos*. Hitherto the only assemblies at all comparable to the newly-created bodies were the provincial assemblies of the nobles, and in any case the similarity of these was but very slight, for though with energetic self-assertion their meetings might have assumed some importance, they were practically of very little significance.

When the creation of the new bodies was ordained these were not superseded, but they continued to lead an uneventful and almost purely ceremonial existence contemporaneously with the local governing bodies set up by Alexander II. in 1863.

These are of two grades, the smaller (district) Zemstvo-Assemblies, and the Zemstvo-Assemblies for whole provinces or "Governments." The district Zemstvo-Assembly consists of representatives from three orders of electors, each of whom chooses a fixed proportion of the members. The three orders are (1) the landed proprietors who become electors in virtue of a property qualification; (2) the rural communes which elect their members not directly but through the volost assemblies, representing the peasants, and (3) the municipal corporations.

The Provincial Zemstvo-Assemblies are elected by the members of the District Zemstvo-Assemblies, each of the latter bodies being represented in the former by seven or eight members.

The functions of the Zemstvo-Assemblies are somewhat analogous to those of our own County Councils. They have to look after the maintenance of roads and bridges, to care for primary education, sanitary affairs, etc. Till recently too, they had to elect Justices of the Peace.

From the very first the Zemstvos have been handicapped in their monetary arrangements; the taxation that they have been empowered to impose has been but a small percentage of the total paid by the inhabitants, and even what has resulted from this limited power of taxation has not been at the free disposal of the Zemstvo-Assemblies. Certain matters, notably education, and measures for public health have been *permissive* objects of expenditure, but permissive only if sufficient funds were left to carry them out after the obligatory objects of expenditure had been fully attended to. These last were matters concerning the central government especially having to do with the army and police, quartering troops and the like, and they have swallowed up such a large proportion of the incomings from local taxation that in spite of the very general anxiety of the Zemstvo-Assemblies to look after education and other intimate needs of the peasantry, very scanty funds indeed have been left in their hands to carry out such objects.[1] Yet at the initiation of the

---

[1] The Statesman's Year Book (for 1893) says that of the local taxation 37 per cent. is spent in "obligatory" expenses. There

reform there was more possibility of advantageous effort in these directions than has since been the case.

In the matter of local government indeed as in other departments of State activity, the effect of the period of reaction has been experienced. The legislation of the last years of Alexander II. diminished the prerogatives of the Zemstvos. The Government was anxious above all things else to reinforce the authority of the provincial governors, to whose power it confided the confirmation or rejection of the election of the Justices of the Peace for rural districts nominated by the Zemstvo-Assemblies, so that the elections by them became nominal affairs.

Sometimes, as for instance in educational matters, the representative bodies are frustrated from headquarters. The Zemstvos have shown a most laudable desire to further primary education, and they have been energetic in founding primary schools in spite of the money difficulties I have spoken about. Probably Russia with all her deficiencies has no sorer need than this. M. Leroy-Beaulieu says:—

"During almost the whole of the second half of Alexander II.'s reign, the ministry of public education at the head of which was Count (Dmitri) Tolstoi was less bent on increasing the number of schools than on supervising and weeding out the *personnel* of the teaching staff. Here as everywhere else, political uneasiness and official anxieties took precedence of all other things. Dominated by the fear of seeing ways opened up for the revolutionary propaganda, Petersburg watched the humble foundations of the provincial Zemstvos

---

is available for hygiene and medical help only 23 per cent., and for education only 17 per cent.

with a distrustful eye. And so it came about that the minister closed most of the seminaries or normal schools for teachers that had been opened by the Zemstvos, and abolished supplementary courses of study which had been organised by them for vacations. The action taken by the central authority was of such a nature as to cause an august personage to say that all the efforts of the minister of public instruction were directed against popular education. Many a time in fact has the zeal of the Zemstvos and the Communes been paralysed by the bureaucracy of St Petersburg, whose timorous watchfulness is more awakened by their schools and their schoolmasters than by anything else. This suspicion has made the position of the unfortunate schoolteachers a miserable one, and by wounding the feelings of a great number of them and embittering them, has done much to encourage in many of them revolutionary aspirations, the very thing from which it is sought to preserve them. The action of informers encouraged by the minister's inspectors, and the petty harassments to which they are subjected at the hands of the police, have had the most grotesque and the most lamentable consequences. Let him be ignorant, lazy, and drunken, and the teacher may safely count on the indulgence of his superiors, who only treat with severity masters who have made themselves suspicious by their zeal in teaching the people" (Vol. II. Book III. chap. ii. p. 205, French edition; English edition, pp. 184-5).

The sessions of a Zemstvo-Assembly are short, and during the rest of the year its business is carried on by a permanent committee appointed by it. This permanent committee or board was formerly freely elected by the whole of the Zemstvo-Assembly, but the administration has recently usurped powers which materially alter the confidence with which the people can look upon the constitution of the board. The whole assembly can now only choose a certain number of *nominees* for this position from amongst their number, and the central government appoints a certain number of these to constitute the board. Sometimes it ventures on still more flagrant aggressions as for example when it recently appointed as chairman of a board a man who had sought election as one of the Zemstvo-Assembly's nominees but who had not been accorded sufficient votes for this. During the last reign too the franchise regulations for the election of the Zemstvo-Assemblies themselves underwent restriction, and the numerical direct representation of the peasantry was reduced.

In 1870 a system of municipal councils was introduced for the three great municipalities of St Petersburg, Moscow, and Odessa, and it was afterwards extended to other large towns. These Doumas as they were called differed in many particulars from the Zemstvo-Assemblies elected for departments or rural districts. The electors were not divided into orders according to their social grade, but into three orders dependent on the amount of taxes paid, classed in such a way that about a third of the total taxes was paid by each order whilst each order returned a third of the members. The effect of this was that the political power, such as it was, was largely concentrated in the hands of the richer classes. Thus in St Petersburg in 1873 whilst of the third order there were 17,479 electors, of the second there were only 887, and of the first only 224; but the 224 electors returned as many members to the council as the 17,479. As electoral meetings, and organisation beforehand were practically forbidden very little general interest was taken in the elections, and as there was no division of the cities into wards, and the nomination of candidates was carried on without limit, the actual returns were almost a matter of chance, except that the substantial merchant class generally obtained the preponderating position, which they used to further their class interests.

A new electoral law promulgated in 1892 has not improved matters, for whilst it has done away with the orders, it has effected this by stringently restricting the franchise which is now dependent on a high property qualification, so that those who before belonged to the third order of voters are for the most part disfranchised altogether.

The Municipal Councils are in some respects subject to the authority of the Provincial Zemstvos and can be taxed for certain purposes of mutual concern by them. This is not the case however in the two capitals and Odessa whose councils have themselves been created Municipal Zemstvos.

### Legal Reforms.

The years 1863 and 1864 saw the initiation of a third great reform. Besides setting in motion the first measures which were to lead to the emancipation of the serfs, and the establishment of Local Councils, the Government determined to reform judicial procedure. Russian law consists of a mass of imperial official pronouncements, ukázes as they are called. These are disconnected, often they are inconsistent one with another. Under Nicholas I. the accumulated mass of ukázes was reduced to a sort of code but without any attempt's being made to inform it with symmetry or to do away with its incongruous superfluities and contradictions. This "*Svod*" as it was called consisting of more than 60,000 articles, and divided into more than 1,500 chapters, remained and remains the working body of law for the Russian Empire, and in spite of its unwieldy dimensions is an improvement on the chaos that obtained before its compilation.

It was to a reform of the way in which the laws of Russia should be administered, not to a remodelling of the way in which they should be presented, that the ministers of Alexander II. directed their attention in 1864. They aimed to effect the separation of the judicial from the administrative power so as to secure the independence of the judges whether in the lower or the higher courts. They aimed too at making all subjects of the Tsar equal in the eye of the law, to secure publicity in the administration of justice, and even in the participation of the people themselves in that administration by the introduction of the jury system and in the creation of elective Justices of the Peace, who were to be chosen by the Zemstvo-Assemblies in the country, and by the municipal corporations in the town.

We cannot say, any more than we can in the cases of the other two great contemporaneous reforms, that of all these lofty ideals nothing at all remains extant of permanent gain. M. Leroy-Beaulieu indeed gives it as his opinion that whilst corruption has found a nidus in the communal tribunals where peasant custom rather than law is still administered, in the reformed courts venality has almost entirely disappeared (Vol. II. Book IV. chap. ii. (French edition), p. 314). One is almost surprised to hear that in the opinion of so competent a judge so great an advantage has been secured, when one gathers from his pages how the reforms of 1864 have gradually been whittled away.

Alexander III. by creating the Cantonal Chiefs brought functionaries into being who were simultaneously invested with administrative and judicial powers and so far as the rural districts were concerned the principle of keeping them separated was abandoned. Again ministers are now careful not to appoint as judges men of independent mind; these excite such distrust that they are kept out in the cold and the fact that when good appointments are to be made their claims are put on one side makes them the readier to give ear to revolutionary politicians. The irremovability of the judges too has been tampered with by a legal device, for under the pretence of appointing them *on probation* they are kept for many years without their positions' being confirmed, so that a very small minority actually enjoy the privileges of irremovability. Other guarantees of justice are withdrawn by the placing of all political offences, and more recently all cases in which any official is concerned in connection with his duties, in a category apart from those tried by the ordinary tribunals and the ordinary law, and in withdrawing them from the judgment of a jury, and still more flagrantly by the action of the political police who have the power when they think that even these exceptional tribunals are not drastic enough for their ends, in political cases to imprison or exile persons merely on suspicion or simply because they are obnoxious, by what is called "administrative process," entirely without trial and without any opportunity of proving themselves innocent. The resemblance to the hated "Lettres de cachet" of the ante-Revolution period in France is very close.

In 1889 a new ukáze was issued withdrawing several categories of cases from the cognisance of juries.

## LEGAL REFORMS. 135

Another popular guarantee of justice has been tampered with by depriving the Zemstvo-Assemblies of the right of electing the Justices of the Peace. The establishment of popularly elected Justices of the Peace was perhaps the most notable of the judicial reforms. These Justices had under their jurisdiction all petty criminal cases punishable up to a certain limit,[1] and also minor[2] civil cases. Their establishment at once wrought an enormous change in the conditions of Russian life. Like the so-called Arbitrators of Peace, the first persons who allowed themselves to be nominated to these offices were of an exceedingly high type. It soon became understood by the peasantry, and resentfully realised by those who had till lately been their lords, that before these tribunals one man was regarded as absolutely the equal of another in legal rights. There was probably nothing else which did so much as this to make the peasantry realise that they had entered upon the full dignity of free human beings.

Unfortunately the high type of the *personnel* of the magistracy was not maintained; it degenerated in a similar way to that in which the *personnel* of the Arbitors of Peace had done. Still the institution remained, and was fairly well administered. But in 1879 a ukáze was issued which instructed the provincial governors to give a confidential report on the character of those nominated for the magistracy by the provincial assemblies. The recommendations of these secret reports have hardly ever been disregarded so that practically the nomination of these magistrates has since then rested with the Governors of the Provinces. The recent years at the end of the past reign have

---

[1] Three months' imprisonment.
[2] Where not more than the value of 500 roubles was in question.

seen the completion of this retrograde change of policy; the Government has, except in the two capitals and in some large towns, swept away this popularly elected magistracy which has done so much for Russia, and has on the whole worked so well, and has superseded it by nominees of its own called District Commanders.

Some curious features of the administration of justice in Russia were illustrated in the trial in 1878 of Vera Zasúlitch. I translate the account given of the matter by M. Leroy-Beaulieu:—

"It was the last political trial[1] adjudicated upon publicly and with a jury. The high social position of the victim of the attempt; the sex, the youthfulness, the coolness, and the exaltation of mind of the prisoner; the daring eloquence of her counsel; the evidence of the witnesses, which almost made it appear that it was the prefecture of police that was on its trial; the jury's unexpected verdict; everything even to the sudden disappearance at the door of the courthouse of the woman who had been acquitted, combined to throw a romantic glamour over this memorable trial. It will be remembered how the affair arose. A young Russian woman living on the banks of the

---

[1] Vera Zasulitch and (five years earlier) Serguis Natchaiev were brought before the ordinary tribunals because the Government refused to recognise the prisoners as political offenders and wished them to be considered ordinary malefactors. Moreover in the case of Natchaiev extradition from Switzerland was only obtained on the Russian Government's formally pledging itself to treat the prisoner as a non-political offender. The case of Leo Deutch extradited by one of the German principalities in 1884 is similar. When the authorities have professedly regarded offences as political they have always tried them (if any trial at all has been vouchsafed) before the exceptional tribunals created for the purpose, in which of course juries have no part.

Volga three or four hundred leagues from the capital had read in a newspaper that a political prisoner not personally known to her had been flogged by order of General Trepov, then Prefect of Police at St Petersburg. Like a new Charlotte Corday the girl constituted herself the avenger of humanity. What she did was to journey half across Russia to mete out punishment to this Prefect who could not control his temper; she obtained an interview with him, fired at him with a revolver wounding him seriously. There was no doubt about the crime's having been committed, or about its having been premeditated; the admissions of the prisoner made this perfectly clear. Yet in spite of the efforts of the prosecution the jury acquitted amidst the applause of the audience and of the crowd outside the court."

That is M. Leroy-Beaulieu's account of the matter. (Vol. II. Book IV. chap. vi., French edition, pp. 409-10; English edition, pp. 374-5). The story can also be read in Mr Stepniak's "Underground Russia."

The case is interesting as showing in the first place a strong sense that the personal dignity at all events of political prisoners should be respected. The after results too are characteristic. The verdict was quashed and Miss Zasulitch would doubtless soon have found herself dealt with by the secret police had she not succeeded in escaping to Switzerland.

The action of the girl was certainly heroic and that of the jury hardly less so. Yet an attempted assassination followed by the return of a false verdict in the teeth of the evidence does not at first sight seem a very ennobling effort in the direction of securing popular liberties. Yet in its essence it may have been informed with very much the same spirit that caused Hampden to refuse to pay ship-money, or dictated the acquittal of the seven bishops, for it was felt to be a notable protest against a tyranny which thought itself perfectly secure.

### Army Reform: Short Service, and Education for the Soldiers.

I must not omit to mention another reform of this period; comparatively little is heard of it, but it has had far-reaching results. General Count Dmitri Miliutin was appointed Assistant Minister of War in July 1860, and in June 1862 became Minister of War, retaining the post during the rest of Alexander II.'s reign. He reformed the Russian army, introducing general conscription and short service. Nicholas had extended the period of service to twenty-five years, but Miliutin introduced annual levies, nominally for eight years' service, but the soldiers had in reality to serve not more than five, and sometimes as short a period as three years. The commissariat was reformed and some of the barbarous corporal punishments of the old regulations were abolished. But what we should perhaps note more than any other point is that every subaltern officer was compelled to instruct the men of his own company or battalion in reading, writing, and arithmetic. By this administrative act, the Russian army became a vast institution for primary education for the male population, one that affects far more than the schools through which only a certain proportion of the peasants have passed as children. The percentage of men who know how to read and write when they leave the ranks of the army is materially higher than amongst the recruits.

One is glad to know that this reform is not one of those which has been subsequently nullified, so that in this instance the title of my chapter (" Penelope's Web ") does not apply.

## The Press and its Censorship.

M. Leroy-Beaulieu, speaking of the control exercised by the Government over the Russian press at the end of the reign of Nicholas, says: "Nothing in Europe equalled the severity of the regulations which had been in force since 1828 unless it were the Roman *index* before the Italian Revolution (for the Russian autocracy being a lay authority had never exercised so much vigour against speculative thought and science as against political writings). Every single periodical, pamphlet, or book, whether in Russian or in a foreign language, whether ancient or modern, was submitted to the censorship before it was published. Ordinary censorship alone seemed insufficient; a censorship of two or three degrees was contrived. In 1848 a superior committee was appointed whose business it was to censure the censorship. Side by side with the ordinary censorship the Emperor Nicholas appointed special censorships whose business it was to watch over each branch of human activity; one of these was the military censorship (abolished by Alexander II.), another was the ecclesiastical censorship which is extant to-day, and conferred as it naturally is on ecclesiastics, extends their jurisdiction to all works dealing with the clergy and religion" (Vol. II. Book V. chap. i., French edition of 1893, pp. 479 and 480; English edition, pp. 438 to 439).

With the press censorship the same sequence of phenomena is observable as with so many other things. Once more it is Penelope's Web. Strides are taken in the direction of a liberal and enlightened policy in the early reforming years of Alexander II., followed in the next decade by reactionary measures which were made more stringent in the deadening years of the last reign.

Under Alexander II., with the exception of the ecclesiastical censorship, the various *departmental* censorships were abolished and in 1865 the "preventive" censorship (that is censorship before publication) was done away with. This last relaxation however took effect in the capitals only and even there only for works which attained a certain importance in size, viz. more than ten printed sheets. Further a copy of each book had to be put in the hands of the censors some days before publication, and although it was not necessary to await their consent before the issue of the book, if in their opinion it were objectionable in tendency they might order the edition to be seized. But the important concession granted by the ukáze of 1865 was that such a seizure was to be confirmed or quashed *by the law-courts*.

In 1872 appeared the first of the inevitable reactionary ukázes. Decision as to whether the publication should be suppressed was taken out of the hands of the law-courts and the matter was henceforth to be settled by a committee of ministers who were to have sovereign authority over thought and pen, and were to pronounce their judgments without trial or debate. From them there was no appeal.

The periodical press of the two capitals is for the most part relieved from preventive censorship if it submits itself to what penalties may be adjudged suited to its trespasses against the views of the authorities. These penalties are very efficient for the end in view. There is a system of warnings; after three of these a paper is liable to total suppression. Falling short of this capital punishment, newspapers are suppressed for periods of three, six, or twelve months, or they are subjected to heavy indirect fines by being forbidden to print advertisements for a specified time, or they are not allowed to be distributed by sale to any but their regular subscribers.

Even English readers used to be familiar with the name of the great Russian newspaper, the *Golos*. This is what M. Leroy-Beaulieu says concerning its suppression :—

"The *Golos* was a periodical which in any other country one would have been tempted to take for a semi-official publication, but the story even of this paper was but one long series of warnings and suspensions. M. Kraievsky's organ had been condemned to silence many times during the latter years of Alexander II., and in July 1881 it was once more suspended for six months by Alexander III. When it once more saw the light in 1882 its second number was assailed by a warning, and it was forbidden to be sold in the streets. In 1883 it was again suspended and this time it was not allowed to come to life again. According to the regulations a journal that does not appear for a whole year loses the right to reappear altogether. In order not to be sacrificed to this rule M. Kraievsky had had specially printed for the censorship a single number of the *Golos* made up entirely of extracts from the *Official Messenger* and the *Moscow Gazette*. The precaution did not save the existence of the fated sheet. The Minister of the Interior had the management of the *Golos* warned that it must not appear again unless the proprietorship and the editorship passed into the hands of people agreeable to the Ministry. The plan was to turn the liberal journal of St Petersburg into a branch organ of M. Katkoff's *Moscow Gazette*. Offers were made to buy it up. The *Golos* which was then the organ that enjoyed perhaps the widest circulation in the country, represented considerable capital. M. Kraievsky its owner, preferred losing all to giving it over to his political opponents" (Vol. II. Book V. chap. i., French edition of 1893, p. 485; English edition, pp. 443-4).

In 1882 appeared a further edict. For the suppression of any publication all that was now necessary was the concurrent decision of the ministers of the Interior, of Justice, and of Education, and of the Procurator of the Holy Synod. By this committee of four the *Moscow Telegraph* was suppressed in 1883, and in 1884, *The Annals of the Country*, edited by M. Soltykov. Both of these were important publications. The *Moscow Telegraph* was the most popular, advanced, and talented of any of the daily papers that have been issued in Russia, and *The Annals of the Country* was the journal which represented advanced thought in politics, philosophy, literature, and art.[1]

The early years of the last reign saw other extensions of the power of the Executive over the press equally deplorable. Thus at certain times the Governors-general who under the dictatorship of Loris Melikov were to suppress Nihilism were allowed to suppress any publications "whose tendencies were recognised as being dangerous."

One very curious result of all this tyranny against the press has been the development of a particular oblique style of writing in the Russian pressman, so

---

[1] Mr Noble says ("The Russian Revolt," page 234) that the tales in this journal were not only witty but immoral, the object of the editor (who was also their author) being "to show that so long as political topics were avoided almost any excesses might be indulged in." The suppression which followed was not on this account, but for the "dangerous" political opinions of the *Annals* "and the alleged connection of members of its staff with secret societies."

that anyone accustomed to write much for the Russian newspapers finds it a little difficult when writing without restraint to put down perfectly directly what he means to say. Like the protective colours observed by Darwin in small birds which shield them in some measure from the observation of birds of prey, the writers have acquired a manner of composition which sometimes enables them to escape the Censor-Vulture. M. Leroy-Beaulieu says :—

"No country has pushed further the art of making ingenious allusions which direct people's thoughts to the points about which the journalists dare not write directly; of making insinuations which cause people to suspect to exist the very things the existence of which is called in question; or giving hints which lend force or point to what is actually expressed" (Vol. II., Book V., chap. i., French edition of 1893, p. 475. Compare translation given in English edition, p. 434).

For foreign languages there is a special censorship, and many of the foreign publications and books admitted to Russia are mutilated by the scissors, or disfigured by the blacking-brush used to blot out those parts to which objection is taken.

But the chief rigours of the censorship for non-Russian languages have been reserved for those spoken within the Empire whose use is deemed to cherish nationalistic dreams inimical to the unity of the whole country; notably the Polish, the Lithuanian, and the Ukrainian (or Malo-Russian) languages. Whole branches of the literatures of these have been entirely suppressed.

The provincial newspapers printed in Great Russia are with one or two exceptions reduced to a state of contemptible **impotence** and insignificance. This it is not hard to understand when one remembers that they have not (like most of the papers of the two capitals) been relieved from the preventive censure. The vexations and delays of the system must indeed be hard to endure. Censors are only found in large towns and the editors have to await their good pleasure before they receive back their proof-sheets. If any difficulty arises the question must be referred to a censorship committee. Of these there are only eight or nine in the whole Empire, so the delays involved in a reference to one of them may easily be imagined.

I must again quote M. Leroy-Beaulieu. His pregnant criticism of the state of things is:—

"This bondage of the provincial press is one of the principal obstacles in the way of the reforms' becoming practically efficacious, and in the way of any control of government by public opinion. It is one of the things which deprives the new administrative self-government, the Zemstvos and the Municipalities, of much of their usefulness. Again here we have one of the causes which account for the ignorance of the Russians of the capital, of highly placed functionaries, and of the Government itself, concerning what is going on in the interior of the Empire. How can the evils from which the people suffer, the abuses of the Administration, the illegalities of local authorities, be brought to the knowledge of the higher authorities by a press which has hardly more independence than the telegrams or reports of the governors? In Russia the Provinces are dumb; the weakly organs which essay to speak in their name have nothing about them either of liberty or spontaneity; their mechanical language tells nothing to anybody" (Vol. II. Book V. chap. ii., French edition of 1893, pp. 503-4; English edition, p. 459).

The following may be read in amplification of the contents of this chapter:—

*Local Government:*—Leroy-Beaulieu, Vol. II. Book III.; Wallace, chaps. ix. and xiv.

*Legal Reforms:*—Leroy-Beaulieu, Vol. II., first six chaps. of Book IV., especially chap. vi.; Wallace, chap. xxxiii.; Stepniak, "Underground Russia," pages 116-126.

*Censorship:*—Leroy-Beaulieu, Vol. II., first two chaps. of Book V.; George Kennan, "Blacked Out," *Century Magazine,* May 1890.

# CHAPTER VI.

## RELIGIONS AND RELIGIOUS PERSECUTIONS.

## Chapter VI.—*Contents.*

THE official theory of "toleration"; how its interpretation has varied with the reforming and the retrograde periods; effect on the Jews, Roman Catholics, "Uniats"—Dominant characteristics of the Greek Orthodox Church—Schism of the Raskolniks in 17th century — Growth of the sects; mysticism; interesting religious ideas—Influence of German Protestantism; sects of the Dukoburi, the Molokani, the Stundists—The policy of extermination applied to the Stundists and to the Jews.

# CHAPTER VI.

### RELIGIONS AND RELIGIOUS PERSECUTIONS.

WE have now spoken of the reforms attempted in the status of the peasantry, in the system of local administration, and in administration of the law; we have seen how to a great extent they have proved abortive; and we have observed how first with the rise, and then with the ebb of the tide of reform there has contemporaneously been an increase and a diminution of the amount of freedom enjoyed by the press, by public meetings, and in general in public and even in private speech. It will here be a convenient place to discuss what amount of religious toleration is exercised in Russia and how much truth there is in the allegations of ruthless and cruel persecutions. Difficult as it is to get reliable information on Russian affairs in general, on no subject does there at first sight seem to be so much discrepancy in the evidence offered as on this. On the one hand we are told that nowhere does such complete toleration exist as in Russia; walk down the Nevskoi Prospekt in St Petersburg and in that one street you will find the great Kazan (Orthodox) Cathedral, a Lutheran Church, a Dutch Church, a Roman Catholic Church, a Jewish Synagogue, and a Mosque. "Does this" it is asked "look like intolerance?" The theory by which the Russian ecclesiastical authorities are supposed to be actuated is that all shall be tolerated in the profession of their religions whatever they may be, so long as they are the creeds of their fathers, but that no change from any religion to another is allowed. There is however one important exception to this rule, for the Greek Orthodox Church is enjoined to make as many converts amongst those professing other religions as it is able. Now observe that this theory of "tolerance" would have justified the ruthless stamping out in the Catholic countries of Europe of the budding Protestant Reformation of three and a half centuries ago, and in fact does justify the Russian Government in their own eyes, in their cruel persecution of the Molokani, the Stundists, and other reforming sects of South Russia. The Stundist persecution is directly instigated by the Holy Synod, and is entirely consistent with the officially avowed theories.

For a fairly frank exposition of the Russian Governmental theory of "toleration" the reader may for example be referred to an article by Madame Novikoff in the *Contemporary Review* for February 1889. It is a review of Mr Stead's "Truth about Russia" and is called "A Cask of Honey with a Spoonful of Tar," the "cask of honey" being the somewhat fulsome account Mr Stead gives of the Russian Government, the "spoonful of tar" the gentle remonstrance he ventures upon with regard to the religious persecution. Madame Novikoff boldly asserts :—

"Russia tolerates all religions and prosecutes at law only sects who propagate immoral and criminal doctrines, which would not be permitted, in fact, in any part of the world where Christian morality is accepted as the basis of legislation.

"Russia established perfect religious liberty long before many of her civilised neighbours."

This sounds well; but next we are enlightened as to what the expression "perfect religious liberty" means:—

"In England and in America, where the Christian faith is 'splittered' into a hundred sects, it may be not only possible but necessary to allow liberty of religious competition, or propagandism. The sporting propensities of those countries discloses itself even in the field of religion. With us it is not so. Our church prays daily for the unity of all the churches. . . . We consider every schism a plague whose infection has to be stamped out. We have no hankering, I assure you, after the ideal of possessing as many creeds as there are sign-posts. . . . As for us, we are content with one absolute Truth, based on the Gospels, and explained by the seven Œcumenical Councils. . . . Before even the duty of defending the frontier from invasion of hostile armies, is the duty of defending the orthodox faith from the assaults of sects and heresies. . . . Hence, while we permit every man to practise freely in Russia whatever creed he professes, we cannot permit attempts to pervert others from the Orthodox faith.

"In Russia you may be Protestant, Catholic, or Mahommedan. You may practise your rites, and worship God in your own way, and also bring up your children in your own creed; but in mixed marriages, with a Greek Orthodox, the law of the country insists that the children shall belong to the established faith. Besides, you must keep your hands off other people's creeds and other people's children. . . . Nowadays every quack soul-saver thinks himself entitled to pervert our simple-minded peasants, by filling their hearts with all kinds of nonsense, in the name of religious liberty. Now, why should there be more liberty given to spiritual quacks than to medical quacks? . . . Imagine a splendid hall, brilliantly illuminated with numerous electric lamps. Suddenly a grotesque tatterdemalion rushes in with a small tallow candle, which he insists is far superior to the electric installation! Surely, it will be his own fault if he is summarily shown the door."

The governmental theory of tolerance thus expounded, imperfect as it is, would seem to afford some sort of protection to believers in the older forms of religion. Unfortunately it is necessary to distinguish between the theory and actual practice in this matter. The Jew has always been made more or less of an exception, and has not enjoyed the privileges accorded to members of other non-orthodox bodies; he has been treated sometimes with less, sometimes with more completeness as a species of religious outlaw.

There have been comparatively favourable and comparatively unfavourable times for religious liberty. During the last two reigns the periods which have been progressive or retrograde in this respect, have corresponded pretty much to the political reforming and retrograde periods.

For the Jew, as for the dissenting sects of South Russia, the beginning of Alexander II.'s reign brought some cheer, and in each case before his death the prospect was excessively gloomy. But the full force of the pitiless storm they have all alike been compelled to pass through was reserved for the past reign, and the principal instrument to compass their misery has been Pobiedonoststev, appointed Procurator of the Holy Synod soon after the accession of Alexander III. Of the details of the persecutions it will be necessary to say a few words later on, but here we must only pause to remark that besides the intensity of the measures for the suppression of heresy, Pobiedonoststev has still further trenched upon the area supposed to be covered by the official theory of toleration. The Roman Catholics are not left unmolested, more especially the Roman Catholics of Poland. The latest instance of outrage on a large scale occurred in the autumn of 1893; it is typical of very much that had taken place before. In the middle of October of that year a terrible onslaught was made on a congregation who passively resisted the arbitrary closing of their church, in a small town near the Russo-Polish frontier (Krózhe). It was cleared by the Cossacks; at least 20 were killed by them, 100 were wounded, the remnant was pursued across a neighbouring river, where a large additional number were drowned. To a milder extent, too, many of the Lutherans of the Baltic Provinces and of Finland are now sharing in the persecution.

Pobiedonoststev was anticipated in his policy in the preceding reigns by Count Protasov and by Count Dmitri Tolstoi. An instance is furnished of the drift of the influence of these men in the treatment experienced by the Uniats.

This sect had its origin in 1595. Its characteristic in the first instance, was that it retained with but very slight alteration the ritual of the Greek Orthodox Church, but at the same time, acknowledged the supremacy of the Pope of Rome. It formed a very curious connecting-link between the two great Churches.

In 1838-9[1] (Nicholas's reign) signatures were ex-

---

[1] For a full account of the earlier episode see in "Distinguished Persons in Russian Society," translated from the German by F. E. Bunnett, Chapter VII., entitled "Count Protassoff."

torted by brutal intimidation from 760 out of 1057 of the Uniat clergy on strictly Russian (as opposed to Polish) soil, for reunion with the Orthodox Greek Church, and the Uniat Church in those parts was immediately completely destroyed. In Alexander II.'s reign, however, there still remained more than a quarter of a million of Uniats in Poland.

After a good deal of harassment of these people, chiefly on minor points of ritual, in 1875 another bogus petition (signatures to which were obtained by fraud and force, and even then representing but a small fraction of this religious body), was arranged, and it was again represented that by means of this petition the Uniats were themselves praying to be received into the bosom of the Greek Church. An Act officially binding them to the dominant Church was issued, but thousands refused to accept it. Cossacks were quartered upon them, and their subsequent treatment is thus described by M. Leroy-Beaulieu:—

"Everything was put in operation against them; fines, imprisonment, flogging, confiscation of their property, exile, and torture—the only thing that was spared was the scaffold. The refractory priests were ruined and exiled. Many hundreds of laymen were transported, some to the province of Kherson, some to that of Orenbourg on the confines of Asia; those who have not recanted are there still. Their families are often separated from them, the father being interned in one country, the wife and children in another. The lands of these rebels have either been confiscated or sold up by auction. As to the old Uniats who have been left in their country, if they do not observe the orthodox feast-days, or receive the sacraments from the hands of the orthodox priests, they are fined.

Their Church has been abolished, and they are forbidden to join the Roman Church. They must satisfy their religious needs at the official fountain; it does not matter that to them its waters seem poisoned; of the neighbouring spring, the only one that they believe to be pure, they are forbidden to drink" (Leroy-Beaulieu, Vol. III. Book IV. chap. ii., French edition, pp. 607-8).

The antipathy that the Uniats feel to their enforced embodiment in the Greek Church is shown by the widespread refusal amongst them to allow their children to be baptized by the Orthodox priests. The children accordingly go altogether unbaptized, and are thus, according to their belief, placed in the gravest jeopardy.

It is to be observed that in the course of the three centuries during which this sect has existed, they have drawn closer and closer to the Roman Church, so that, although at its inception they had more in common with the Eastern than with the Western communion, the reverse is now the case.

Now although, as we have already seen, and as we shall see still further, the portions of the Russian people who are not of the Orthodox body are very considerable, the great majority of them belong to the Greek Church. What then strike one as the dominant characteristics of the Church to which others are compelled to assimilate themselves by such means as are described above? So far as I can ascertain, nothing is so striking about it as its utter spiritual lifelessness; its whole energy is concentrated on securing accurate, punctual, and mechanical ceremonial observance. This for example is how it strikes a Scotchman who has devoted a good deal of his life to the study of Russia.

"Primitive mankind," he says, "is everywhere and always disposed to regard religion as simply a mass of mysterious rites which have a secret magical power of averting evil in this world and securing felicity in the next. . . . The tendency to regard religion as a mass of ceremonies which have a magical rather than a spiritual significance . . . is only too general amongst the Russian people. It must be admitted that the Russian people are in a certain sense religious. They go regularly to church on Sundays and holy-days, cross themselves repeatedly when they pass a church or Icon, take the Holy Communion at stated seasons, rigorously abstain from animal food—not only on Wednesdays and Fridays, but also during Lent and the other long fasts—make occasional pilgrimages to holy shrines, and, in a word, fulfil punctiliously all the ceremonial observances which they suppose necessary for salvation. But here their religion ends" (Wallace, chap. iv. pp. 62-63).

The first great secession from the Orthodox Church took place in the reign of Alexis; and if it furnishes additional proof of how great stress the members of the Eastern Church lay upon ceremony—it also gives evidence of the grim earnestness with which these superstitious beliefs are held by some parts of the community, and shows the willingness to undergo unlimited suffering for conscience' sake which continues to the present day to enlist our sympathy and admiration.

The following is the account Mr (now Sir Donald) Wallace gives of the matter :—

> "When the art of printing was introduced, it became necessary to choose the best texts of the Liturgy, Psalter, and other religious books, and on examination it was found that, through the ignorance and carelessness of copyists, numerous errors had crept into the manuscripts in use. . . .

## THE OLD BELIEVERS. 157

Certain irregularities had likewise crept into the ceremonial. The chief of the clerical errors lay in the orthography of the word 'Jesus,' and the chief irregularity in the ceremonial regarded the position of the fingers when making the sign of the cross. In order to correct these errors, the celebrated Nikon, who was then Patriarch, ordered all the old liturgical books and the old Icons to be called in and new ones to be distributed; but the clergy and the people resisted. Believing these 'Nikonian novelties' to be heretical they clung to their old Icons, their old missals, and their old religious customs as the sole anchors of safety which could save the Faithful from drifting to perdition. In vain the Patriarch assured the people that the change was a return to the ancient forms still preserved in Greece and Constantinople. . . . An Anathema, formally pronounced by an Ecclesiastical Council against these Nonconformists, had no more effect than the admonitions of the Patriarch. They persevered in their obstinacy, and refused to believe that the blessed saints and holy martyrs who had used the ancient forms, had not prayed and crossed themselves aright. . . . The decree of excommunication pronounced by the Ecclesiastical Council placed the Nonconformists beyond the pale of the Church, and the civil power undertook the task of persecuting them" (Wallace, chap. xx. pp. 308-9).

The persecution became particularly severe during Peter the Great's reign, and in the succeeding period. According to official accounts, between 1719 and 1736 more than 440,000 men were dispersed in every direction. Their flight into forests and deserts was followed by the soldiery who had orders to seize them, knout them, and throw them into prison. The Old Believers took refuge in wholesale suicide, their method being to shut themselves into large buildings and fire them, or to make a large fire and then jump into the flames many hundreds together. In 1679, 1700 thus threw themselves into the fire; in 1680, in one province alone 1920 peasants burnt themselves. In 1687, 2700 shut themselves up in a convent and immolated themselves. In spite of this self-destruction *en masse*, communities survived, the most important being amongst the lakes of North Russia. (See " La Russie Sectaire " par N. Tsakni.)[1]

The Old Believers themselves split into different sects; partly through their influence too, but largely independent of it, there sprang up a number of other sects. The rites and beliefs of these were in many cases extremely fantastic—dancing, leaping, flagellation, and self-mutilation being mingled with mysticism. On the other hand, in some instances religious ideas of great interest appear. Thus one sect held as its fundamental idea that in each man divinity lay hidden. Each in his degree may contain God, just as Christ contained Him altogether. Consequently this sect is called that of The Christs, and one of their principal rites is mutual adoration, for adoration of man they say is adoration of the image of God.

The filiation of the independent religious sects of South Russia is a blend of descent from such ideas as these and the influence of German Protestantism. In consequence of the neighbourhood of Poland and Austria, and especially as a result of the influence of numerous colonies of German Baptists scattered through the country, the ideas of Luther and of Huss have penetrated there. Nevertheless it would be a mistake to regard the South Russian Dissenters as

---

[1] This book is referred to in future pages as " Tsakni."

purely Protestants, and to hold, as an extremely able little book about the Stundists ("The Stundists: The History of a great Religious Revolt") does hold, that they owe their origin entirely and exclusively to the influence of the Germans. The descent of many of their ideas can be traced from the older Nonconformist bodies of the North, though there has in one respect been a sweeping reaction from the ritualism of the older religions with their unyielding formalism. In the teaching of this group of sects on the contrary "is shown an endeavour to do away with every kind of formalism and ceremony; and a predisposition to follow after a religion in some respects unprecedentedly concerned with spiritual and moral matters only" (Tsakni).

Take for example the sect of the Dukhoburi (the word means seekers after the spirit of religion). Their fundamental dogma is "the abrogation of all ceremony and religious pomp—and the insistence on the worship of God 'in spirit and in truth' of the 'spiritual God whom each one bears within him in his heart.' Hence their tendency to recognise divinity in man himself. The Dukhoburi say that God is inseparable from man, and dwells constantly within him" (Tsakni). Here we have the idea of The Christs repeated. "As to the army and war they look upon the latter as cruel work, bloody and impermissible; accordingly they steadfastly refuse either to enter military service or to take the oath, considering it an act opposed to human dignity."

"As a matter of course, their anti-governmental tendencies have brought down serious persecutions on their heads on the part of the Government." In the times of Catherine II., Paul, and Alexander I. they were comparatively leniently treated, but "in the reign of Nicholas I. the Government set itself energetically to work to combat the heresy and completely uproot it. Orders were issued to banish to Siberia or to make soldiers of such of the peasants as embraced the schism. The sectarians' propaganda in Siberia was an immense success; it carried away the soldiery and even the prisoners, and was the despair of the Siberian authorities. Then the most prominent amongst their teachers were sent to the most far-removed mines; a good many of the sectarians too were exiled to the Caucasus." They were pillaged by the officials and settled in strange lands under conditions incompatible with existence. Their fate would indeed have been a dreadful one had it not been that the Prince of Mingrelia, whose country had to a great extent been depopulated by war, knowing the excellent qualities of these people as colonists, offered to settle them in his country under very favourable conditions. The Russian Government gave its consent.

"This," writes Tsakni in his account of the Russian Sectaries, "was thirty or forty years ago. In three years' time Mingrelia was occupied with a mass of sectarian communities which proved most serviceable to the country; agriculture did well with them, they introduced many trades, established active commercial relations, and began to grow rich rapidly. . . . At the present time almost all the Dukhoburi are to be found in Siberia, the Caucasus, and the Eastern provinces of European Russia, and they are estimated to number about 150,000."

From the Dukhoburi sprang another sect, one that is much more developed than its prototype, viz. that known as the Molokani or milk-eaters (their name arising from the fact that in spite of the express prohibition of the Orthodox Church, they drink milk during Lent). In many parts they have engulfed the Dukhoburi and entirely taken their place. Some of their ideas and customs are so interesting that I cannot forbear quoting from Tsakni's account of the sect.

"Both in public and private life the Molokani avoid all formalism and ceremony. They have no churches; the nearest house, an open court, or even a field will serve as a place of prayer for the faithful . . . When the leader enters all present receive him by bowing their heads. The leader seats himself and begins to read aloud. After the reading, psalms are sung to tunes adapted from the popular folk-songs, then there is discussion on what has been read. . . . Every Molokani enjoys absolute liberty about religious ceremonies. No obligatory dogma or ceremony exists. For instance marriage amongst the Molokani is confined to a simple civil formality, a mutual pact which may be ended by the mutual consent of the two spouses or on the expressed wish of either of them. The initiative in marriage belongs to the young people. 'When parents force their children to contract a union against their will' say the Molokani 'they commit an action contrary to the will of God.'" Marriage "only takes place before the whole commune which decides whether those to be married are competent properly to establish a family both from the moral and material point of view, and satisfy themselves that the marriage is entered upon of their own freewill and that there is no coercion on either side."

The parents have no ability to oppose the marriage or to disinherit their children if their wishes are unobserved.

". . . The husband can neither mortgage nor sell his goods without the consent of his wife. If the husband dies childless all his property goes to his wife; if there are children the wife, the sons, and the daughters all receive equal parts. The outcome of these customs is that one does not find unhappy households amongst the sectarians, nor illegitimate children. The Molokani woman is accustomed to independence from her earliest childhood; and in the family circle she is not a slave, but her husband's companion, enjoying the same rights as he. . . . Whilst almost all Russian peasants are illiterate the Molokani with hardly an exception know how to read. . . . The Molokani consider war simply brigandage and assassination. No severity or coercion on the part of the Government avails to compel a Molokani to take part in a battle; at the first collision with the enemy he throws down his arms."

The Molokani have been subjected to minute police surveillance; they have been forbidden to assemble for religious service or to meet together in private houses at all. An assembly of *three* is illegal. Whole villages of them have been exiled to Siberia and the Caucasus, where, however, they have developed and improved their new surroundings something in the same way that the Dukoburi have done.

There are several other sects with characteristics not unlike those we have been speaking about, for instance that with which Count Leo Tolstoi's name is now particularly associated, but perhaps it would be out of proportion with the scope of this handbook to describe any other except that of the Stundists concerning which so much interest has been excited in England. The best account of this sect and the persecutions which they have endured appeared in a series of articles in the *Christian World*, now republished as a little book entitled "The Stundists: the Story of a great Religious Revolt." For those who prefer to acquire their knowledge of such matters through the medium of a story "The Highway of Sorrow" written by Miss Hesba Stretton and an anonymous collaborator who writes with great authority on the subject, gives accurate and touching pictures of Stundist life.

The author of the *Christian World* papers does not follow some of the authorities in considering the Stundists as one of a *group* of sects in revolt against the wooden formalism of the Russian Orthodox Church. His view is that the colonies of Suabian peasants planted by the Empress Catherine amongst the imaginative and impressionable peasantry of Little Russia have acted as a ferment in a susceptible environment. Doubtless German influence has been all important in founding the sect and in moulding its ideas. Yet if one loses sight altogether of the other religious movements amongst the peasantry which preceded it, one hardly obtains a complete view of the question, and one does not realise that a great part of the religious revolt among the South Russian peasantry has been independent of the influence exercised by German religious thought. Such a revolt was especially likely to arise at the time when the people of Russia were extremely excited after the emancipation of the serfs. The Stundists are now beginning to spread northwards, but until quite recently they were found entirely in South Russia, and for the most part, in the territory of the Little Russians. The two principal centres of their activity have been the neighbourhood of Kherson (the sect originated in a village near this town), and in the country surrounding Kiev.

"'The Bible and the Bible alone is the religion of Protestants' is a saying attributed to an English divine of the last century. The Stundists are probably more circumscribed still. The New Testament, and the New Testament alone is the religion of the Stundists. Theoretically, they pay the same reverence to both Old and New Testaments; practically the New Testament is their only [1] rule of faith and conduct" ("The Stundists: the Story of a great Religious Revolt," p. 55). The "doctrine of the right of every man to interpret Scripture for himself is also tenaciously held by the Stundists. Not the Church, not a priest, or a commentator, but each individual man has the right and incurs the duty to search the Scriptures for himself. . . .

"Those who have not been in Russia can form no idea of the prominent place" the superstition of icon-worship "occupies in the religious life of the people. Every peasant's cottage—the very poorest even—has one or two of these painted representations of Divine beings, the Saviour, the Virgin, God the Father, or some of the principal saints. They are hung up in all public offices, from the ecclesiastical consistory to the bureau of the petty police official; they are before your eyes in banks, merchants' offices, shops, railway stations, steamboats, drinking shops. . . . To their icons peasant and noble do obeisance; before them they prostrate themselves in prayer. The people call them 'God' and burn holy oil before them. If happiness is a Russian's lot in life he ascribes it all to the icon;[2] if misfortune follow him, it is because he has omitted some duty towards it— either the oil has not been replenished, or the frame

---

[1] This is becoming less true than it was: as educated people are now identifying themselves with the Stundists, the Old Testament is being made more use of.

[2] It must not of course be understood that such superstition as this is universal amongst the Russians; what is here represented however prevails very largely.

has not been kept bright, or he has sworn, or got drunk in its presence. Favourite icons in churches receive the adoration of thousands, and are prayed to in every emergency of life. Icons follow the armies on their march, and victory is always sure when they are propitious. This is idolatry pure and simple, but it is, nevertheless, a vital part of the national sentiment. The courage, therefore, of the Stundists, isolated and unprotected peasants, in rebelling against this, in raising their voices against the national degradation, is worthy of the highest praise. . . . Another tremendous power in Russia, against which the Stundists have steadily set their faces, is sacerdotalism. . . . In general it may be stated that Stundists do not hold the generally received notion, that it is desirable to maintain a distinct ministerial office." Refusing to pay the dues claimed by the priests, denouncing "the sordid, grasping man who asserts spiritual authority over him; his own life the sternest reproof that the priest can have, is it any wonder that Stundist and Pope are embittered enemies, and that the priest with all power and authority in his hands, resorts to those terrible reprisals, that policy of persecution which has of late years so stained the Russian Church?" (*Ibid.*, chap. x.).

It is clear that the Stundist sect came into being at a fortunate time. The years from 1858 to 1871 were as favourable for its inception as any that could be found, for these were the very years which covered the progressive and reforming period of Alexander II.'s reign. During the first years there was no persecution, and the new religion spread rapidly and obtained a firm grip on many of the people. The first arrest we hear of is that of the Ratushni brothers, which appears to have taken place in 1867. In this and the following year attacks on the idolatry practised towards the "Icons" or holy pictures began. "A number of prominent Stundists were arrested in consequence, but they only suffered imprisonment for a few weeks." Up to 1870 the position of the Stundists in relation to the Orthodox Church had been something akin to that of the Methodists in relation to the English Church at the beginning of Wesley's mission. But about 1870 "the Stundists were gradually severing themselves from all connection with the Orthodox Church."

This appears to have been a good deal attributable to the influence of a minority of the body who had adopted the doctrine of adult baptism. They seem to have been formed of more sturdy fibre than the rest. Their influence "did much to make the ordinary Russian Protestant more vertebrate. Until the Baptist set his face sternly against the Orthodox Church, and all its corruptions and defilements, the Stundist was satisfied to steer diplomatically between his new and his old faith. Afraid of giving offence and of consequent trouble, he adopted a line of action and a mental attitude,—outward conformity to Orthodoxy and inward contempt for it,—which was suicidal,—destructive of all true spiritual progress. The Baptists rebelled, and it is to their rectitude on this point that the present lofty position of Stundism is due. . . . The Baptist wing of the Stundists is undoubtedly the best organised and equipped. But if the German Baptists were at first so friendly and sympathetic, it is a matter of deep regret that latterly, when the storm and stress of persecution has beaten alike upon both sections of the Russian brethren, the Germans have held themselves studiously aloof. Secure in their own rights to worship God in their own way, they have proved themselves lacking in sympathy for their Russian co-religionists."

In 1877 or 1878 the Stundists began to feel the real weight of persecution. They were raided and deprived of their New Testaments and hymn-books; they were prevented from meeting for worship in their cottages, and their presbyters and deacons were forbidden to leave their localities for the purpose of confirming the more remote and weaker churches. But all these difficulties the brethren contrived to surmount.

When however soon after the beginning of the reign of Alexander III. the power of Pobiedonoststev became supreme in all matters relating to religion it is needless to say the crusade was carried on with the greatest cruelty and barbarity.

1882 marked the first stage of the new measures which as an ecclesiastic expressed it, were to succeed "the gentle and paternal pressure of the worldly powers" hitherto exercised. The "local commissaries of police,—men generally of a common and rough type, whose tyrannical methods are proverbial,—were empowered to levy arbitrary fines on peasants who continued to attend Stundist meetings after a warning to absent themselves." There followed evictions, and eviction sales, and imprisonment in default of the payment of fines.

The next step (1884) was to subject the leaders to severe penalties: imprisonment for long periods with common criminals, banishment with their families to distant provinces which often meant death for numbers of them, especially the children, on the terrible foot journeys, or arrival at their destination only to find themselves faced with economic ruin.

"From 1888 onwards the policy of extermination

seems to have taken the place of simple repression, and wholesale banishment and imprisonment, not only of the leaders but of ordinary members of the Stundist community, was of constant occurrence."

Our writer remarks that "The nations of the West ... do not seem to realise that they have at their gates a Power more intolerant of religious liberty than was Spain in her worst days, and persecutors as unscrupulous and narrow-minded as Alva and Torquemada. How can they know it? Russia works in secret; her methods are underground, and her victims are voiceless. There is no press in Russia, worthy the name, to report and denounce each case of persecution as it occurs. The trials of heretics are conducted with closed doors, the public being carefully excluded. Russians themselves do not know a tenth of what is being done." . . . .

"Religious intolerance is just as rampant in Russia to-day as it was in England during the reign of the Tudors" (*Ibid.*).

When he goes on to say "It is only prevented from going to the extremes of personal torture and the public stake by the dread of Western opinion," he gives what is equivalent to an exhortation to all those engaged in studying Russian questions and enlightening public opinion concerning them, to continue in their course. Yet the case does not appear a hopeful one at the moment, for as he remarks, since 1888 the policy of suppression has been supplanted by one of extermination, and the new reign has as yet brought no relief.

In the persecution to which heretics in Russia are subjected the authorities have been accustomed to distinguish between the "less obnoxious" and the "most obnoxious"—the latter being treated with far more harshness than the former. A circular issued by the Council of Ministers in the autumn of 1894 for the first time classified the Stundists amongst the "most obnoxious." It was possibly in consequence of this that a few months later the Russian news concerning the sect brought further discouragement.

A telegram printed in the London *Daily Chronicle* of 5th February 1895 says:—

> "Our Moscow correspondent learns, from the provinces of Kiev and Kherson, that large bodies of Stundists are returning to the Orthodox Church, worn out with their long struggle for freedom of worship. The Greek Church has a large number of Orthodox missionaries at present engaged in districts where there is a considerable Stundist population, and report has it that nothing in the way of scruples hinders the zeal of these priests. There is still no sign of any grace or amnesty being extended to Stundists in gaol or in banishment."

From the persecution of this quarter of a million of sturdy peasants of the South, we must turn to that of the five or six millions of Israelites of the Empire:—

Of the persecution of the Jews it is necessary to speak distinctly. It is said that there is properly speaking no religious persecution here; that what is done is done from political motives. Now to a certain extent it is true to say that all the persecutions of non-orthodox bodies in Russia are undertaken from political motives. The bigots who wish to harry everybody into the Orthodox Church simply because it is the Orthodox Church, obtain their main strength and support from alliance with the idea that Orthodoxy is one of the most potent political unifying forces at work to make all the outlying Russian peoples of the same assimilated mass as the Great Russians. Hence mainly arises the opposition to the Lutheran Church in the Baltic

Provinces, and to the Roman Catholic Church in Poland. One of the principal reasons that make the Stundists and the other reformed sects of Southern Russia excite the hatred and alarm of the Government, is that these religions tend to separate the peoples who profess them from the mass of the Orthodox subjects of the Tsar, and to create bonds of sympathy between them and Protestant Germany and England.

With the Jewish as with the other religions the two reasons for persecution exist side by side. Notwithstanding what is said to the contrary a certain amount of it seems to be attributable to pure religious bigotry, to the old spirit of Torquemada which for example dwells within the breast of the Procurator of the Most Holy Synod, the notorious Pobiedonoststev. Turning to the political motives for persecution these appear to be stronger in the case of the Jews than in that of the other religions with which we have to do. For in the first place the Jewish religion like that of the Mohammedans is inflexible; conversions from either to Christianity are of very rare occurrence. Then the Jews exhibit certain economic qualities which may arouse popular enmity, especially the enmity of an ignorant populace, so that it is more easy than under most circumstances for the Government to stir up a crusade backed by the support of the body of the people. This is a phenomenon that has been seen in other countries besides Russia. In the year 1290 Edward I. expelled all the Jews from this country, and it was not till the Commonwealth that the decree of banishment was rescinded so that it is very probable—as has been pointed out in an interesting essay by Mr George Radford—that Shakspeare delineated the character of Shylock without ever having seen a Jew. Even to-day in Germany the *Judenhetze* (Jew - hatred) which possesses a portion of her people is with difficulty kept in check. The peculiarity in Russia is that no effort is made to keep these popular prejudices in check, but that on the contrary the people are hounded on to attack and maltreat the unfortunate Jews by the very authorities who ought to be instructed enough to wish to restrain them. For this popular dislike of the Israelites a good many writers even amongst our own countrymen hold that there is cause. I do not share this opinion. I think it is to be admitted that whilst the Jews often make admirable mechanics their bent is rather towards commerce, trade, and finance than to laborious physical labour, especially such as agricultural labour. Jewish writers seek to show that this is merely a consequence of their having been denied access to the land in so many countries for so many centuries, but they hardly prove their case. In England for example where no such trammels now exist, the proportion of Jews amongst agricultural labourers must be quite insignificant whilst the proportion of Jewish pawnbrokers is considerable. It is of course difficult to say where cause ends and effect begins, but it is clear that in Russia as in other countries such unpopular functions as those of the money-lender are apt to be undertaken by the Jews. In a poor country like Russia too where the security for debt is frequently very bad, and where capital is not plentiful, the rates of interest will become so high as to be ranked usurious. But to hold that because they often receive a high rate of interest the Jews do a real injury to the country is a view unsupported by the facts. In parts of the country from which they are expelled native money-lenders take their place, but being apt to be less expert business men than the Jews, and capital and competition amongst capitalists being both withdrawn, the current rate of interest rises enormously. M. Errera mentions that after the expulsion of the Jews from Moscow the rate of interest in private pawnshops rose from 25 to 200 per cent. per annum. It is in fact the Jews who keep the rate of interest from being even higher than it is; they are often too the only expert organisers of business in the country, and those parts of the Empire which are denuded of their presence undoubtedly suffer largely in prosperity. To give one example—it was by the Jews that a system of insurance for peasants' cattle was introduced into Russia. The harrying of the Jews during the last reign is at any rate one of the causes of the alarming growth in the economic poverty of the people.

It is further to be noted that though the persecutions were inaugurated under the pretext of protecting Russian labour from the "exploitation" of a class of drones, its full weight has not in fact fallen on the capitalist class amongst the Jews, but has been reserved for the artisans and the classes amongst which the greatest poverty prevails.

For many of the other accusations that have been trumped up against the Jews in Russia there is no foundation. It has been said for example that they are ignorant, uncleanly, and unchaste; in all three particulars they are superior, and in the first and third very markedly superior to the average of the Russian nation. Their desire for education amounts to a passion which is kept in check with the utmost difficulty by the ingenious devices of the Ministry of "Instruction." The accusation that amongst the Jews there is marked disaffection towards the Government is unfortunately equally untrue; their fault is excessive meekness under insult and injury.

The most authoritative book on the whole subject is Leo Errera's "Les Juifs Russes; Extermination ou

Emancipation?" now translated into English under the title "The Russian Jews: Extermination or Emancipation?" It is perhaps less effective as an appeal to the emotions of horror and indignant disgust which the cruelties of the religious persecutions must produce, than Mr Harold Frederic's "The New Exodus," but it gives a better bird's-eye view of the whole question.

An important authority largely depended upon by M. Errera in the evidence concerning the facts of the case is the report addressed in 1892 to the American Government, by Messrs Weber and Kempster, the two Special Commissioners charged by it with a mission to Europe to enquire into the causes of the growing immigration of penniless aliens into the United States.[1] It contains nothing but facts personally verified by these gentlemen during a long journey through Russia and Poland.

The principal features of the persecution of the Jews in Russia during the last three years, as given by M. Errera, may be summed up as follows: With insignificant exceptions they were permitted to settle and live only in Old Poland and the so-called " Pale of Settlement," forming together a stretch of land along the German, Austrian, Hungarian and Roumanian frontiers, *not exceeding one-eighth of the whole territory* of European Russia (Finland and the Caucasus included). Thousands of them succeeded however in settling throughout the Empire, and have been tolerated there since 1865. In 1891 they were suddenly compelled to break up their homes, to give up their business and work, and to go to the Pale. The overcrowding of the Pale which

---

[1] This is the report mentioned in the April (1894) Number of *Free Russia* (p. 30) as having been placed on the Russian Censor's prohibited list.

results is appalling and leads to the most horrible insanitation, and to the most terrible economic difficulties. One statistical note will suffice to illustrate this. In the Province of Kiev (within the Pale) the average number of inmates in Jewish houses is now almost three times what it is in Christian houses. In the town of Berditchev it is about five times as great. The position is still more aggravated by the fact that Jews who have for four years lived in the smaller towns and villages have, to the number of about half a million, been driven into the larger towns.

Many honourable and lucrative professions have been closed to the Jews who are besides excluded from the navy and from the higher grades of the army.

Since 1886, the number of Jews that may be admitted to the universities, to the higher schools, or to the gymnasiums,[1] has been restricted. This is with the object of preventing their obtaining diplomas which admit them to the " privileged classes " who may live outside the Pale. It is an example of the enforcement of the policy of " Russia for the Russians," *i.e.* for orthodox, imperialistic Great Russians, or those who identify themselves with them and imitate them. One has not unfrequently in connection with educational questions, come across official pronouncements of the Russian Government which would fittingly find a place in one of Mr W. S. Gilbert's topsy-turvy plays. Here is an example:—In December 1886 the Minister of Public Instruction promulgated with the Imperial sanction a decree which opens thus:—

" Whereas many young Jewish people most anxious to take advantage of superior classical,

---

[1] Intermediate schools for classical education. Only the graduates from these schools are entitled to enter at a university.

technical and professional teaching, present themselves each year for admission to the universities, and pass their examinations, and continue their studies in the various schools of the Empire, it has appeared desirable to put an end to so unsatisfactory a state of things."

Jews are not allowed to enjoy the privileges resulting from public institutions or charities although they subscribe to them, and in some cases have actually founded them. *They are even excluded from the hospitals.* Difficulties are put in the way of the Jews in the exercise of their religion. Jews are continually exposed to the violence of subsidiary officials, to the extortions of the police, and to vexations of every kind. Side by side with this, all foreign Jews have been pitilessly expelled from the Empire, even though they may have been born within it, and though they may have strenuously endeavoured to secure naturalisation. These 'foreigners" have for the most part been nominally either Turkish or Roumanian subjects. The expulsion has pressed especially hard on the latter who are not admitted into Roumania, that country also disowning them.

Taking a general view of the religious persecution in Russia, one is struck by nothing so much as the absolute insecurity against the prevalence of such a terrible state of things so long as an arbitrary autocracy exists. For example, M. Errera in speaking of the expulsion of the Jewish artisans from Moscow, remarks that the privileges which were accorded to them by Alexander II. were cancelled by a stroke of Alexander III.'s pen. Nor is it only a difference of disposition in the Tsar himself that may make all the difference between prosperous living and miserable death to millions of his subjects. The caprice of the autocrat's subordinates becomes an all-important element in the lives of his down-trodden subjects. Thus the last year of Alexander II.'s reign was marked by an ordinance of toleration towards the Jews issued by Markov, the Minister of the Interior. The first year of Alexander III. saw Ignatiev in that position. The policy of tolerance was sharply reversed; Jewish riots were fomented, and the terrible "May laws" were passed in May 1882. But in the following month Ignatiev was succeeded by Dmitri Tolstoi. Markov's ordinance was reaffirmed, and the "May laws" became a dead letter for a time. But it appears that whether they remained a dead letter or no depended purely on the capricious chances which preside over the attainment to the chief offices of state in Russia. The growing influence of Pobiedonoststev was enough to secure that by the present decade, without any re-enactment, operations under these terrible "laws" should come into full operation. Surely no more striking object-lesson could be given to illustrate the dangers of a despotic system of government.

The following may be read in amplification of the contents of this chapter:—

> Leroy-Beaulieu, Vol. III. gives very full account of religions, whether Orthodox or non-Orthodox—see especially Book IV.; Wallace, chaps. iv., xix., xx., and xxvii.; N. Tsakni, "La Russie Sectaire"; Stepniak, "Russian Peasantry," Vol. II.
> 
> *Concerning the Stundists and their Persecution:*—"The Stundists: the Story of a great Religious Revolt."
> 
> *Concerning the Persecution of the Jews:*—Leo Errera, "The Russian Jews; Extermination or Emancipation?"; Harold Frederic, "The New Exodus."

# CHAPTER VII.

## DRAMATIS PERSONÆ ON THE POLITICAL STAGE OF MODERN RUSSIA.

## CHAPTER VII.—*Contents.*

THE peasantry numerically preponderant — Different views concerning the peasantry; comparison with that of France before the Revolution and that of Bulgaria to-day—The instructed classes; analysis of their political sentiments — Government employ—The Slavophils; Panslavism; the Russian Liberals; the so-called "nihilists"—Nihilism begins as a revolt of the soul of the Russian against the political and intellectual yoke to which it is subject, first manifested in private relations only, then developed into militant socialism; there follows the period of terrorism and the duel between the Government and the revolutionists, which is in its turn now giving way to an appreciation of the value of constitutionalism—Reasons for hoping that a *rapprochement* is possible between the new "nihilism" and Russian "liberalism"—Mr Lazarev's experiences; his support by the Saratov bar—The professions generally (except the priesthood) have liberal sympathies.

Great personages: Alexander III., Pobiedonostetev, Katkov, Nicholas II.

# CHAPTER VII.

### DRAMATIS PERSONÆ ON THE POLITICAL STAGE OF MODERN RUSSIA.

WE have now supplemented the historical sketch given in my second and third chapters by a rapid review of what has taken place in several of the chief departments of internal political activity during the reigns of the last two Alexanders. In every subject that we have investigated we have found a very similar sequence of events. Whether it has been the economic condition of the peasantry, local government, the administration of the law, the conditions under which the press can disseminate instruction, or the state of religious freedom, everything at the beginning of Alexander II.'s reign seemed pushing vigorously forward towards the light, everything at the close of that same reign appeared to be benumbed and blighted. The reign of Alexander III. was a long and tedious prolongation of this winter of discontent interspersed with many a terrible frost.

The subject I now propose to investigate is the scope and power of the principal forces at work on the political stage of modern Russia.

One cannot help turning at first instinctively to the peasantry; they are so overwhelming in numbers that by mere physical preponderance they claim our first attention for of the many millions that inhabit Russia some eighty to eighty-five out of every hundred persons must be counted as peasants. Of this great mass of the people we get the most diverse views presented to us. On the one side we are given a highly idealised picture. In him the early revolutionists saw the nobility of the natural man uncontaminated by the artificiality and vices of civilization. The bulk of the revolutionists have outgrown their rather naïve illusion, but it is still presented with picturesqueness enough to be interesting, though hardly with force enough to be convincing, by the self-rusticated philosopher who is probably Russia's greatest living man of letters. On the other hand, not a few depict the Russian peasant as being the most squalid and debased of the dwellers upon earth. For example, this view is presented with all its repellent force by the literary firm who write under the name of "Lanin." We are not for the first time confronted with the contrast between the idealistic and the realistic description of a nationality or a class; and when we have nothing before us but a bare enumeration of current facts, the realist seems to carry things before him. But the position of the idealist is not so untenable as might at first sight appear to be the case. His conception indeed is actually revealed from time to time in bright exceptional characters which stand forth to measure the height which their comrades may some day reach. Insight into the possibilities of attainment is of the greatest importance when we are looking forward to the future development of a people or a class. Lanin's sordid conception of the Russian peasant is likely in the long run to be at least as far removed from the truth as is Leo Tolstoi's glorified picture of him to-day. There are influences at work which may within a comparatively short period very materially modify the characteristics of the Russian poor man; one is education, the woeful incompleteness of which has even under the most reactionary periods tended to diminish. If liberal governmental tendencies were for even a short time to remove the hindrances placed in its way great steps would be taken in this direction. There is very little doubt that another most potent cause of modification will be the growth of large towns; the economic movement which transformed the face of England a century ago is in Russia only just beginning, but it has now set in. It may be that fifty years hence as many will belong to the poor-man class as now, but it is extremely unlikely that there will then be anything like eighty-five per cent. of the population still engaged in agricultural pursuits. The agglomeration of large numbers of the people in towns will bring with it far greater opportunities of political thought, political education, and political action. But even taking the problem as it now stands, the existence of the mass of the peasantry is no such absolute bar to great political reforms as is sometimes assumed. Let me call to mind two historical situations which may be regarded as in some respects parallel. Might it not before the French Revolution have been said of the French peasantry as it is now said of the Russian peasantry, that they were utterly sordid and debased? that they were quite without political intelligence, and that therefore free political institutions were altogether unsuited to their circumstances? That aspect of the case might then have been put forward with much plausibility, but whatever view we may take of the sequence of historical events in France during the last century we should hardly now found our conclusions on any such assumption. But there is another parallel in contemporary politics which is in some respects very much closer. Between the size and importance of Russia and of Bulgaria there is of course no sort of comparison, but apart from the different scale that must be applied in considering the extent of the two countries, Bulgaria presents in many respects striking resemblances to Russia. Like it, it is essentially "a peasant state." It is true the peasants who form the great bulk of the nation have not been subjected to three centuries of serfdom, but they have on the other hand been for four centuries under the Ottoman yoke. Their communal institutions and their religion are like those of the Russians, and ethnologically they seem to be almost identical with the inhabitants of the southern parts of the Empire, for they are described as being of Slav stock, dashed with an admixture of Tatár blood. The general resemblance of their characteristics to those of the Russians is striking. Those who read Mr Edward Dicey's extremely interesting book about this people ("The Peasant State: an Account of Bulgaria in 1894"), will find that after the last Turkish war the principality was granted a constitution which though it is described as being a mixture of absolutism with democratic institutions, has bestowed popular political rights which would be accepted by the reform party in Russia as a very fair instalment of their demands. The powers of the prince are certainly extensive, but on the other hand there is universal manhood suffrage. There is a one-chamber parliament (the Sobranje), to which all citizens not less than thirty years old are eligible for election if they can read and write. One deputy sits for every 20,000 electors. "The members of the Sobranje are guaranteed absolute freedom of speech, and are not liable to arrest or trial during the sitting of Parliament without the previous consent of the chamber. . . . . The Parliament thus constituted possesses absolute authority to pass laws, to impose taxes, to provide the funds required for the administration of the State, either by loans or by taxation, and to discuss and modify the budget." On the other hand the prince has the right of veto.

What account then does Mr Dicey give of the results of bestowing such political institutions as these on Slav peasants? In the main he says the constitution is worked fairly; the worst thing the book mentions (certainly serious enough), is the tampering with the results of the polls at elections, but the author thinks that if the returns were falsified so as to go seriously against the wishes of the electors on any question which they considered vital, the irregularities would not be tolerated. It is true that since the publication of his book the murder of Stambulov has exhibited in a lurid light the dangers which are being brought on their country by the conspiracies of the pro-Russian party and by the criminal lack of energy of the prince and his present Government in administering justice and securing order; yet Mr Dicey's argument is in the main unaffected. He points out that amongst the officials there is no corruption that can for a moment be compared to that which is rampant in Russia, though he considers that the standard maintained is not so high as in English public life. Commerce and industry are growing with healthy steadiness; the finances of the country are not only sound, they are regulated with almost excessive caution. The army is efficient; "if the necessity should arrive, Bulgaria could at once mobilise an army of 100,000 men, well provided with arms, ammunition, and means of transport, and ready to take the field at very brief notice." "The men are well fed, well clothed, and well housed."

The Sobranje votes about one-seventh of the whole of the nation's expenditure for public education, which is gratuitous and compulsory up to twelve years old, with a further gratuitous course (if desired by the parents), up to eighteen years old. The whole country is well provided with primary schools, and some of the secondary schools are such that any country might regard them with satisfaction. This is what has been attained for education under the Bulgarian constitution. It will be remembered that under the Russian autocracy those who can read and write, or indeed even those who have the chance of going to school at all are still quite a small minority.

With the results before us of this experiment, which seems to have been conducted in the political laboratory for our especial benefit and instruction, I think that even now there is no cause to say that the Russian peasantry are utterly unfitted to receive any kind of free political institutions; they have for example chosen their representatives to the district zemstvo assemblies, in a very intelligent and capable manner. What is so often overlooked is that the very endowment with such institutions inspires an interest in political affairs which may very well have previously lain dormant, and that this interest itself becomes the best assurance of ability to take part in political life.

But after all the peasantry though they are so preponderant numerically, are not by any means the only people we have to consider in connection with this problem. Even in countries which possess universal or almost universal suffrage, the political influence of one active and instructed citizen is of more avail than that of a dozen illiterate voters, often of more than 100 or so, for he becomes the leader of a group of men. This is much more the case in a country like Russia where for imperial purposes there is no suffrage at all. So that it would be quite a mistake to suppose that because the "intelligent and instructed classes" in Russia number perhaps but some fifteen per cent. of the population, that their wishes and ideas are insignificant and negligible, that they in fact are entirely swamped by the mass of the people. To assert the converse of this would be grossly incorrect, but of the two assertions it would be the one least removed from the truth.

It is important then to attempt some sort of analysis of the political sentiments of educated Russia.

We know of the Russian army as one of the great military hosts of Europe. Side by side with this armament for foreign service there is another army whose work it is to administer the internal affairs of the Empire. Russia is governed by an enormous bureaucracy; there are everywhere to be found innumerable officials, " Tchinovniks " as they are called. So it comes about that a very considerable proportion of the educated classes in Russia are in Government employ, either as officers in the army or navy, or in the huge system of the civil service. There are in fact hardly any other openings to employment for gentlemen's sons. For some classes in Russia it is more a matter of course to enter the army, or become officials, than it is for a certain social grade in England to go to Oxford or Cambridge. Government employment under a bureaucracy is not a good nidus for the inception of free political ideas. The whole of the individual's material interests are weighing down the scale opposed to that which supports aspirations towards political liberty. This is true both directly and indirectly: directly, because any suspicion of political untrustworthiness would be enough to deprive an official of his position, and his livelihood; indirectly, because there has grown up associated especially with officialdom, a system of wellnigh universal corruption out of which the great majority of officials thoughout the Empire get some sort of a picking or other. Under these circumstances it is not surprising that a great number of them, perhaps the bulk of them are officials and nothing more. They regard it as their business to maintain the autocracy and the power of the bureaucracy; there their political ideas end, and as to political aspirations they have none. What is more surprising perhaps is that to a great number of those who are in Government employ, this description does not apply. We have seen how as early as 1825 there was a great military revolt which was headed by officers of the army, who represented the most enlightened political views of their time. There is many an officer in the army and navy to-day who thinks for himself in political matters, who when the occasion arises, may also act for himself. In the civil service, amongst the Tchinovniks properly so called, independence of political thought is probably still more frequent.

But to what can independent minds attach themselves? Is there outside of official circles any formulated political thought? Can one distinguish for example in Russia any approach to political parties?

Of one party at least in Russia one has certainly heard a good deal; I mean the Slavophils. It is in fact the only party of which there has been very much opportunity to hear, because it has been the only one that has been permitted to raise up its head into publicity, to publish and insist on its own views in the newspapers, and during the most influential but least creditable period of its existence, to have as its particular organ a newspaper of extraordinary activity, influence, and power. Its ideas on the subject of internal policy are substantially those which Japan has recently abandoned, which China too may now be forced to abandon. In Russia the party is the modern embodiment of that conservatism by which Peter the Great found himself opposed and against which he hurled himself with all the might of his personality.

"In the eyes of the Slavophils," says M. Leroy-Beaulieu (Vol. I. Book IV. chap. i. p. 227 in English edition, p. 213 in French edition), "Russia is substantially different from Europe. Having received from the past peculiar institutions, she is by her origin and bringing up, by the elements of her culture, called to entirely different fortunes. In the manner in which her land has been peopled, in her conception of family, property, and authority, Russia possesses the principle of a novel civilization, and naturally, if local patriotism is to be believed, of a better-balanced civilization, more stable and harmonious, more really capable of progress without definite end, than the senile and effete occidental civilization, threatened as the latter already is, with decomposition as a result of its internal conflicts."

The foreign policy of the Slavophils may be described generally as being Panslavistic; that is to say their ideal has been to embody with their country the smaller Slavic states, especially those of the Balkan peninsula and of the border-lands of the Austrian dominions. Short of effecting an actual union of these with Russia they would look to establishing a kind of protectorate over them. The ideas of the Slavophil-Panslavist party appealed to strong if not to very enlightened patriotic tendencies in a large section of the Russian people; their mouthpiece was Katkov the editor of the *Moscow Gazette*, who attained a position of remarkable influence. The whole movement had the strong support of the late Tsar when he was heir-apparent, and so far at any rate as internal policy was concerned after he was monarch, and it was perhaps partly in consequence of his powerful patronage that the party were able to obtain the position of independence so remarkable in Russia which they enjoyed. In the time of Alexander III. however the apogee of their power had passed. They had attained their greatest triumph in 1875-7 when they aroused the country to enthusiastic support of their policy and practically forced the hands of the Emperor Alexander II. and his Government compelling them to adopt their ideas.

Mr Charles Lowe says ("Alexander III. of Russia," chap. ii. p. 34): Alexander II. "was much less bellicose than the party of extreme Panslavists, but he was hurried along by the national movement and in spite of all his autocratic power, he found it impossible to stem the current of the popular tide, which was setting deep and strong for a war with the 'unspeakable' Turks."

Although Slavophilism when actively embodied in a line of policy such as the brutal one formulated by Katkov, must be described as unenlightened and retrograde, there is of course a modified sense in which the word is sometimes understood which must not be overlooked, a sense in which it was adopted by some of those who were disgusted with Katkov's later policy. If by Slavophilism is meant that disposition of mind which seeks out all that is worthy of appreciation and honour amongst the distinctively Slav institutions and characteristics, the strictures are not applicable. The policy which would suppress all good coming from without is quite distinct from that instinct which would nourish all good springing up from within. Understood in this latter sense however Slavophilism ceases to be the badge of a particular party, for Russians of every party have possessed this nationalistic sentiment. It was especially strongly, sometimes indeed passionately developed amongst almost all the great men of independent mind in the middle of the century and during the reign of Alexander II., though very many of these were bitterly opposed to the Katkov policy.

Similarly the word Panslavism may be taken to have two significations. In the one it merely means a strongly sympathetic feeling amongst the Slavs for all peoples of their race. In the other it implies the aim actually to absorb all minor Slav nationalities in Russia and their thorough *Russification* after they have been absorbed. By "Russification" is understood amongst the Panslavists of this hectoring order, complete assimilation to the Great Russian or Muscovite type. The Polish type, the Ukrainian type, and it is hoped in the future the Bulgarian type are to be completely superseded. Panslavism indeed when thus interpreted becomes Panmuscovisation.

The other great school of political thought amongst educated Russians may be called that of the Russian Liberals though those who compose it have perhaps hardly been organised enough at any time to be denominated a party. Of the Russian Liberals one hears a good deal less than their importance demands: they might almost be called the silent party for they have never forced themselves to the front as the Slavophils have done, nor have they ever been inclined to work clandestinely like the revolutionists and thus gain notoriety. It is more difficult than in either of these other two cases to get authoritative statements of their views, to find out for what they are working, and how they are working. Yet it is not impossible that in the political development of the country their importance has been greater than that of any other section of the people. They like the Slavophils had their militant hour. It came 15 years earlier when they surrounded the Tsar Alexander II. with their influence and through his instrumentality instituted that great series of reforms of which we have spoken in earlier chapters. Not only were the Russian Liberals the inspirers of these reforms but to a large extent they were the instruments by which they were carried out. The reversal of their fortunes dates from the outbreak of the Polish insurrection in 1863. Never after that event did Alexander II. so completely surrender himself to their ideas. It was followed in April '66 by an attempt on his life when he was fired at by Karakasov, and in the following year another attempt was made by a Pole named Berezovski, while Alexander was on a visit to Napoleon III. at Paris. The influence of these events led him to turn his back on his early Liberalism and though all the years in the decade of the 'sixties may perhaps be counted as his reforming period he began after the suppression of the Insurrection and still more after the attempt of 1866 to reconsider his policy in many directions, and there slowly developed in his mind and in his actions the stubborn reactionary policy which is the feature of the decade of the 'seventies. The idea of the Liberals was to work *with* the Tsar, not against him; with this change in his personal views then their influence in the country seemed entirely to disappear; and the field was left clear on the one side for the Chauvinism of the Slavophil party, on the other for the underground activity of the revolutionists. The Liberals indeed made through the medium of their Zemstvo sittings and on one or two other occasions elsewhere some remarkable protests against the abandonment by the Tsar of his Liberal policy; but further than this they were not prepared to go. If the Tsar were bent on following the reactionary path, their course seemed to them to be simply gloomy acquiescence and retirement from the political arena. So that at this period the Liberals did really for a time become almost a negligible quantity in Russian political life, and for anything different from the blatant and ignorant policy of the Slavophils and the looking-backward policy of Alexander II. and his ministers, we have to look to the group of extremists, who although when compared either with the Slavophils or the Liberals were numerically insignificant, made themselves felt by their energy and unbounded devotion to their purposes. This group is the one we know under the name of the nihilists. But the name "nihilists" describes them very badly; it is a name that has as little descriptive value as the popular name which designates the great Conservative party of England as the successors of a wild and lawless clan of Irish.

M. Leroy-Beaulieu says (Vol. I. Book III. chap. iv. pp. 182-3 in French edition, pp. 197-8 in English edition):—

> "As it was first understood 'nihilism' implied hardly any connection with politics at all. It was little more than a certain way of bearing oneself, thinking and talking,—a mannerism, a fashion, an affectation one might say that came into favour among the young people of 1860 to 1870, among the pupils of the universities and the girl-students with their cropped hair, living abroad or in the provinces.
>
> "These were the outward symbols of a spirit of revolt against all traditional authorities

and antiquated religious or political dogmas, of a spirit of negation stamped with an intolerant materialism and naïve radicalism, which at bottom was nothing more than a violent reaction of the soul of the Russian against the governmental system and the intellectual yoke under which it had long been bent. This was the first and properly speaking, the true nihilism, the nihilism which has been depicted in immortal strokes by the most famous Russian novelists " (Tourguénev, etc.).

"After this theoretical and abstract nihilism, often taken up merely in an amateur and dilletante manner, sometimes made up of nothing but posing and outward show, a nihilism which did not attempt to put its maxims into practice except in the individual life and in private relations, there came about 1871 under the twofold influence of the Paris Commune and the International, a nihilism of action and agitation, transformed into a militant socialism."

The early nihilism here referred to was in fact most important, for it was the outburst of the revolt against the iron rule of authority which permeated the family, as well as social and political life in Russia.

What the so-called Nihilists really were in the early 'seventies was a body of enthusiastic socialists who felt laid upon their shoulders the mission of a propaganda of their ideas amongst the common people. Accordingly thousands of ardent young men and young women laid aside their culture and in many cases the ease of wealthy positions, to go amongst the people, to assume their dress and employments, and to work with them in order to persuade them that they were genuinely of their number, the object throughout being merely that they might have opportunity of acquainting themselves with the peasantry and preaching their doctrine to them.[1] Their teaching was not seized upon with any avidity by the peasantry but it was continued both in country and town till about the year 1878; the Government then released from the occupation of the Turkish war, resolved to put an end to the propaganda which it considered a dangerous one.

M. Leroy-Beaulieu's view is that it was this determination of the Government to interfere with a peaceful socialistic propaganda that was the actual determining cause of the formation of the terrorist section of the party. However that may be, the wrongs which they conceived themselves and their country generally to suffer did induce a certain part of the old socialist party to determine to have recourse to violence, and from '78 to '81 they carried out a terroristic policy with extreme firmness and self-devotion.

The contest between the revolutionists and the Government from the year 1878 to 1881 can only be likened to a duel; a duel however in which the measures resorted to were so terrible that each side appealed to the public opinion of Europe to justify it in the course it took on the grounds that the deeds of its adversary had placed it outside the pale of civilisation or any ordinary reprisals. Mr Noble in "The Russian Revolt" gives the following account of the matter:—

> "The repressive measures of the Government had been growing in severity. The slightest offences against absolutism were met with the most disproportionate punishments. For an insignificant disturbance in Kiev one hundred and fifty students were dismissed from the University, and thirty banished to a northern province. The

---

[1] See Noble's "Russian Revolt" pp. 200-1.

courts had grown vindictive and partisan. The law of trial by jury was daily ignored. Prisoners acquitted by the ordinary process were systematically brought under administrative procedure and banished or imprisoned afresh without trial. The spy and denunciation system had become intolerable. The crusade against the revolt was carried on by a secret and unscrupulous organization of police, known as the Third Section. Prison life was unendurable. Revolts broke out in the Fortress of Peter and Paul at St Petersburg and in the central prison at Kharkov. So badly were the prisoners fed in these places that numbers of them refused to partake of nourishment until a more humane treatment had been introduced; some resolved to die of starvation, others had food forced down their throats. Cumulative irritations like these worked minds up to a pitch of frenzy. On the 2nd (14th) of August 1878, Kavalsky was shot at Odessa by order of a military tribunal."

General Mezentsev, chief of the Third Section had been warned that if this sentence was carried out he would be killed; accordingly, two days after the execution, although he was at the other end of the Empire, he

"was stabbed to death in the Nevsky Prospect in full daylight. The reply of the Government was to hand over all political crimes of violence to a military tribunal, to strengthen the spy and repressive system, and to appeal to society for aid and sympathy. . . . . General Orenteln, succeeding Mezentsev, cast nearly two thousand persons into prison in St Petersburg alone. In February, 1879, Prince Krapotkin, Governor of Kharkov, was shot by Goldenberg for ill-treating prisoners under his care. Two months later on the 2nd (14th) of April, 1879, came Soloviev's attempt on the life of the emperor. The would-be assassin fired five shots at the Tsar, but none of them took effect. Absolutism was now fully awakened to its danger. The country was divided into six divisions, and a general governor, armed with extraordinary powers, detailed to each. The pass system was enforced with new rigours. In St Petersburg, General Gurko converted the *dvorniki*, or house porters, into a body of spies charged with regular police duty.

"The reply of the revolt was characteristic. .... The terrible 'Executive Committee,' came into existence."

Alexander II. was sentenced to death if he would not consent to introduce a constitutional form of government. There followed the mine at Moscow, the explosion at the Winter Palace at St Petersburg, and finally (1881) the emperor's death was compassed by the throwing of bombs.

It was however only a section of the socialist party that pursued the course of violence; something like a schism had occurred in the party on the question of whether terrorism should be resorted to or not. Those who could not prevail upon themselves to adopt these measures continued to act very much as they had done before. But two fresh influences very soon made themselves felt in connection with these parties, or fractions of a party. The hopelessness of the task which the peaceful socialists had placed before themselves became more and more evident, and the party dwindled down into insignificance practically into extinction just as the liberals had done before. The liberals had had definite and practical aims before them, but they had lacked the boldness and self-reliance to insist on pursuing them in the teeth of the Government. The socialists did not lack for boldness or self-reliance but the aim which they had set before themselves, viz., the conversion of a stolid and backward peasantry to the idealised theories of an exalted Socialism was one that was unpractical and unrealisable. Many no doubt as they became convinced of this, drifted into the ranks if not of the active terrorists, of those who sympathised with them and could be relied upon as allies in the background. Incidentally we may note that terrorism was *passively* backed by a considerable portion of the liberals, and even indifferentists, so intolerable was the reaction of Alexander II. felt to be after the dawn of liberalism.

Meanwhile the terrorist group itself was being permeated with ideas that were entirely new to the so-called nihilist party, and these ideas deserve our very careful attention as they are of great importance in the political situation of to-day. Up to this time the socialists had not meddled with politics properly so called at all: they had concerned themselves only with the condition of the people. To them it was indifferent whether they lived under an autocracy or under a constitution, indeed many dreaded "bourgeois" constitutionalism more than autocracy; any considerations of political machinery appeared to them to be beneath their notice; those were things which they would leave to the bourgeoisie. But when a part of this body of socialists descended from its castle-in-the-air to the realities of life which were for it peculiarly grim, it began to realise, not yet indeed that its theories of social reform were very crude, but at least that its methods of trying to bring them about were crude.

Here is M. Leroy-Beaulieu's account of the matter:—

"In the bloody struggle with authority which the revolutionists had entered upon, they had not only changed their tactics and method of procedure, but their point of view also. Till now so disdainful of the 'bourgeois' liberties of Europe, which they had regarded with contempt, they discovered that political liberty at which they had turned up their noses, might be of value, if for nothing else, as a guarantee against the arbitrariness of the administrative, and a pathway to lead to freedom of propaganda. This conception was a new one to 'nihilism' and radically modified its character. The struggle against authority had glided from the vague and misty domain of Utopia to the firm ground of practical politics. The aim of the revolutionists had now become the destruction of the autocracy. Their terrible campaign against the sovereign and the Government had a well-defined end in view: the putting down of absolute power. And so it happened that at the very time when they were revolting society by the terrible nature of their deeds, they were drawing near in their point of view to that of the public and the liberals. In their manifestoes they declared themselves ready to disarm on the condition that the sovereign would consent to convoke a national assembly. So by this singular right-about-face it has come about that nihilism has ended in constitutionalism, the very thing it had treated with most disdain" ("L'Empire des Tsars et des Russes," Vol. II. Book VI. chap. ii. pp. 562-3, French edition).

The importance of this development of "nihilist" opinion will be at once seen when we consider that for practical immediate political ends the programme of

the nihilists and that of the liberals was now to all
intents and purposes identical. This point was dramatically illustrated when ten days after the assassination
of Alexander II. the manifesto of the "Executive Committee" of the revolutionists was conveyed to his son
and successor. The chief points in this document
besides a demand for the amnesty of political offenders,
were the insistence on the necessity for the convocation
of a National Assembly freely elected on a popular
suffrage, and freedom of the press, of speech, and of
public meeting. The liberals so far as they expressed
themselves put forward almost identical objects as
being those which were of most importance for the
welfare of the country. But was it possible in the
nature of things for these two parties to coalesce and
take common action for common objects? There lay
behind them a long tradition of mutual distrust and
contempt; besides this the liberals might argue: "True,
the revolutionists now seek as their immediate end,
political liberty; but they do so only as an instrument,
that they may be in the better position to bring about
their ultimate object of introducing socialism; with this
ultimate object of theirs we have no sympathy." The
revolutionists on the other hand might say—"What
sort of allies are these who will desert us at the very
moment when we have gained the preliminary advantage which will place us in some sort of a position to
attain to that which we think really of importance in
itself, and not merely a means to an end?" Mutual
distrust of this kind seems in fact to have prevented
any very cordial co-operation between the two bodies of
reformers during the whole of the reign of Alexander
III. Is there any reason to think that the reign which
has just begun opens with a better chance of a *rapprochement* between the liberals and the nihilists? I

think there is. The two great hindrances as we have seen have been the tradition of mutual disdain, and the insistence by one of the parties on socialism as the paramount end, the only end in fact of real importance. Now with regard to the first,—mutual distrust and contempt,—time has done a great deal to soften it. The other question presents more difficulties, for as far as I can judge it is unquestionably true that the bulk of the so-called nihilists are still socialists, whilst the vast majority of the 'liberals' are not so. But here again I think there is some reason for hoping that a still further development is going forward in the opinions of the nihilists. To their socialist ideal indeed they still cling; but their attitude of mind towards political liberty is undergoing a further change. Political freedom is ceasing to be regarded as merely an instrument for social reconstruction; its value in itself to the dignity, the independence, and the civic happiness of the individual is beginning to be appreciated, and by some of the nihilists it has even come to be regarded as of more importance than social reconstruction. One of the little booklets widely distributed in Russia by clandestine means is a tract written by Sergius Stepniak about three years ago. It has been translated, and forms part of the little volume published in the autumn of 1894, called "Nihilism as it is." As an address to fellow-revolutionists it is of peculiar interest and value. I will quote some sentences from it to illustrate my point.

> "We believe that political liberty gives all that is needed for the solution of the social question. . . . .
> 
> "But while regarding the solution of the labour question in Russia as a problem that will be brought prominently forward in perhaps the near

future, we emphatically protest against the habit which has grown up amongst us of treating political liberty exclusively as a means to 'the solution of the social question.' We feel as an insult that we should look upon liberty as a mere tool with which to obtain something else, as though the needs and feelings of free men were strange to us, as though our duties to the people have blinded us to our duties to ourselves and our human dignity.

"We think, moreover, that this timid phrase may lay us open to a danger, the possibility of which is probably unsuspected by many of the wise persons who repeat it. From the constant harnessing, as it were on principle, of political freedom to the solution of the labour question, there is but one step to democratic imperialism. From the point of view of narrow labour interests, it may appear more advantageous to uphold the huge power already established, once it offers immediate economic reforms, than to follow the long and difficult path to general freedom. . . . . We admit of no compromise on this point, and, in case of a conflict between civil liberty and imperial socialism, we should take our stand on the side of 'bourgeois' liberals against the 'peasantist' socialists, who allowed themselves to be caught in such a snare.

"We do not believe in the possibility of making the people prosperous by decrees and edicts from above. . . . .

"It is only by guaranteeing liberty to our opponents that we can secure our own. The science of liberty" consists "in developing the faculty of tolerating what is unpleasant or even injurious, whenever it is the result of the use of rights equal to our own.

"We do not see why all persons of a progressive turn of mind who are our opponents on the economic questions should not pay us back in the same coin. There is not in our view a single point which could hinder us from working in common with them.

"We acknowledge without equivocation that, as regards the political question, which for us is the question of the day, our programme is just that of the advanced section of Russian liberals. . . . .

"The Russian revolutionists, . . . . protested for a long time against 'politics'; and when at last they accepted it, they avoided the beaten track and, wishing to find out for themselves something new and original, went by round-about by-paths. . . . .

"The liberals on the contrary, went straight towards their end without any hair-splitting, and thus attained to a simpler, more logical, and more practical standpoint in politics."

The pamphlet concludes with a strong appeal for mutual tolerance in the face of the common enemy (pp. 34-38).

As if in response to this appeal there is clandestinely promulgated in 1894 the manifesto of the "Popular Right" (Narodnoe Pravo) Party, and an excellent pamphlet entitled "The Burning Question." The former is translated in the same little volume as Stepniak's appeal (pp. 118-121). Clearly, as we shall see, this emanates from a section of the socialist party but it is also clear how closely they are approximating to the political ideal put forth by Stepniak. The manifesto sets forth that:—

"In the opinion of the party, popular right includes in itself alike the conception of the right of the people to political freedom and the conception of its right to secure its material needs upon the basis of national production. The party considers the guarantees of this right to be—

"Representative government on the basis of universal suffrage.

"Freedom of religious belief.

"Independence of the courts of justice.

"Freedom of the press.

"Freedom of meeting and association.

"Inviolability of the individual and of his rights as a man."

. . . . .

"Thus understanding Popular Right, the party sets itself the task of uniting all the oppositional elements of the country and of organising an active force which should, with all the spiritual and material means at its disposal, attain the overthrow of autocracy and secure to every one the right of a citizen and a man."

Here we have what I think may at any rate be accepted as symptoms of a better prospect that the determination and heroic self-sacrifice of the nihilists will at last effect a junction with the sobriety of judgment and perseverance, as well as with the numerical and material importance of the liberals. There is nothing that might do so much for Russian freedom as such an alliance as this.

Such a consolidated party of reform would attract to itself a very large proportion of the most educated and energetic amongst the Russians. Here and there one comes across symptoms of public spirit in rather unexpected quarters, which seem only to require focussing to make them effective. I recently heard a speech by an escaped Russian exile, Egor Lazarev in which he gave a short sketch of his life so far as its political aspects were concerned in Russia, which for example illustrates the attitude of the legal profession. Part of his story is told in George Kennan's book "Siberia and the Exile System," Vol. I. p. 268.

The story of Mr Lazarev as told by Mr Kennan is an admirably illustrative instance of the arbitrariness of the Russian political police, but to my mind perhaps its most interesting part is in the sequel. This concerns his relations with the legal profession at Saratov. Mr Lazarev after suffering severe persecution from the Government, had studied law and begun the practice of his profession; when he claimed admission to the bar the officials at St Petersburg indicated to the Saratov courts that he was a persona ingrata and that his application to be admitted should be refused. In the Saratov courts however the cause of legal rights found sturdy champions; they found no flaw in his legal claim to practise as a barrister and he was duly admitted. It was then that he was exiled without trial to Siberia by administrative process for three years the first of which he spent in imprisonment in Moscow waiting for the exile party to be made up. After the expiration of the period of three years he again returned to Saratov, and in spite of the still stronger representations made to the bar authorities by the St Petersburg tchinovniks he was again admitted, the court actually having the boldness to write to one of the ministers that there was no evidence before them to show that Mr Lazarev had been otherwise employed than in travelling for his own pleasure. Five months later he was again put in prison, and spent a year in solitary confinement. His crime was bringing a letter from Siberia to a Stundist. His case was reported to the minister, who brought it to the notice of the Tsar. The Tsar said, "Send him back for five years to the remotest part of Siberia." Again he was sent from Moscow on foot to Siberia. He spent two years in Siberia, and then escaped by Japan and America.

The lawyers of America are said to be the most conservative and (in the general sense) most undemocratic class in the country; the Russian lawyers do not seem to be open to the same reproach. Indeed of the professions generally it may be said that their sympathies are for the most part on the liberal side. An exception must however be made of the priesthood. Where historical facts are in question it is not desirable to use tales and works of fiction as authorities; the case is sometimes otherwise where general characteristics have to be delineated. It would be difficult to give a more real impression of the sordidness, the absence of spirituality, the pettiness, and the narrowness of the general run of the Russian priesthood than is given in the beautiful little tale in Mr Fisher Unwin's Pseudonym Library "A Russian Priest." Its tragedy, as that of many Russian stories, lies in the gradual disappointment and disillusionment of an ardent soul who enters a sordid walk of life under the firm conviction that he can make a great and decisive impression upon it.

It is necessary before leaving this sketch of the dramatis personæ on the modern Russian political stage, to say something of its great personages, for though descriptions of kings and emperors doubtless usually take a quite disproportionate place in narratives of contemporary history, in Russia at least, the character, disposition and attainments of the Tsar and those immediately around him have great importance quite apart from the snobbish gossipry which revels in such details.

The character of the monarch who died in 1894 is now pretty generally understood in well-informed circles.

The flood of exaggerated eulogy which filled our newspapers during the autumn of 1894 will be remembered; now that it has subsided it may be permitted to speak with more frankness than was shown at that time by our journalists; they were perhaps entrapped in what Mr Meredith calls "the pit-fall of sentiment." Probably the most salient characteristic in Alexander III. was the low level of his mental equipment. To naturally poor parts was added the disadvantage of no preparation during his earlier life for his post. He was educated exclusively as a soldier, for until the death of his elder brother in his twentieth year he had no prospect of ascending the throne. The character sketch in Mr Harold Frederic's "New Exodus" (chap. viii. p. 136) seems to me to sum up rather well what was seen of him by those who had closer opportunities of observation than most.

> "Alexander III. is a man of rather limited mental endowments and acquirements, who does not easily see more than one thing at a time, and who gets to see that slowly. . . . He has no idea of system and no executive talent. He would not be selected to manage the affairs of a village if he were an ordinary citizen. It is the very irony of fate that he has been made responsible for the management of half a million of villages.
>
> "He has an abiding sense of the sacredness of this responsibility and he toils assiduously over the task as it is given to him to comprehend it. Save for brief periods of holiday-making with his family, he works till two or three o'clock in the morning examining papers, reading suggestions,

and signing papers. No man in the Empire is busier than he.

"The misery of it is that all this irksome labour is of no use whatever. So far as the real Government of Russia is concerned, he might as well be employed in wheeling bricks from one end of a yard to the other and then back again. Even when one tries to realise what 'Russian Government' is like—with its vast bureaucracy essaying the stupendous task of maintaining an absolute personal supervision over every individual human unit in a mass of a hundred millions, and that through the least capable and most uniformly corrupt agents to be found in the world—the mind cannot grasp the utter hopelessness of it all. . . .

"Alexander III. simply struggles on at one little corner of the towering pyramid of routine business which his ministers pile up before him. Compared with him Sisyphus was a gentleman of leisure.

"This slow-minded mercilessly-burdened man knows very little either of the events close about him or of the broader currents of contemporaneous history outside. . . . He was a man grown before his elder brother's death pushed him forward as heir to the throne. A belated effort was then made to engraft upon his weak and spindling tree of knowledge some of the special fruits of learning which a future Emperor should possess. He was docile and good. Some of his teachers established a powerful personal influence over him, the effects of which were afterwards to be of such terrible moment, but they accomplished little else."

Possibly this account of the late Tsar is a little too tame; it does not quite give the idea of the exceedingly passionate and rather coarse nature that the last Alexander possessed.

Mr Lowe the *Times* correspondent in his recently published book " Alexander III. of Russia " thus sums up his conception of the drift of the political ideas of Alexander (pp. 183-4):

"It was known that he was by far the most ardent champion in all Russia of the three Slavophil principles of Autocracy, Eastern Orthodoxy, and Nationality—'one king, one faith, one law'—and it soon became apparent that he had set his heart on carrying all these principles into practice in the most energetic and uncompromising form.

"He had three alternatives before him : either to maintain the *status quo*; or to move in the same direction as Austria—*i.e.*, towards decentralisation; or, finally, to endeavour to nationalise the Empire at the expense of the subject races and in favour of the most important—the 'Great Russians.' He chose the third of these and his watchword became 'Russia for the Russians.' Whoever stood in the way of the fulfilment of this design, whether Jew, German, or Swedish Finlander, must go to the wall. To carry out this policy, however, time was required, for, should war break out, and an enemy gain foot on Russian soil, a revolution might possibly ensue, and this would not only endanger the process of union, but might even imperil the cohesion of the state. It was therefore essential to the Tsar's policy that there should be peace, so as to afford leisure for the innovations he contemplated at home; and if Alexander III. gained so much credit for keeping the peace of Russia abroad, it was only at the cost of the civil strife into which he now prepared to plunge a large portion of his own people."

One of the most important personages under Alexander III. was Pobiedonoststev then and still the Procurator of the Holiest Synod, that is to say a sort of Minister of Public Worship for the State Church. He is a "sincerely and fanatically pious man as the Greek Church understands piety. . . . His religious fervour contemplates without blinking the prospect of ten millions of Jews, Lutherans, Catholics, and dissenters generally being despoiled, evicted, harried by Cossacks and driven like criminals from their homes" (Harold Frederic). He was the chief of the advisers who inflamed Alexander's Panslavistic tendencies till they led to the most terrible results: the harrying of his border countries till all their national and religious individuality should be assimilated to the Muscovite model, the infringement of the Finnish constitution which he had promised to respect, the persecution of the Russian Protestants in the South and of the Jews throughout his Empire, the suppression of education and intelligence, and of the freedom of the press, thus cutting off from himself the only possible means he had of ascertaining what was going on in his country, and of combating the enormous abuses that had grown up there.

A still mightier personage whilst he lived, though not in the service of the Tsar, was Michael Katkov; although he died in 1887 one has to say a word about him when considering the forces at work in the Russian political world of to-day just as one still has to say something of Alexander III., for "the evil that men do lives after them." Katkov began his political life as an ardent member of the most advanced party the comrade and friend of Herzen and Bakunin, and (after editing the *Moscow Gazette* for five years) as one of the editors of a literary magazine *The Russian Messenger*, in which appeared for the first time some of the masterpieces of Tourguénev, Saltykov, and Leo Tolstoi.

"At that time there was nothing to indicate that Katkof was in any way unworthy of the friendship and confidence of such men. . . . The change of front came like a thunderstorm. . . . One of the points in the liberal programme was to effect a reconciliation between the Russian and the Polish people on the basis of substantial justice and mutual concessions. . . . A small fraction of the liberals however, were at variance with the majority respecting the Polish question. They were eager enough to obtain political freedom for their own country, but they would not willingly see it extended to the Poles. The drift of the party was represented by individuals of little influence, until Katkof was inspired with the idea of putting himself at its head."

In 1863 Katkov for a second time became editor of the *Moscow Gazette*:

"He devoted his attention wholly to the Polish question, doubtless with a grim satisfaction at the thought that to frustrate the plans of the Poles would be to score an important victory over the Russian Liberals. He denounced the preparations that were being made in Poland, foretold a speedy insurrection, and stigmatized as traitors all his fellow-countrymen who remained unconvinced by his arguments and unmoved by his appeals. When his predictions were at last fulfilled all the passions of his nature broke loose in wild disorder. His style of writing resembled that of a Hebrew prophet; the measures he advocated were as cynical as any to which Marat ever affixed his name; and the immediate result he sought to bring about in Poland was such as no man with a vestige of humanity would dare to avow to himself. Those who are not acquainted with the details of the Polish insurrection, with the sickening scenes of bloodshed and fiendish cruelty which marked every step in the work of repression, and with the part that Katkof played in that horrid drama, are not qualified to form an estimate of the man's character or of his work." . . . He appealed "to the worst passions of the people, whom he at last worked up into such a state of frenzy that every deed of violence, every cold-blooded act of cruelty perpetrated against the Poles, seemed a distinctly meritorious act. And the passions he then so successfully inflamed have not yet subsided. A Pole is still, in the eyes of millions of the common people of Russia, an object of loathing, a malignant being of an inferior order whom it is an act of great self-denial in the State to tolerate."

After the Polish insurrection Katkov "claimed to be considered as the official mouthpiece of the Russian people." No minister was powerful enough to stand up against this journalist. On one occasion the Minister of the Interior ordered the suspension of the issue of his paper, but the command was absolutely ignored and the Minister himself was attacked in the paper; he had to acknowledge himself defeated, and meekly to submit.

The immense power Katkov now wielded he used exclusively on the reactionary side. Greatly to his influence was due the suppression of such publications as the "Golos" and "The Annals of the Fatherland," the new fetters placed on the education system, the whittling away of the privileges of the Zemstvoes, and the curtailment of the popular franchises for local government purposes.

(This account is taken from an article on Michael Katkof by "An English Resident in Russia," *Contemporary Review*, Oct. 1887.)

Of the new Tsar Nicholas not a great deal is as yet known. That a Tsar in his position might do a good deal for the liberation of his country there seems to be no doubt. For example his personal discountenancing of the religious persecution would do much; so too would his personal insistence that the press should enjoy some liberty. During the first two or three months of his reign we observed what symptoms we were permitted to hear about with some degree of puzzlement, so ambiguous did they appear. Nicholas, we were told, moved more freely about amongst his people and with fewer guards than his predecessors.

If this was so it was at any rate so much to the good, but it was not after all clear whether the gentleman who was seen buying gloves in a shop like any ordinary mortal was not his cousin the Duke of York.

It was said on his accession that he had promulgated an important amnesty, but it is found on examination that those imprisoned or exiled without trial by administrative process, are simply left as they were before, to the tender mercies of the Minister of the Interior. One would have hoped that the victims of arbitrary disregard of law would have received relief before murderers and thieves.

"We must further note," says *Free Russia*, "that all reference to an amnesty for those whose offence consists in holding religious opinions which are not those of the Orthodox State Church is omitted from the manifesto. No ray of hope is held out to the Stundists, the Old Believers, and other dissenting bodies. The continuance of persecution upon the old lines proves that the manifesto is not understood by the Russian administrators and officials to mean any large measure of tolerance. The Jews are harassed now as they were before. Political arrests are continued on an extensive scale" (*Free Russia*, January 1895).

This darkness is but faintly illuminated by the spark of grace shown in the edict, which orders those who persisted in going to their ancestral Roman Catholic church at Krózhe after they had been officially informed that they had joined the Eastern Communion and that their old church would therefore be closed (such of them at least as had escaped being sabred by the Cossacks. or being drowned in the river when being pursued by them), should no longer be imprisoned but should have their sentences commuted.

Finland has obtained a ratification of her constitution (the Finns delaying to take the oath of allegiance till this was conceded).

On the other hand no relief has been given from the rigours to which the press is subjected. A Reuter's telegram dated from St Petersburg, April 20th, 1895, says:—

> "The Tsar has rejected the petition recently presented by seventy representatives of the press and literary men, praying for a relaxation of the laws governing the press in Russia; the Commission consisting of the Minister of Justice, the Minister of the Interior, and the Chief Procurator of the Holy Synod, to which the document was referred having adversely reported upon it."

The use of the Russian language is still insisted upon

in Poland, and a new crusade has been set on foot against the Ukrainian language and literature.

It is true that Gourko, the embodiment of brutality, was removed from the government of Poland, but Pobiedonoststev the arch-persecutor remained head of the Synod. Sævitia has gone, but Crudelitas remains.

All this left us mystified enough, till at the end of January the young Tsar made a notable declaration which removed all doubt from our minds as to whether we were henceforth to regard him as a friend or as an enemy of freedom. To this incident I shall have to refer at some length in my next chapter.

The following may be read in amplification of the contents of this chapter :—

> Leroy-Beaulieu, Vol. I. Book III. chap. iv. ; Book IV. chap. i. ; Vol. II. Book IV. chap. vii. ; Book VI. chap. ii.
> Wallace, chaps. xxvi. and xxviii.
> Stepniak, "The Russian Storm Cloud," Part I., and "Nihilism as it is."
> Ed. Dicey, "The Peasant State ; an Account of Bulgaria in 1894."
> Potapenko, " A Russian Priest."
> 
> For accounts of such interesting and important personages as Schuválov, the brothers Miliutin, Gortchakov, Ignatiev, the Aksákov family, Koshelev, and Bilinski, the reader may be referred to "Distinguished Persons in Russian Society" (published in English in 1873), and Samson-Himmelstierna's "Russia under Alexander III. and in the Preceding Period" (published in English in 1893) both translated from the German.

# CHAPTER VIII.

## "HOW LONG THE MANY MUST ENDURE THE ONE?"

## Chapter VIII.—*Contents.*

The political forces at work and the phenomena observable; the bureaucracy supreme; its *personnel* very numerous and very corrupt; red-tapism. The results of being governed by such a body: "Administrative process"; Russian prisons and exile system; army contracts and commissariat; "the crusade against culture." What chances are there of the overthrow of the bureaucracy and the introduction of constitutionalism?

Recapitulation of ground already traversed; the racial problem; the peasantry numerically overwhelming; why this need not be regarded as an insurmountable obstacle to progress; the new forces that are coming into play in Russian life. Turning to the historical aspect we find in the past the ideas of (1) consolidation and (2) Europeanisation; both alike have striven to establish Russia as a great maritime power and have followed a policy which would willingly find its consummation in the acquirement of Constantinople. But with the Decembrist Revolt of 1825 there becomes noticeable a new political idea and the struggle for political freedom begins. It ripens during the reign of Nicholas and has a wonderful outburst of activity at the beginning of that of Alexander II. But the political privileges then accorded are afterwards largely rescinded. How can the Russian people fail to read the moral that popular liberties must be founded not on the will of a prince, but on the will effectually expressed of the people?

The different elements which make for progress in Russia now drawing closer together. Madame Tsebrikova's letter to the Tsar. General agreement as to necessity of granting constitutional reforms; some of the difficulties considered. Attitude of Nicholas II. towards the question; his declaration of January 29th, 1895; the *Times* commentary thereon; the futility of the position there put forward. Constitutionalism the only road to good government.

## CHAPTER VIII.

### "HOW LONG THE MANY MUST ENDURE THE ONE?"

In our last chapter we have marshalled before us the *dramatis personæ* on the political stage of modern Russia; our task is now to consider the drama that they may be called upon to play.

We have seen the persons of the play to consist of the Tsar himself hedged round by the impervious ranks of the corrupt bureaucracy; of the great mass of peasantry (who as yet remain for the most part loyal to his person, believing that their misfortunes spring not from his action, but from that of the officials); of the educated classes, including the army and navy officers, and the bureaucracy, and the professional people, and the well-to-do amongst the traders; most of these (where the interests of Government employment leave their choice unfettered) sympathise either with the Old Russian Slavophil ideas, or have liberal tendencies; amongst the various sections of the last there is now noticeable a predisposition towards consolidation. Occasionally there arises a notable personality in the army or amongst the ministers, or on the other hand in literature, whose influence is felt in the country.

These being the political forces at work what are the phenomena observable?—Well we must now realise if we have not realised it before, that the government in Russia lies for the main part in the hands of the bureaucracy. In many directions an enlightened Tsar could doubtless do much, but if he wished his reforms to be of real value, above all if he wished them to be of permanent and reliable value, he would have to set his mind to the overthrow of the power of the tchinovniks, and consequently he would necessarily have to call in to his aid some governing power extensive enough to grapple with it. Such a one could only be found in some form of constitutional government. But the Tsardom during the last reign did exactly the contrary to this; it delivered itself over bound hand and foot into the power of the bureaucracy, for it was on these terms alone that the bureaucracy would accept the responsibility of guarding its personal physical safety. What sort of personal safety was actually secured for the prisoner of Gatchina it is perhaps more for his son Nicholas than for any one else to judge. Yet as we shall see the son announces his determination to follow in the path of his father!

It is an important investigation for us to make, to ascertain what sort of a *personnel* this bureaucracy to which the government of Russia is for the time being delivered, presents. As we have seen, it is to a large extent independent of control from above, both because the monarch is afraid to maim his own instrument of government, and because he is physically unable to grapple with the mass of affairs that every hour brings to the ministries of St Petersburg for decision. If he takes pains to inform himself as to what is going forward in one department, so many of the twenty-four hours are occupied; there are not enough hours in the day for him to be able to possess the most superficial knowledge of what goes on in all those departments over which he is supposed to exercise supreme control.

Neither from below is there any restraining power, for not only is there no representative government which is allowed to approach however remotely imperial affairs, but public opinion itself is choked to death. The press is gagged and under the direct control of the bureaucracy itself, there is no right of public meeting, even conversation between a knot of friends on political matters or on the doings of the officials is dangerous. The *personnel* of the bureaucracy is immensely numerous; and monetary corruption is so prevalent amongst them as to be almost universal. M. Leroy-Beaulieu attempts to dissect the causes of this corruption :—He says that it is a service that has been thrown open to the adventurers of all nations and that since the time of Peter the Great theft and fraud have been their traditions. "Then" he says "one must take account of the demoralising influence that the institution of serfdom had on all classes of society, of the ways of an Eastern despotism, which survive more or less beneath the surface of European reforms." Then there is the extent of the Empire and the ignorance of the bulk of its inhabitants, giving a magnificently free field for the exercise of abuses. Lastly there is the insufficiency of remuneration. "In many branches of the administration the inadequacy of salary has been so notorious that it has practically been accepted as an authorisation to have recourse to illicit sources of remuneration." These predisposing causes are quite enough to account for the growth of abuses where the environment is so favourable. One might, perhaps, be disposed to add to them that as any manifestation of individuality is persecuted and submissiveness is regarded as the highest virtue — *fear*, rather than honour and self-respect, becomes the main impulse of conduct. Hardly any body of men would withstand the temptations of being vested with the enormous uncontrolled powers of the Russian tchinovniks, and it appears that there are reasons that make them little adapted to make any stand against them. Whether we examine the army or the civil service, the corruption we find is of the most appalling and hopeless kind. The evidence on this point is practically universal. But this great body of officials so loose in what they actually do, are usually apparently strictly regular in their methods of setting about work; nowhere is red-tapism carried to such a pitch. Minute and multifarious regulations have been devised in the vain hope of putting some check on the cupidity, incompetence, and tyranny of the officials; but they have served only to shelter them more completely than ever from any chance of being efficiently held in control. The author of "Revelations of Russia," says:—

"This system originally devised as a check on those employed, by placing on record, in black and white, the minutest details of everything connected with their duty, has had the contrary effect of insuring impunity, by burying every transaction in such an inextricably voluminous mass of documents, as to prove an effectual shelter for every species of fraud, which is protected, not here and there, or occasionally, but by high and low, and with a nefarious order and regularity similar to that with which, in great capitals, associations of thieves are conducted" (Vol. I. p. 24).

This is a just description of the instrument of government to which the millions of the Russian people are subject. If such is the arrangement for conducting the business of the nation we can hardly expect it to be done well. It is in fact done terribly badly.

Many instances will at once occur to the mind. I may mention as examples the system by which those suspected of political disaffection are suddenly and arbitrarily exiled or imprisoned for long and indefinite periods of time without any sort of trial on the mere fiat of a policeman of superior rank.

From this point the mind naturally reverts to another instance—viz. the terrible state of the Russian prisons, and the conditions of transportation of prisoners and exiles as revealed by Mr Kennan's investigation. The prison structures are very bad and the sanitary arrangements unspeakably abominable; overcrowding exists to a frightful extent; for the whole Empire, about one-fifth as many persons again as there is officially declared room for, are in prison, or were so according to the last available information; but the deficiency of room is not of course spread evenly throughout the country, so that in some localities it is infinitely worse and the number of prisoners has mounted up in some provinces to two-and-a-half and in one province actually to five times the number that there is certified room for. This must practically mean a death sentence to very many of the prisoners; the sick-rates and the death-rates are accordingly very high, and such diseases as typhus and scurvy are prevalent. In Tomsk forwarding prison in 1886 more than half the prisoners had typhus, and in the following year nearly two-thirds suffered from the disease (62·6 per cent.) nor is even this the worst case given in Mr Kennan's tables.

The effect of official corruption on the arrangements for the army may be read in Stepniak's "Russian Storm Cloud" where an account is given of the terrible sufferings of the soldiers in the Russo-Turkish campaign consequent on the bad supplies or absence of supplies of food, clothing, and medical appliances. The author says that it was to the Russian army contractors and commissariat officers that Russia owed the enormous losses of that terrible war, in which it is calculated that there perished not fewer than 100,000 of her children.

The same writer in his book "Under the Tzars" gives an account of what he calls the "Crusade against Culture." We have already touched on this subject when speaking of the restrictive regulations put in force against the Jews. But the whole nation and especially the great mass of the peasantry suffers from regulations of the same sort though not carried to such an extreme.

In the primary schools a maximum, instead (as in other countries) a minimum, is prescribed to education. "It is strictly forbidden to the little peasant children to acquire more than an elementary knowledge of the catechism and of sacred history, of reading and writing, and of the four first rules of arithmetic." It is persistently arranged that the number of schools in which even this poor education is given shall be ridiculously below the demand of the people. As to the secondary schools, large numbers of them are actually suppressed, and when attempts are made to add to their numbers by local effort (by the action of the Zemstvo-Assembly for example), such attempts are crushed. The curriculum is deliberately designed to stupefy the pupils. Thus the explanatory appendix to the regulations says that the "less history is studied in the gymnasiums the better": general geography is proscribed by the Minister of Instruction on account of its "dangerous tendencies." It may "suggest conflicting conclusions and give rise to useless reasonings." The Minister of Public Instruction in fact "opposes by every possible means the diffusion of secondary education. When resistance becomes impossible he tries to exclude from its benefits the professional classes (to whom it is a matter of life and death) in order to confine it as much as may be to the higher nobility and richer citizens. The privilege once granted to these classes, he makes the instruction given as sterile as possible, and arranges matters so that it may be imparted to the fewest numbers." In the universities the same sort of thing goes on with even more force. The number of students is thinned by wholesale expulsions and by closing important institutions; those that are left, and even the professorial bodies, are subject to police officials who are introduced amongst them under the designation of "inspectors" and so forth. Amongst students all clubs and unions are forbidden.

An interesting dispatch dated February 1895, from the Minister of the Interior Dournovo, addressed to the Minister of Public Instruction Delyanov, will serve as a recent example of the governmental attitude towards the spread of public enlightenment. It was of course intended to be private but it leaked out and a translation was published *in extenso* in the *Daily Chronicle* (London) for April 27, 1895. The following passages from the document will show its tenor :—

"Among the social phenomena which came to the front during the last year, the tendency to raise the level of popular education by means of organising popular lectures, libraries, reading-rooms for, and free distribution of, scientific, moral, and literary publications among the factory and rural population, which was so strikingly manifested, must be specially pointed out."

. . . . . . .

" But while the libraries and reading rooms are, though not under sufficient, yet still under some, control, the free distribution of books escapes any governmental control. Still more must it be noticed that the distributors of these books are intelligent young people of both sexes, very often still pursuing their studies, who penetrate into the midst of the people in the capacity of teachers, statistical agents, organisers of soup kitchens, and the like.

"The failure of the crops in 1891, and the cholera in 1892-3, caused an exceptionally large influx of educated young people into the villages, and as a result they have revived the tendencies of Russian young persons to raise the level of the people by the initiative of the intelligent classes, which had somewhat decayed during the eighties."

. . . . . . .

"Taking into consideration all that has been said, it appears probable that the above-mentioned movement, which was called into being by the popular calamities of the last few years, being led by such experienced and clever men will develop systematically in a way which will not be in accordance with the views of the Government, and that in the near future it may lead to very undesirable results.

"In view of these considerations, and being preoccupied with the safeguarding of security and order, I should think it urgent at once to take serious measures to the effect that the help of the public to the cause of popular enlightenment, always valuable and honourable in principle, should not become, under the influence of ill-intentioned persons, and under the condition of uncontrolled interference by private persons and societies in this important department of State affairs, the source of the perversion of popular ideas and of the estrangement of the people from historical traditions made sacred by past centuries. My opinion is that the active help of private persons and private societies to the cause of popular enlightenment may be useful and permissible only on condition that this help is carried on in accordance with the system adopted by the

Government represented by the Ministry of Public Education, and that the work of all such societies and persons should be under the watchful control of its organs."

Action in the direction desired by M. Dournovo followed his dispatch with the result that all the agencies for popular education referred to by him are now placed under the "watchful control" of the reactionary Minister of Public Instruction.

We now come to the great question which is the natural objective of any systematic work on Russian politics such as this. The present situation appears to be intolerable. Before any alleviation can be obtained must we wait several centuries for historical development to ripen? or may we expect quicker relief? Let us very rapidly recapitulate any conclusions we may have come to in the course of this book bearing upon the point.

Firstly I think we have concluded that racially there is no cause for despondency. The ethnological element which has imposed on the others its language, its religion, and its national feeling and sentiment is that of the Slavs, that is to say a purely Aryan stock. If it has been superimposed in the North on an important substratum of Finnish races we remarked that those races whenever they have been placed in near relations with others more advanced than themselves, have shown a singular aptitude for assimilating themselves to them, whilst the higher types of Finns, such as the Magyars of Hungary, compare favourably with any Indo-European race. The admixture of blood to the South with Tatár or Mongol-Tatár races does not alter the conditions sufficiently to make us depart from our inference that the ethnological *material* with which we are concerned throws no bar across the path of progress.

On the threshold of our subject we are confronted with the problem of the peasantry, overwhelming in numbers, and as yet for the most part, loyal to the person of the Tsar. The importance of mere numbers may be overrated but still where the ultimate sanction of governmental authority is a huge army, and where this can ever be recruited from an unfailing source such as a loyal peasantry would supply, we recognise that the element in the case is not one which can be treated lightly.

Well, we must remember that the effects of the emancipation are being felt; that the peasantry are becoming more alive to political, as opposed to merely communal, thoughts and ideas, and that the terrible weight of imperial taxation under which they are crushed, furnishes a constant incentive to them to grapple with the problem of the conditions which govern their existence, and to make them endeavour to make their yoke less hard. Not a little weight is to be attached in this connection to the new aspects that Russian life presents, even since the date of the Emancipation.

We have to note that many of its conditions are entirely new; that each new year sees the introduction of a new state of things such as has never been extant before and of a nature that may very probably bring into action new political aspirations and activities. For we have found that South Russia is practically a colony, and one that has been comparatively recently settled. During the last half century the Empire has something like doubled its population, industrial and manufacturing developments have begun though they are still in their infancy; the railway system has a great future before it, and large towns are (with the exception of half a dozen or so, including the two capitals) only now beginning to spring up.

All these considerations encourage us to hope that the time to entrust the Russian peasants with political privileges, is not far distant, and that they may show themselves at least as capable of wielding them, as their cousins of Bulgaria.

Turning now to our historical survey, it disclosed to us in the first place the inception by the Muscovite Princedom in the fourteenth century of the idea of consolidation of Empire. From that time to this, that Russia shall be great, that she shall be solidified, and that she shall be homogeneous have been accepted as governing precepts.

In the time of the immediate predecessors of Peter the Great, and much more emphatically during the reign of that monarch himself, these rudimentary ideas of government began to be supplemented by others of not less importance. Peter entered into a combat against the laziness, the roughness, and the ignorance he found rampant within his realm. It was ordained that Russia was to be rescued from her position of semi-Asiatic isolation, and that she was to be established as an important member of the great European family. The idea of Europeanisation was added to that of Consolidation of Empire, and both alike found a great means to their establishment in the founding of a great Russian *maritime* power with a formidable navy. Accordingly the aim to which the fighting and diplomacy of all Peter's reign lead up, was the Russianising of the Baltic, and the founding on its shores of a maritime capital which would be in closer touch with Western Europe than Moscow was ever likely to be. What Peter did for the Baltic, his successors have in great measure done for the Black Sea, and at the present moment ports have been constructed on the far distant Pacific coast to be connected with the

Western capital by a railway 6666 miles long. The ideal which Russian statesmen have placed before themselves to round off and complete this policy of maritime growth is the acquisition of Constantinople, and the command of the Bosphorus and the Dardanelles. (It is not my intention to discuss here whether the realisation of such an ideal will ever meet with acquiescence from England.)

We had to wait till the present century before the growth of a third set of political ideas became noticeable. The struggle for popular political liberty, to the idea of which Englishmen are so accustomed that they hardly understand how history can be written or formulated without it, makes in Russia its first serious demonstration in 1825. Even then it was for the most part confined to the army, and even to the upper ranks of the army. It was crushed with the greatest ease and ruthlessly punished. But from this time forward we have more numerous and to us far more interesting forces at work in the Russian political arena. The stern repression of the reign of Nicholas I. keeps them below the surface for a time, but on his death there breaks out under his son the extraordinary liberal movement, which was signalised by the emancipation of the serfs, the establishment of local government, the reform of the law-courts, and the introduction into the army of short service, and an educational system. There is no doubt that in spite of the absence of any outward manifestation of the kind great progress was made during the reign of Nicholas I. in political education; and this progress seems to date from the revolt of the Decembrists in the first days of his reign. Herzen says ("My Exile," Vol. II. p. 167):—

"Comparing the Moscow Society before 1812, with that which I left in 1847, my heart beats with joy. There is no doubt, we have made an (*sic*) immense progress since that time. Then, a society of malcontents existed likewise, but it consisted of the dismissed, the sent-away, of those kept quiet by force; now it is a society of independents."

M. Leroy-Beaulieu says the same thing. He emphasizes the important part that public opinion and public spirit played in the reforms of Alexander II.'s reign and shows how the way for all this was paved during the reign of Nicholas, not a little by the writings of Tourguénev, Gogol, Herzen, etc. Speaking of the emancipation of the serfs, he says :—

"Here we behold a national movement, comparable though at a long distance to the movement from which the French Revolution issued. This phenomenon is a new one in Russian history, and is worthy of as much attention as the Emancipation itself and the reforms which accompanied it" (Vol. I. Book VII. chap. i., French edition, pp. 413-4; English edition, pp. 419-20).

But if such was the progress that was made under Nicholas and those that preceded him, what was it compared with the strides forward made in political education during the reigns of the two Alexanders who succeeded him? For what was it that happened during these two reigns? An extraordinary series of political privileges were accorded, and then they were to a large extent taken away again! For a few years the people were allowed to accustom themselves to some of the sweets of liberty, and then they were roughly reminded that these liberties were not in any real sense of the word theirs at all, and that they could be taken back as easily as they had been bestowed. To a sensitive nation just beginning to feel the strength and vigour of independence infuse the young blood in its veins, what series of events could possibly have been devised better than this to foster patriotism and the growth of enlightened political instincts? The moral is so obvious that it may plainly be read by the whole people. Popular liberties must be founded on popular will and popular strength. The Government has written in large letters plain for all Russians to see—" Put not your faith in Princes."

What then has been the influence at work which has prevented a stronger demonstration's being made ere this against the reactionary policy of the last twenty years?

One main cause has undoubtedly been that the liberal and enlightened part of the people has been split in twain, the one section following after an impracticable socialism, the other section allowing their shrinking from that policy to induce them to a policy of non-resistance when their political privileges were being taken from them. The traditions of the Russian liberals are of too fine a character for it to be possible to accuse them of obsequiousness to the Government, but I think there can be very little doubt that they have carried the policy of conciliation which they appear deliberately to have adopted, a great deal too far.

To use the pithy phrase of an Englishman made indignant by the meek attitude of some of his fellow-countrymen, we may say of them with equal applicability that they have thought " Let us repeat no tales and allow no outcry against this terrible Russian Government, and *by civility we may coax it into an occasional act of humanity.*" They have even at times been inclined to go so far in this direction as to join in the hue and cry against the socialist-nihilist party who should be their closest and most valued allies. If all this has caused much bitterness in the past between the different sections of Russian reformers we have seen reason for hoping that a common policy may be possible for them in the near future. The tribulations of the late reigns have taught lessons to both parties alike. We have seen how the socialists are beginning to grasp the value of purely political as opposed to socialistic privileges, how some of them are even placing the former before the latter. This at once opens the door for an alliance. The liberals too we may hope, are shaking off that listless inertia which one is sometimes inclined to think has usurped the place of their former splendid energy.

Early in 1890, Madame Tsebrikova, who had always been opposed to revolutionary measures, went out of Russia for the purpose of sending an open letter to the Tsar setting forth some of the grievances under which her country-people suffered. The terms of the letter were perfectly respectful but also exceedingly frank: she sent it not only to the emperor himself but to the foreign press by which it was published. Some of the passages in this letter are very striking especially when one remembers that it was written by a quiet literary lady of fifty-four years old who was opposed to the extreme revolutionary party and had taken not a little pains to dissuade young people from identifying themselves with it :—

"The Zemstvos," she said, "asked for freedom of speech, the abolition of administrative exile, public justice, personal security, and the right of meeting for the discussion of their general needs. If, at the present time, the Zemstvos silently submit to new measures still further invading their rights, that is no guarantee for the slavish submission of future generations, nourished with the suppressed discontent of their fathers. Power of resistance gathers slowly through generations, and at last bursts forth. . . . Blood is horrible to me on whichever side it is shed, but when bloodshed on one side is rewarded with a decoration, and on the other side with a gallows-rope, it is easy to understand which bloodshed will have for the young the charm of heroism. Besides the punishments by sentence of a court, we have 'administrative' sentences by means of which the Government disposes of its enemies when there is not evidence enough to try them. But what is this if not arbitrary lawlessness? Political prisoners are the defenceless victims of arbitrary despotism that reaches downright brutality. . . . Freedom of speech, personal security, freedom of meetings, full publicity of justice, education easy of access for all talents, suppression of administrative despotism, the convoking of a National Assembly for which all classes can choose their delegates—in these alone is our salvation."

In such noble sentences, not unworthy of a place beside some of the utterances of our defenders of liberty in the times of the Stuarts, did this woman assert not only the rights of her countrymen but the determination of the Russian liberals no longer to play the part of passive spectators whilst they were being trampled upon.

After the issue of her letter she openly returned to Petersburg to face the consequences of her action. She was immediately arrested and banished without trial to a distant province from which however she has recently been permitted to return.

On the general necessity of granting constitutional

forms of government in Russia all moderate people are becoming agreed. Let us hear what the judicious M. Leroy-Beaulieu has to say on the subject. In the last chapter but one of his second volume he dwells in the first place on the mistake as he views it of considering the peasantry alone as the people who have a right to a voice in this matter.

"Can one," he asks, "say that in the peasantry consists the whole of Russia? Can one apply to it Louis XIV.'s saying 'The State—I am the State'? . . . In whose interests should Russia be governed? Solely in those of the lowly born, the unlettered plebs? Solely in those of one class? and that the most ignorant and the one that makes least demands? Yet at bottom this is the advice given by those who invite the autocracy to rely on the masses of the people alone, and to oppose itself to the educated classes."

This is not the view taken by M. Leroy-Beaulieu who regards the instructedness, and the superior political intelligence of the educated classes as being entitled to a great deal of weight. He goes on to say:—

"Russia without a constitution and without political rights, is not yet to be considered a modern state; like Turkey it can hardly even be considered a European state. Now is there either in the descent or in the character of the Russian people, in its history or in its religion; is there in its social organisation, or in the foundation on which as a nation it is based, anything which makes it so distinct from other Christian peoples as to forbid it from enjoying any part in those political liberties which are enjoyed to-day in greater or less degree by all other European nations? . . . Is Russia so radically different from the rest of Europe, does it belong so little to our continent, to our civilisation, that it must be destined by nature, or by the fatality of racial origin to a type of social governance and a form of political government radically dissimilar?"

We have recapitulated enough of M. Leroy-Beaulieu's opinions, and the grounds upon which they are based to know that he must answer these questions in the negative. He says:—

"There must be some outlet to the burning and tumultuous hopes which under the inspiration of Europe are bubbling over amongst the youth and the educated classes, there must be an outlet, and such an outlet can only be found in political rights and privileges, in a charter or a constitution. Words matter little, it does not matter what things are called: what is wanted in Russia is the thing, national representation. Officially this country has for centuries been mute; it is now necessary to give it a voice; if this is not done one knows not what catastrophes may follow; on the vast stage monopolised till now by the Government and its agents, it is now time to make room for a new actor, an enigmatic personage about whom little is known, talked about incessantly in some quarters, but as yet neither seen nor heard.

"We are told however that amongst enlightened people there are some who though they are liberal and even for the East radical, are opposed to any constitutional experiments' being tried in their own country for some time to come, or regard any prospect of their being introduced with the most melancholy apprehensions. 'What are we to understand?' say they, 'are you under the pretext of cutting short our difficulties going to precipitate us into new ones which may perhaps be even more serious? What is the good of undertaking a task for which we are so ill equipped? and for which we are without even the materials to work upon? It is to claim to be able to complete and crown the edifice of reforms, before the lower stories shall have been built. What constitution would work with our inexperience and ignorance, with our indolence, and cut-and-dried way of going to work? What we want is a sound and honest administration, justice given freely and without favour in the suppression of corruption and of the arbitrary conduct of the officers of the State. Imperial self-government would not become us, but local self-government would; what we want is the development of our provincial and municipal institutions, of our Zemstvos and our doumas; in fact the consolidation and completion, or perhaps we might better say the sincere carrying out of all the reforms of Alexander II. Russia would then be happy, peaceful and strong.'

"This unassuming and discreet language has but one fault; beneath apparent wisdom and the cloak of practical common sense, is really concealed a naïve, I will venture to say a childish deception. It is certainly true that what is wanted above all things else in Russia is a sound administration and justice without favour; the deception is to think that such advantages can be obtained and that one can enjoy them in security without anything to guarantee them; to argue thus is to be blind to the exact thing from which Russia is suffering, the thing which deprives of their result the best-conceived reforms, the absence that is to say of control and of guarantees, and these can be found in popular rights alone. . . . The Russians who profess to put their faith in administrative reforms (alone) are to my mind comparable to people trying to make a clock go without its pendulum."

Thus does this writer who is looked up to by all Europe as perhaps the greatest authority on Russian politics, pronounce unhesitatingly in favour of constitutional reform.

He completes his chapter by considering some of the difficulties of the situation. What is to be done he asks with all the frontier regions where the populations are imperfectly assimilated to the homogeneous Great Russian people?

"How find for all these conquests of the Tsar, a place in a liberal constitution, and in a Russian Assembly?

"The objection is a serious one. The dimensions of the Empire, its centralistic traditions, the variety amongst the populations to be found within its borders, these are certainly some of the chief obstacles in the way of the establishment of a free system of government.

. . . . . . . .

"With the provinces of the Vistula—the kingdom of Poland properly so called, the simplest course would perhaps be to have recourse to the same usage as in the case of Finland, to restore to it its automony and at the same time give it a constitution. For Russia that would be the best means of guaranteeing its western frontier, to wean its subjects of the West from the revolutionary spirit and protect them from the intrigues of ambitious neighbours at the same time that they secured for themselves a free government. To think as some people blinded with national prejudices do, that the Russian people could themselves enjoy political emancipation, and at the same time keep a broad zone of European provinces in a sort of political serfage or helotism is a delusion to which events would soon give the lie. On the other hand to attempt to apply identical institutions to all the peoples of the Empire to compel them all to take their places in a constitution exactly on one pattern throughout would be dangerously to complicate the working of the new system of government and at the same time to entangle the results beforehand.

"Wishes for autonomy will probably sooner or later exhibit themselves in the Baltic Provinces, Lithuania, White Russia, Little Russia, and Bessarabia, and further (on account of the remoteness of their situation) such regions as those of the lower Volga, the Ural, and Siberia."

I may perhaps be allowed to touch on another difficulty with which M. Leroy-Beaulieu does not as far as I remember grapple. In looking backwards over the constitutional history of England one witnesses a gradual growth of the widespread political privileges of the present time. The democratic suffrage has not been the growth of a day, but of centuries; long before the working people enjoyed political power, the trading classes had obtained a share of it—and long before that a curb was put on the power of the monarch by the nobles. Is growth on lines somewhat similar to these possible in Russia ? That such will be the course of events there, seems to be exceedingly improbable. The grading of Russian society is too abrupt, and it is not sufficiently stable to make one hopeful for such a course for the growth of constitutionalism. Are we to conclude on the other hand that a sudden proclamation of universal suffrage with all the equality of political rights enjoyed by American citizens is the only alternative? For if that is the case the difficulty of first introducing constitutionalism is immensely increased. I think another door is open to reform, viz. that of indirect representation with a popular suffrage at its base. So far as constitutionalism can be said to be a familiar subject at all to the Russian, this is a device perfectly well known to the mind even of the Russian peasant. The smaller local Zemstvo-Assemblies already send delegates to the larger ones of the second grade; it would seem a very natural development that the first Russian parliament should be made up of representatives from these larger district assemblies.

Now I think that the whole summing up of our argument has made it perfectly clear that by far the most important question which faced us at the beginning of the new reign in Russia, was "Will Nicholas do what in him lies to help the introduction into his country of constitutional forms of government?" Self-abnegation, and a resolve to surrender some part at all events of the full measure of his autocracy, would be the only thing which being of itself of value, would bring with it assurance of *permanent* improvement.

We had not to wait long for a reply to our queryings concerning this matter. On Jan. 29th 1895 the young Tsar made a public declaration of the utmost importance. I quote from the account that the *Times* gives of the incident the next day:—

> "Whatever doubts may have been felt or affected as to the policy of Nicholas II. were yesterday very decisively settled by a particularly clear and unequivocal announcement from his own lips. St Petersburg is at present crowded with delegates from every part of the Empire charged with the duty of congratulating the Tsar upon his

marriage. More than six hundred deputations, each composed of three or four members, represent the nobility, the military classes, and the Zemstvos, or local representative councils of every part of the Tsar's wide dominions. One hundred and eighty-two of these deputations were yesterday received by His Majesty, whose speech upon the occasion is a model of vigour and brevity. Advancing a few steps the Tsar pronounced in a strong clear voice, and with a remarkably resolute manner, the following words:—

"'I am pleased to see here the representatives of all classes assembled to express their feelings of loyalty. I believe in the sincerity of those sentiments, which have always been characteristic of every Russian. But I am aware that in certain meetings of the Zemstvos voices have lately been raised by persons carried away by absurd illusions about the participation of the Zemstvo representatives in matters of internal government.

"'Let all know that, in devoting all my strength to the welfare of the people, I intend to protect the principle of autocracy as firmly and unswervingly as did my late and never-to-be-forgotten father.'"

Our great English newspaper allows itself to comment on this event as follows:—

"This uncompromising assertion of the autocratic principle will excite no surprise in Russia, or in the mind of men fairly conversant with Russian affairs, though it may give a shock to people who have indulged in vague expectations of some kind of new departure. Our readers have never been led to suppose that the change of rulers would bring about any change in the principles upon which Russia is governed, or that Nicholas II. would be found any more willing than his father to delegate to popular assemblies any portion of the centralised authority which controls every detail of Russian life. Representative institutions in Russia exist in a somewhat rudimentary form, their powers are limited in theory and yet more restricted in fact, and, notwithstanding sporadic claims for a larger share in administration, they have, upon the whole, little real vitality. When the Zemstvos were established by Alexander II., for they can boast no higher antiquity, a wave of reforming zeal was agitating the surface of Russian society. It was a time of rather extensive theorising, in which numerous adaptations of Western institutions, and perhaps yet more numerous deductions from first principles, were brought forward for the regeneration of the Russian people. The district Zemstvos, representing communes rejoicing in emancipation from the power of the great landlords, were expected by eager reformers to effect impossible transformations of Russian life. They were to send delegates to provincial Zemstvos charged with wider and more general duties of local administration, which it was hoped would prove nurseries of advanced ideas. They in turn were to send representatives to a central assembly in Moscow or St Petersburg which it was thought might properly assume the advisory powers of an ancient Russian institution which, before the time of Peter the Great, was wont very humbly and submissively to lay its opinions at the foot of the throne. However humble and submissive it might be at first, the advocates of reform thought it probable that in course of time a popular assembly resting on so broad a democratic basis would gradually acquire sufficient authority to offer something more than timid suggestions. Alexander II. disliked the distant possibility of such an innovation, and the parliamentary idea languished under his rule. His successor disliked the idea of representative interference even more strongly, and interfered even more decidedly. By methods administrative rather than legislative, the use of which is extremely well understood in Russia, he greatly curtailed the powers even of the provincial councils in local affairs; while dreams of political activity on the part of a germ of a parliament in a central assembly were practically annihilated. It is now made perfectly clear that they cannot be revived under the rule of the Tsar Nicholas II., who has formulated with unsurpassable firmness and decision the most absolute theory of autocratic authority.

"Russian institutions are not to be judged from a western standpoint, nor is it much better than an impertinence to condemn them for want of conformity with ideas springing from widely different circumstances and a wholly dissimilar history. Judged by all the ordinary tests of national prosperity, the absolute rule of the Tsar seems to suit Russia very well, and it is not for foreigners in any case to presume to affirm that something else would suit her better. The mode of government which the Tsar has just asserted his determination to maintain can at least show a history of achievement in the building up of States which its rivals cannot pretend to equal. In Russia, at any rate, it must for the present be accepted as an ultimate fact."

Now it is well that we should have the case for

maintenance of the autocracy clearly put before us as it is in this article, though one would perhaps have preferred that its exposition should have been left to one of the reactionary compatriots of the Tsar himself, such as the ingenious Madame de Novikoff, than that it should have become apparent that a great English journal had forgotten those political principles which it is the pride of the English Conservative party to preserve intact, and the ideal of the English Liberal party to carry to still more glorious results than they have already attained.

But what is the contention? That although political liberty is essential for our welfare, in Russia it is superfluous; there, the autocracy can be relied upon to carry out satisfactorily all the functions of government. But the whole lesson that we derive from our study of the subject leads us to conclusions the direct opposite of these. It would be tedious once more to recapitulate and insist upon them; we have seen by what an irresistible chain of logical necessity, autocratic rule (because of the limits of one man's time and bodily vigour) implies government by means of a bureaucracy; how such a government must in self-defence suppress criticism; how therefore it comes about that public opinion is annihilated, its means of finding utterance by free speech and a free press not being allowed to exist; the environment is then the most favourable that can be conceived for the growth of all kinds of political evils; the first to come into existence are official corruption, tyranny, and selfishness; corruption brings in its train the neglect of the interests of the nation in every material direction; money is apportioned for the army, but the soldiers are not given adequate food and clothing; money is allocated for the rebuilding of prisons, but the old infamous dens still

# EFFECTS OF AUTOCRACY.

exist; all sorts of reforms are projected and the money carry them out is wrung from a peasantry that are taxed so highly that unlike every other peasantry in Europe their material condition is becoming more and more depressed in spite of the increasing facilities for material production; and when the money is thus collected at the cost of terrible sufferings the projected reforms are for the most part not carried out at all; the funds stick to the fingers of the official class. These are the evils that follow in the train of corruption. But the spirit of unbounded tyranny and oppression of the people is also without a bridle; the result here is that no Russian can call his personal freedom and happiness secure from one day to another. The whole country is watched by an immense body of secret political police and a whole army of spies in their employ. To do anything displeasing to this organisation is to run the risk of being thrown into prison or exiled to a distant part of the Empire for an indefinite period, without any trial, and therefore without any opportunity of justifying your deeds, or obtaining redress from the grossest injustice. Seeking after religious truth is met with ruthless persecution; even the exercise of their ancestral religion by the Jews has led to a wholesale expulsion from certain parts of the country which killed thousands and ruined hundreds of thousands during the last reign. All this seems to be apparent to any one who has only a superficial knowledge of the subject yet the *Times* tells us that—"Judged by all the ordinary tests of national prosperity, the absolute rule of the Tsar seems to suit Russia very well, and it is not for foreigners in any case to presume to affirm that something else would suit her better." If, as the *Times* in its preceding sentence teaches us, "impertinent" is a proper term to apply to one's adversaries in controversy, it is not to the contentions of the Russian reformers whether by nationality Russian, English, or American, that the adjective would seem most fittingly to apply.

Further, we may ask, is it really possible for the advocates of Autocracy to ignore the great historical lesson that was exhibited to us in Russia only thirty years ago? If the experiment of benevolent autocracy was to be tried, what better circumstances could we possibly hope for, what fairer and more prosperous surroundings could it possibly have, than those that existed in the reforming period of Alexander II. The Tsar himself was working for certain great ameliorations. He was enthusiastically backed up by the most intelligent and the most unselfish part of his subjects, who carried out his designs in an admirable manner. It is true that these reforms have left some impress for good even on the Russia of to-day, but what a large proportion of them have been lost to the country by subsequent reaction! Is it not perfectly clear that if reforms are to depend on the initiative of an absolute monarch they may also be swept away at his wish? If this were not evident from the nature of things, does it not become so in the light of history? You may laboriously wind up a bucket from a deep well, but if you have no stop-catch to put on your windlass the bucket will rush down once more to the bottom immediately you release the handle. Russian reformers wish not only to effect reforms but to *secure* them. There is no evidence before us to show that Nicholas II. is likely to attempt the inauguration of a reforming period of anything like the vigour or importance of that of his grandfather; but even supposing he were to try to do so, if it should happen that subsequent deaths in the Royal family resulted in the accession to the throne of some poor creature of marked moral and mental feebleness, what would become of any progress that might have been effected? Further the question arises (and it is a question of the utmost moment), as to who is to control the arbitrary caprice of the heads of departments? Who is to govern the rulers? for the real rulers they are. If under the firm hand of his father one minister could relax the persecution of the Jews till the influence of the Procurator of the Holy Synod grew strong enough to intensify it once more, is the hand of Nicholas II. expected to be powerful enough to do away with all such inequalities of will or whim amongst his subordinates? One can hardly ask such questions as these seriously. The conditions have grown too immense to be controlled even were there called to the throne another personage as mighty as the great Peter. It is absolutely certain that if they are not prepared to show any measure of trust in the people, his pigmy descendants will fail in the task.

The following may be read in amplification of the contents of this chapter:—

Leroy-Beaulieu, Vol. II., Book VI., chaps. iii. and iv.; Wallace, chap. xiii.; Stepniak, "The Russian Army and its Commissariat" in "The Russian Storm Cloud," and Part IV. of "Under the Tsars"; Kennan, "Siberia and the Exile System" (especially perhaps the appendices).

# CHAPTER IX.

## THE QUESTION OF THE EXTRADITION OF PRISONERS TO RUSSIA.

## Chapter IX.—*Contents.*

GENERAL reasons for refusing the extradition of political prisoners—Reasons particularly applicable to Russia for refusing extradition at all events for political offences—We are dealing with a power that has been habitually treacherous and perfidious, moreover it frequently punishes without trial, and whilst it is known that barbarous punishments exist, it is impossible to ascertain the fate of individuals—There is no stability in any arrangements that may be made, as the way in which prisoners are dealt with is subject to complete alteration at the sudden irresponsible will of an individual—Dishonourable methods of procedure of Russian Government—Endeavours, by making false representations to prisoners to induce them to betray their friends—Spy system: *agents provocateurs*, kidnapping, Russian intrigue in Bulgaria—The "Ungern-Sternberg" case in Belgium—Imprisonment and exile without trial following often upon release after acquittal by the regular tribunals—Barbarity of some of the methods of punishment employed—The American extradition treaty.

## IX.

### THE QUESTION OF THE EXTRADITION OF PRISONERS TO RUSSIA.

One ground on which the dictum that political prisoners should not be surrendered to a foreign state may be defended is sometimes overlooked; political crimes are not necessarily less heinous and less deserving of punishment than other crimes; but every prisoner, however heinous be the offence of which he is accused, is entitled to a fair and impartial trial by an unprejudiced tribunal, and in political cases it is often impossible that this should be available, for in giving the political prisoner up to the government that demands his extradition we deliver him up to his accuser with a knowledge that he will be arraigned before judges who in some countries have direct interest in the result of his trial, and in all countries are in common with their compatriots, subject to national and patriotic bias.

Besides this general reason which with others justifies us in maintaining our historic tradition of refusing to give up political prisoners to another power, there are a number of others which are at present applicable to Russia in a way that they would not be to many of the States of Western Europe. In the first place it is felt to be impossible to have satisfactory mutual arrangements of this sort with a power that is habitually and has been habitually for many reigns, treacherous and perfidious. It is felt to be equally impossible to surrender prisoners to punishment which may be of extreme barbarity and concerning the actual form of which it is not possible to obtain accurate information in particular cases. Nor can we give up men who may be sent to exile or to prison without any trial at all. Finally the conditions of an agreement should be binding on both parties alike; and each party should know exactly to what it itself and the other party to the agreement are pledged. This cannot be the case with an autocratic power which can and does alter at the sudden irresponsible will of a single individual the whole conditions which surround the way in which prisoners are dealt with.

The first point I take is that Russia is a power that we cannot trust; we cannot be sure that she will act in a fair and honest way or that she will carry out what she has engaged herself to do. The importance to be attached to this part of the subject is quite clear. When a demand is made for the extradition of a prisoner it is supported not by direct evidence; practically it is impossible to transport all the witnesses that would be necessary to hold anything like a preliminary trial in the foreign country which happens to be the venue; all that is sought then is to make out a *prima facie* case; and this is done by the production of depositions by the government which makes the demand; now if that government is not a scrupulous one such depositions may easily be forged or tampered with, possession of the prisoner may be obtained on trumped-up charges, and his person being once secured he may eventually be punished for an offence of which no mention has been made to the surrendering country, and though it is true that it is improbable that such action would be taken *immediately*, whilst the case was still liable to supervision, it would be quite possible to keep the *eventual* fate of a surrendered person so secret that remonstrance would be impossible.

We see then the great importance of the nature of the preliminary enquiry in the surrendering country. On this point I will quote a sentence from the petition presented to their government by the American Society for the Abrogation of the Russian Extradition Treaty (reprinted in the American edition of *Free Russia* for December 1893) :—

"It will be seen that the prosecutor has two great advantages: he need only make out a case of probable guilt; he may use depositions taken in Russia; whereas the fugitive may not" [or rather probably *can* not, as he has no opportunity of working up his case in his own country]. "The only question before the magistrate, after he has decided the identity of the fugitive and that the offence is extraditable, is whether the prosecutor has made out 'a *prima facie* case,' that is, whether there is probable cause to believe the fugitive guilty; or, in other words, such a likelihood as would justify committing a man for trial here. If the magistrate deems the evidence sufficient to sustain the charge under the provisions of the treaty, he certifies that fact, together with a copy of all the testimony taken before him, to the Secretary of State, and commits the fugitive to prison to await action by the State Department upon a requisition from the Russian Government. These proceedings may be reviewed by a United States judge under a writ of *habeas corpus;* but upon such a review the judge has merely to decide matters of law, and has no jurisdiction to review the decision of the magistrate as to the sufficiency and weight of evidence."

But it will perhaps be considered that it is making rather a strong assertion to say that Russia cannot be trusted not to use corrupt testimony in procuring the extradition of persons whom it desires to punish. Perhaps it is, but we must remember that we are talking of a government which has for a great number of decades of years been notorious for its unpleasant ways in such matters as these, and so far from there being evidence of its having abandoned underhand and dishonourable methods of procedure, we are unfortunately continually getting pieces of evidence of a contrary character. All the testimony goes to show that the methods of dealing with political prisoners in Russia would be as abhorrent to our sense of honour as the espionage and tell-taling common in some French schools would be disgusting to an English school-boy. For example endeavours are made by making false representations to prisoners to induce them to betray their friends. Herzen in "My Exile" quotes a personally experienced instance of this. During one of his judicial examinations Prince Golitsin said to him, "You are obstinately silent; you evade answering. You spare through a false sense of honour, people of whom we know more than you do, *and who have not been so discreet as you.* You will not help them but they will ruin you." Now it was of course quite untrue that any confession had been made by Herzen's friends implicating him; equally of course Herzen was too alert a man to be entrapped by such a ruse. This happened some half century ago but from that time to this hardly a single Russian political prisoner recounts the experiences he has undergone without referring to some similar incident which has happened either to himself when under examination, or in some case of the kind which has come before his notice.

This is an instance of what may happen to a political prisoner if brought before a tribunal for one of the numerous examinations that take place, (unless indeed they are dispensed with altogether, and he is sent to captivity or to exile at the dictate of the secret political police). No whit more scrupulous are the methods employed for getting possession of the persons of those who are regarded by the Government as being inimical. The constant employment of an enormous army of spies both at home and abroad, arbitrary domiciliary visits and searches very often at night, and the employment of "agents provocateurs," that is of people who pretend to be themselves engaged in the crimes they are placed to check, holding out inducements to others to enter upon them, are some of the means employed. If these fail and if occasion is favourable, no scruple is made to having resort to positive lawless violence, and prisoners have actually been kidnapped from foreign soil where they are supposed to be protected. The periodical *Free Russia* has done very good service in keeping a watch on these doings. Five years ago it quoted several of the Roumanian papers to shew the state of things in that country then. (See *Free Russia*, October 1890, pp. 8, 9.) Not only Bucharest but the whole country was swarming with the spies of the Russian Government, they employed themselves in devising plots and in practising bribery of the local officials to the advantage of the Russian Government. The names of the generals of this spy-army were given by the Roumanian papers.

Let us give a particular instance of the work of these persons:—A Russian named Dobrogeanu had been living as an emigrant in Roumania for fifteen years.

He had left Russia after having been banished by the administration (without trial) to the shores of the White Sea for reading some forbidden books and expressing disapproval of the Government. He now sought naturalisation as a Roumanian citizen. The idea was exceedingly displeasing to the Russian Government but the bill conferring the privilege was carried by a large majority in the Roumanian parliament. It still however had to be confirmed by the senate. Anonymous letters sent to the senators defaming his character seemed not to be effecting their purpose. A Russian spy named Motylióv then offered to a Polish resident 10,000 francs and certain other advantages if he would consent to introduce secretly into Dobrogeanu's house a machine for coining false money. The Pole however instead of carrying out the proposal disclosed the intrigue to Dobrogeanu who informed the official attorney-general. (See *Free Russia* for January 1891, pp. 11, 12).

It is delightful to read how often these somewhat elaborate plots miss fire through the refusal of those whom the Russian Government seeks to use as its tools, to play such dishonourable parts.

Several instances are recounted by Mr Edward Dicey in his recently published book about another of the Balkan States ("The Peasant State: an Account of Bulgaria in 1894"). In Bulgaria indeed Russian intrigue has been rank. It has kidnapped one of her princes; and it is not clear that it must not be held responsible for the use of the very engine of underground warfare which it calls upon all Europe to denounce when levelled against itself; for there is evidence to connect it with the assassinations of Beltchev (1890), of Vulkovitch (1891), and perhaps with that of Stambulov himself in 1895, and with an abortive plot to kill the present prince (Ferdinand).[1]

The arrangements of the Russian Government for confidential police work are not confined to its near neighbours, to whom it is supposed to stand in the relation of an elder protecting brother. It has establishments in Paris, and even in London and the United States.

Last September there appeared in *Free Russia* (see *Free Russia,* September 1894, p. 73) an account of the doings of a man styling himself Baron Ungern Sternberg. His real name is Jagolkovski. After adopting the passport of another man he received money from the Russian Consulate at Marseilles and again at Nice. He installed himself at Liège in Belgium, where he perpetrated some of the deeds for which he is now charged with being an anarchist, but in the same month travelled to Berlin and was again supplied with money at the Russian Consulate there. He made two more visits to Belgium in 1893 and 1894 to take part in dynamite exploits. *Free Russia* remarks:—

> "The combination of such proceedings with the receipt of Russian official money is certainly most interesting, especially when we take into consideration that the genuine Baron E. Ungern-Sternberg, whose passport was used, was an official of the Russian Consulate."

A Reuter's telegram dated from Liège, March 18th, 1895, says:—

> "The Court of Assizes here to-day pronounced sentence upon the anarchist Jagolkovsky, the so-

---

[1] See especially chap. iii. and chap. xvi. of Mr Dicey's book, and article in "Fortnightly Review" (July 1893) "The Russian Intrigues in South-Eastern Europe" by C. B. Roylance-Kent.

called Russian Baron Sternberg, who is now a prisoner at St Petersburg. Being found guilty of having participated in the robbery of dynamite from an explosives factory, he was sentenced to penal servitude for life" (*Daily Chronicle*, March 19th, 1895).

A point that transpired at the Liège trial was that during his criminal activity the prisoner continually wrote to an address where there lived a subordinate official of the Russian Consulate, who, although of a different name from that used on the letters, we may perhaps presume was their actual recipient.

It is instructive to learn from more recent information furnished by the "Vorwärts" of Berlin, (Aug.-Sep. 1895) that the Russian government (which is at present posing as the upholder of the principle of extradition,) has itself tried Jagolkovski (although he has committed no serious offence in their country) and sentenced him to life-exile in Siberia. This is an excellent method of avoiding handing him over to Belgium; and we note that the St. Petersburg authorities are not without care for the prisoner's comfort, for he has not been sentenced to imprisonment, but only to banishment with deprivation of civil rights. Whether he will in reality suffer any imprisonment at all is in fact doubtful.

Let us turn to some other aspects of the case against delivering over prisoners to Russia.

Political prisoners if tried there at all, are tried by tribunals other than those before which ordinary offenders are brought. These exceptional courts are of the nature of courts-martial, and none of the ordinary safeguards for the prisoners' adequate defence can be relied on in them.

Even more serious is the fact that in a large proportion of cases no trial at all is vouchsafed, and those who are regarded with disfavour are thrown into prison or banished for indefinite periods merely on secret police mandates. As the *lettres de cachet* were one of the faggots that burnt most fiercely in the conflagration of the French Revolution, so imprisonment and exile by administrative process are felt by the Russian revolutionary party of to-day to be amongst the most bitter injuries inflicted on their country. An admirable article in the *New York Evening Post* (quoted in the American edition of *Free Russia* for July 1893) puts these points before the reader. It says:—

"The administration of justice in Russia is, as far as externals go, more orderly, swifter and surer than in Oriental countries, but it wants that feature of the supremacy of law over every other power in the State which is the great distinction between the justice of barbarians and the justice of civilized men. No judicial decision in Russia is final. No acquittal by judge and jury secures a man his liberty. No accusation is necessarily public. Not only may the verdict of a jury be disregarded by the Executive, if the case is held to have a political aspect, but the Executive is the sole judge of the existence of the political aspect. And of what value would acquittal by any court be, in the presence of the fact that transportation to Siberia, without indictment or trial, on mere 'administrative order,' as necessary for the safety of the State, is always possible, and that every man, woman, and child in the Empire is exposed to it. For these reasons it seems to us that although we cannot claim exterritoriality from Russia for our own citizens resident in Russia, we ought, for the very reasons which cause us to claim it in other countries, to refuse to surrender any one to Russian justice without exacting some guarantee that the defendant at the trial shall enjoy the privileges and facilities which he would have in countries governed by the civil law, say in Germany, and that if acquitted he shall have the right to leave the country without liability to arrest and detention on any other charge."

. . . . . .

"There is no crime so heinous as to deprive the criminal of the right to a fair trial. This is probably the only fundamental natural right of every human being as a human being. We cannot conceive of the Almighty himself refusing it. It is because neither political nor any other offenders are sure of it in Russia, that we are bound to be careful about putting any human being, on any charge, into the hands of the Russian courts and police."

In the way they are captured, in the way they are judged, and in the way they are condemned unheard alike we find reasons against entering into relations for the extradition of prisoners with Russia.

There is a final reason in the treatment of prisoners which in some instances makes it as incongruous to deliver up victims to the miseries in store for them as it would be for us to do so to China where torture is openly acknowledged as one of the weapons of punishment.

Everyone is acquainted with Mr Kennan's exposure of the state of the Russian prisons. Russia is not the first country where the state of the prisons has been very abominable; what makes her case peculiarly hopeless is the impossibility of reform under a bureaucracy which is incurably corrupt. A Howard might arise in

# EXTRADITION.

Russia as one did in England, but it would be impossible for his enthusiasm to be attended by the same success there at present. The health-giving breeze which may blow away the impurities from these places can only be fanned into motion by a powerful public opinion. Its first whisper in Russia would be ruthlessly suppressed. So that till we have political reform we shall wait in vain for effective prison reform. There are certain overt practices which are removed from torture by a very fine line indeed. Such are chaining to the wheelbarrow for months together. Others differ in no way at all from torture. Such are floggings with that terrible instrument the plet. I have no wish to horrify my readers with realistic descriptions of what such floggings mean. The plet is a horrible three-thonged whip, and is used in Siberia, and occasionally in European Russia.

Beatings with the cane are common throughout Russia, and are so prolonged as often to be exceedingly horrible affairs.

A curious commentary on the information of those who assert that such horrors are things of the past is furnished by the following newspaper telegram (*Daily Chronicle*, April 18th, 1895).

"From our Correspondent.

"*St Petersburg, Monday Night.*

"Under the new regulations affecting prisoners in Russia and Siberia, women who are condemned to hard labour or to banishment to Siberia will not in future be flogged or chained to wheel-barrows at the mines. Convicts of the first class undergoing hard labour will be both manacled and fettered, but those of the other classes will be fettered only. Women sentenced to hard labour for an indefinite period will still be kept in manacles, but of a lighter pattern. Generally speaking it may be said that corporal punishment is abolished in the case of women, and refractory prisoners will be punished either by their sentences being prolonged or by temporary confinement in separate cells on a diet of bread and water."

The "new regulations" show that women have up to this time been flogged and chained to wheel-barrows, and that the alleviation which is to be granted to them will not even now be extended to men.

Other evidence is furnished by Mr de Windt who has been travelling in Siberia with the object of investigating the alleged horrors of convict life but with the avowed opinion that he should find them much exaggerated. From the island convict station of Saghalien he wrote a letter to the *Evening Standard* (dated May 28th, but received in England only in time to be published in the issue of October 24th, 1894). In this he denies the truth of some of the rumoured atrocities but is obliged to acknowledge that in that island at any rate the plet is still in use. He writes:

"Two men (Vassiliéff and Kalenik) were brought here, tried, and sentenced to ninety lashes with the 'plet,' a terrible instrument, now abolished in other parts of Siberia, and only used here in cases of murder. Vassiliéff (whom I saw yesterday) was found to be insane, and was therefore spared, but Kalenik was flogged, and died a few days afterwards of blood-poisoning arising from the punishment."

It may be urged that the island of Saghalien is an out-of-the-way place, and that the experience there should hardly be instanced against Russia generally.

To convicts however Saghalien is one of the most important places in the Empire. We are now considering the question of whether there should be given up to Russia men who may be sent there. As a matter of fact flogging with the plet is practised throughout Siberia when "vagabonds" are dealt with, and also for certain offences in the cases of prisoners who have been sentenced to "deprivation of civil rights." A recent instance of flogging with the plet is reported from European Russia (from Kasan on the Volga).

The fact of course is that an Autocracy is not in any way bound by any pronouncements it may previously have made, for it may at any moment it chooses reverse its former action. Besides this consideration we have to remember that the Russian Autocracy whatever its inclinations may be, is shown to be quite unable to control its own officials in these matters.

Yet as newspaper readers will be aware, the American Government has recently concluded an extradition treaty with Russia which makes Russian political refugees in that country feel far less secure than they formerly did. I should like to quote a few sentences from a very powerful article written by Mr George Kennan in the American *Forum* (May 1893) concerning this treaty when as yet its ratification was not concluded.

"Suppose," he says, "that under the provisions of the pending treaty a Russian revolutionist who has sought asylum in the United States is accused by the Russian Government of having attempted or conspired to assassinate the Tsar. A *prima facie* case is made out against him on paper, and as the treaty declares that an attempt on the life of the Tsar shall not be regarded as a political offence, he is extradited. The case perhaps attracts so much attention in Europe and the United States as a political case that the Russian Government does not dare to try the accused secretly by court-martial, upon the common law charge of murder or assault with attempt to kill, and it therefore makes a show of fairness and justice by trying him before a specially appointed court of senators and acquitting him on the ground of perjury or insufficient evidence. Does this acquittal ensure the safety of the extradited person? By no means. Although he succeeded in escaping to the United States once, he may be utterly unable to do so a second time, for the reason that he has not money enough to make again so long and expensive a journey. He is watched constantly by the police, and in the course of two or three months from the date of his acquittal by the court he is suddenly arrested by the order of the Minister of the Interior and exiled by administrative process to the Siberian territory of Yakutsk upon the ground that since his judicial vindication he has become 'politically untrustworthy.' Can any remedy be suggested for such an abuse of the extradition treaty as this? It is vain to argue that the Russian Government is an honourable government, and would not act in this way. The Russian Government is *not* an honourable government and it *has* acted precisely in this way. More than half of the 'politicals' acquitted by the court in 'the case of the 193' at St Petersburg in January 1878 were immediately re-arrested and exiled by administrative process. In August of the same year, soon after the assassination of General Mezzentsef all persons in St Petersburg who had been tried by the courts for political offences and had been acquitted were banished by administrative process and put under police surveillance in various remote parts of the Empire." More recently "In January 1891 a Russian subject named Vladimir Lutski who was living in Bulgaria and who occupied there the position of Director of the Marine Branch of the Bulgarian Department of Public Works, was decoyed to Constantinople by means of two forged telegrams purporting to be from his friend Prince Nakashidze, and was there kidnapped by a party of men under the direction of the dragoman of the Russian Embassy. He was put on board the Russian steamer 'Nakhimof' taken across the Black Sea to Odessa and eventually sent to the great prison known as the House of Preliminary Detention in St Petersburg."

Mr Kennan finally sums up the case for refusing to enter into such extradition arrangements with Russia, as follows:

"The maintenance of a state of siege throughout a large part of the Empire for a period of twelve years in a period of profound peace; the trial of civil and political cases by courts-martial behind closed doors; the exile of political suspects by administrative process to the wildest and remotest parts of Siberia without trial or hearing; the burial alive of political prisoners in the bomb-proof casemates of Petropavlovsk and Schlusseburg; the terrible overcrowding and consequent mortality in Siberian *etapes* and forwarding prisons; and the marching of thousands of exiles, men, women, and children across the great Siberian plains in the rigour of an Arctic winter, are all repugnant to the modern sense of justice and humanity, and shameful and disgraceful to a

Government which calls itself civilised and Christian."

The following may be read in amplification of the contents of this chapter :—

> Stepniak, "Under the Tzars," Parts II. and III. For an exposition of the case against the Russo-American Extradition Treaty see Kennan's "The Russian Extradition Treaty" in *The Forum* of May 1893, and for a reply putting the case from a contrary point of view see *The Forum*, July 1893, article by John Bassett Moore.

# CHAPTER X.

## PLEA FOR SYMPATHY WITH THE CAUSE OF FREEDOM IN RUSSIA.

## Chapter X.—*Contents.*

Reasons which justify the existence of an organised band of friends of Russian freedom in other countries; necessity of preventing the conclusion of improper extradition treaties, or the countenancing of Russian political agents in entrapping their victims in foreign countries on false pleas—An informed opinion concerning Russian politics to some extent a safeguard against needless war—The value of an articulate criticism of Russian governmental action, even though it comes from abroad—The intrinsic interest of the subject of the struggle for freedom in Russia—The value to Russian reformers of sympathy from other countries.

# CHAPTER X.

## PLEA FOR SYMPATHY WITH THE CAUSE OF FREEDOM IN RUSSIA.

Such a volume as this may not unfittingly end with an epitome of the reasons which may be given why the subject of Russian Politics may be expected to make a strong appeal to our interest and sympathy. To some these reasons have appeared so cogent, that they have consolidated themselves into a Society whose object it is to study Russian politics and to aid and encourage by every legitimate means those who are struggling to obtain political and religious freedom for Russia.[1] The subject of my last chapter gives a very striking instance of how useful, nay how necessary, the action of a body of instructed and organised people may be in such a concrete case as presenting opposition to the unjust extradition of political or quasi-political[2] prisoners. The American branches of the Society I have mentioned, together with other societies which sprang up by their side, made the most strenuous efforts to prevent the conclusion of the extradition treaty with Russia. Their protest it is true did not avail to prevent

---

[1] For particulars concerning the Society, see Appendix.

[2] The American treaty sanctions the extradition of those who escape from Russia (as almost all refugees do escape) by means of using a forged passport; this offence is not in itself deemed by the treaty political it is merely forging a Government document.

its signature, but the hope of getting it abrogated has not yet been abandoned, and in any case the nation has been so educated by the controversy thus evoked, that gross abuses of the powers given to Russia by the treaty, will be much less likely to be attempted by that power, and if attempted will be far more jealously watched by Americans, than would otherwise have been the case. Yet with America the treaty now exists, and similar treaties exist with almost all the near neighbours of Russia amongst the continental states. It might very well happen at some future time that an English Foreign Minister might be induced by the blandishments of Russian diplomacy to forget the sturdy traditions of his office, and that the English people might be called upon to safeguard their own country from entering into a similar compact.

Nor is the actual conclusion of such a treaty the only danger to which it is possible that we even in England, may be subjected. The existence of the wild anarchist plots of the last few years puts another weapon in the hands of an unscrupulous Government, such as the Russian. It endeavours to cloud the understanding of the politicians of Europe, and to create a confusion in their minds between the political refugees from a fatherland from which it itself has expelled happiness, and the wild enemies of society whose hands are against all government and all social order. The story of "Baron Sternberg" is only one amongst many which illustrate a deliberate line of policy pursued by the agents of the Russian Government abroad, the object of which is if possible, to involve their political opponents in complicity with criminal anarchists. Such a policy may even meet with an occasional instance of success amongst the youthful revolutionists who have been driven out of their sobriety of moral judgment by the persecutions to which they have been subject. The instances of such aberration however are but occasional, and for the great bulk of their prey the bait is laid in vain ; none the less does it often happen that they are victims, for the Russian secret foreign police take advantage of times of national misfortune and panic (such as that which prevailed in France after the assassination of President Carnot) to secure the alliance and co-operation of their brother police officials in other countries. From Paris at the time I refer to there took place at the instigation of the Russian political agents a wholesale expulsion of Russian men and women who were as far removed from being criminal anarchists as any reader of this book can be. Here again we have to keep watch and ward over a very concrete matter. It must never be said that the English detective or regular police hound down as dangerous anarchists Russian reformers who are working only for their country's liberation.

Apart from these perfectly direct political aims, the education of public opinion, and the increase of popular knowledge concerning Russian political conditions, cannot fail to have the most important influences on the policy adopted by this country towards Russia. For example has not the increase of the knowledge of Russian conditions made enormous progress since the time of the Bulgarian atrocities ? Then the English liberal party quite failed to distinguish between the great Russian people and the tyrannical Government superimposed on it: now most of us have learnt to appreciate the people but to regard with the utmost distrust their Government. We now see what some of us did not then see, that the confidence the English liberals placed in the Russian Government was as undeserved as was the rooted antipathy and distrust of the English conservatives of that time towards the main body of the Russian people. We may safely affirm that both English liberals and English conservatives are now better informed.

The influence is immense of such an improvement as this in the public's acquaintance with the subject. Between two great Empires like those of Russia and Britain, questions of conflicting interest are sure from time to time to arise, but we feel more confident than we did twenty years ago that the two countries will not be engaged in war either as the result of some mad misconception, or in consequence of the disillusionment that would be likely to follow crazily-misplaced confidence.

This same growing amount of instruction about things Russian amongst Western peoples has too the most important effects within Russia itself. For the first time the actions of the Government are challenged by an articulate public opinion. Within the Empire as we have seen no criticism of the authorities is tolerated, but the Government are none the less sensitive to the voice of public opinion when it reaches them from the foreign press. This is shown by the pains they take to prepossess the opinions of such amongst their visitors as they consider likely afterwards to try and inform the peoples of Europe and America concerning their Russian experiences, no less than by the care with which they plant literary defenders in America and western Europe who shall be ever ready to take up the cudgels in their defence. It is even possible that some actual reforms have been aided, or at any rate that some outrages on the dignity of humanity have been averted, in consequence of the publicity gained by other peoples' insisting on looking in at their windows. For example if Count Leo Tolstoi were arrested, something like a European scandal would be created, and so Count Tolstoi in spite of his outspoken utterances, and the unwelcome course of conduct he pursues, remains free from arrest and even from serious molestation.

Two more reasons remain to be adduced why Russian politics should be studied, and why the maintenance of such a companionship as the Society of Friends of Russian Freedom is defensible. The one is solely on our part. It is the keen interest, the intellectual delight, of watching the development of the greatest political problem of the day. What Italy was to freedom-loving politicians in the days of Mazzini, what Greece was to them still earlier in the century, that at its close is Russia. It is the battlefield on which the cause of liberty is at gauge to-day, and the course of the struggle there must have a fascination for all friends of freedom which will draw their eyes to that distant arena in spite of the absorbing nature of the pursuit of political questions in their own countries. Unlike Italy, and unlike Greece, there is (if we exclude the Polish question) here, in the main, no foreign domination to be shaken off; it is the fight in its naked simplicity between autocracy and democracy—never before has the struggle occurred on so mighty a scale so that the fortunes of 120,000,000 wait upon the issue. Never before has the world seen so great a governmental power striving to live after the ideals of an Eastern despotism, but using as its instruments the railroad, the telegraph, and the appliances generally of modern civilisation. We see worked out before our very eyes, reported daily (in some mutilated form) in our newspaper on the breakfast table, those problems of mediæval history which we may have tried dimly to realise. The fact that we are having such an historical panorama displayed before us, is only slightly veiled by the modernness of the means of government which the bureaucratic autocracy adopts, and by the equal modernness of sentiment and thought which rules amongst a part of those who are rebelling against its authority.

The other and final article which may be put forward in the apology for the existence of a foreign band of sympathisers with the cause of freedom in Russia, is of more real practical moment. It is said that the fact of there being a company of those who feel for their distresses does much to mitigate the griefs of the exiles in Siberia who after the lapse of months hear of their doings and even read their publications. At first sight this consideration may perhaps be dubbed sentimental, and deemed of insufficient importance to influence our actions. Yet, of how much real moment it may be to them we shall perhaps get a notion if we compare the position of the patient on the sick bed, racked with pain but surrounded by his loved ones, with that of the prisoner condemned to the torture-chamber who sees no faces about him but those of enemies and tormentors. The physical sufferings in each case may be the same, but there is an immeasurable difference in the position of the two men. Sympathy may well make all the difference between hope and blank despair.

Whether the Russian reformers be exiles in Siberia, or whether they are still working in the cause of liberty as yet unnoticed by their Government, the existence of an organised band of sympathisers in other countries must be an immense encouragement and help. Like the sane man immured in error in a mad-house, they need some occasional re-assurance from outside that it is not *they* who are lunatic. Discouragement, apathy, doubt: scepticism as to the actuality of all lofty moral, social, and political ideas; these are the insidious enemies that are apt to creep upon them; these are the enemies whose defeat our alliance can do so much to further.

# APPENDIX.

## The Society of Friends of Russian Freedom.

(Established November, 1889.)

The Society of Friends of Russian Freedom is a body of men and women whose object is to further the cause of political and religious liberty in Russia by legal and legitimate means.

The existence of a Society in England concerning itself with the internal affairs of another country, although by no means without notable precedent, requires a word of explanation.

Russia is said to be an autocracy. But absolutism in Russia does not really mean government by the will of the Tzar. That stupendous task may indeed be undertaken, but cannot possibly be accomplished by one man. The acts of the Government are determined by officials whose decision are enforced by an enormous army of ignorant and often brutal subordinates.

This bureaucracy is in general excessively corrupt and oppressive. Against large classes of the community its members practise cruelties and barbarities, which are an outrage on humanity. The people of other countries would refuse to passively acquiesce in these if they were properly informed concerning them.

As instances may be cited, The Persecution of the Jews, of the Stundists (a million Protestant peasants of a type somewhat resembling the Puritans of the 17th century in England), and of all other Religious Denominations differing from the Orthodox Greek Church, and The Disgraceful Treatment of Prisoners and Exiles, especially of political prisoners.

Since the reaction which followed the reforms in the early part of the reign of Alexander II., the Government has shown itself not only corrupt, oppressive, and cruel, but doggedly retrograde. What possibilities have Russian citizens of struggling in their own country against the terrible yoke laid upon them? There is no freedom of speech, of public meeting, or of religion. The press is gagged. The people have no voice in the Government, and they have no means of resisting the evil deeds of those set over them.

Education is systematically sterilized. Arbitrary arrest for political offences is followed by imprisonment and exile, often without any form of trial (by what is called "administrative process"), and when trial is permitted, it is without a jury, and the right of cross-examining witnesses is absolutely in the control of the court.

The prisoners not infrequently die or go mad in consequence of their sufferings. Sometimes they themselves end their miseries by suicide. Those who pass through the ordeal survive only with shattered health. A large proportion of the best of the intellectual classes—professors, teachers, doctors, authors, and promising students, both men and women—are banished to the wilds of Siberia, their lives ruined, and their talents lost to their impoverished country.

What can the outside world do in so desperate a case? Nothing? On the contrary, the events of the last few years show that it can do a great deal.

The Society of Friends of Russian Freedom—

(1) Aims at supplying accurate information as to the deeds done in Russia, which the strict surveillance of the police in that country succeeds so often in shielding from observation.

Every successful attempt at ventilation does something to dispel the accumulated foul vapours in these dark places. Of this a signal instance has been afforded in the publication of George Kennan's "Siberia and the Exile System."

(2) It aims at encouraging the Russian liberals and also those who are suffering from religious persecution, by giving them some visible proof that the heart of the rest of the civilized world is with them.

(3) It aims at keeping public watchfulness alive lest Europe and America should be induced under false pleas to aid and abet atrocities abhorrent to them. As an instance of the need for such watchfulness

may be mentioned the danger of the extradition of political offenders under false claims.

(4) It aims also at giving such encouragement and aid to Russian political exiles in Siberia as may nerve them to obtain freedom by flight.

To carry out these objects the Society—

(I.) Supplies authentic and recent information concerning the cause of freedom in Russia by publishing a monthly paper, *Free Russia*, in England, by publishing pamphlets, and by organising lectures and meetings.

(II.) Collects money for assisting Russian political prisoners and exiles to escape. (Contributors to this fund should signify that they wish their donations to be applied to this purpose).

For all general purposes subscriptions may be sent to the Hon. Treasurer, Dr Spence Watson, Bensham Grove, Gateshead-on-Tyne.

The publication of the Monthly Paper (which is sent free to all members) is in itself a considerable expense. The Society is anxious to be put in a position to maintain special correspondents in Russia, who would add largely to its value.

Membership of the Society is obtained by a subscription of not less than 5s. per annum. BUT A GOOD MANY SUBSCRIPTIONS OF A LARGER AMOUNT ARE REQUIRED IF THE WORK OF THE SOCIETY IS TO BE DONE EFFICIENTLY.

There are also several Provincial Branches working in close sympathy with the mother Society.

It will be seen that the objects of the Society are to secure for Russia the freedom which this country obtained centuries ago, or perhaps we may more justly say, has always in some measure enjoyed. The Society has the support of persons of all shades of political opinion. Several members of both Houses of Parliament—Conservative, Liberal, and Irish Nationalist alike—are members of the General Committee or of the Society, and subscribers to the Society's funds. In fact, the policy advocated makes a strong appeal to every inhabitant of these Islands, for it is the only alternative to TERRORISM—that policy of despair which it seeks to supplant.

# APPENDIX.

## GENERAL COMMITTEE OF THE FRIENDS OF RUSSIAN FREEDOM.

Those marked with an (*) form the Executive Committee.

William Allan, M.P. ; The Rev. Charles A. Berry, D.D. ; The Rev. Stopford A. Brooke, Percy W. Bunting, *W. P. Byles ; The Countess of Carlisle, The Rev. W. Moore Ede, J. E. Ellis, M.P. ; Miss Isabella O. Ford, *J. Fredk. Green, L. T. Hobhouse, The Rev. Page Hopps, R. A. Hudson, *Miss Mary Hargrave, R. Maynard Leonard, Thomas Lough, M.P. ; John Macdonald, *W. Mackenzie, *Mrs Charles Mallet, S. T. Mander, J.P. ; E. J. C. Morton, M.P. ; J. Fletcher Moulton, Q.C., *Edward R. Pease, *G. H. Perris, *J. Allanson Picton, Miss Ada Radford, Mrs Herbert Rix, *Herbert Rix, Joshua Rowntree, The Rev. Professor Shuttleworth, *Mrs Arthur Sidgwick, *Adolphe Smith, Henry C. Stephens, M.P. ; James Stuart, M.P. ; *Herbert M. Thompson, The Rev. Canon Thompson, *William Thompson, J. S. Trotter, *T. Fisher Unwin, *Mrs Wilfrid Voynich, Mrs E. Spence Watson, Alfred Webb, Miss Helen Webb, M.B. ; Henry J. Wilson, M.P.; Robert Spence Watson, LL.D., *Hon. Treas.*, Bensham Grove, Gateshead ; *Miss G. L. Mallet, *Hon. Sec.*, 132 Cromwell Road, South Kensington, London, S.W.

"*FREE RUSSIA*" is published every month by Messrs *Ward & Foxlow*, 113 *Church Street, N.W.*

---

## BRANCHES :—

CARDIFF.—*Hon. Sec.*, H. M. Thompson, Whitley Batch, Llandaff, Glamorgan.
EDINBURGH.—*Hon. Sec.*, D. W. Wallace, 53 George IV. Bridge, Edinburgh.
LEEDS.—*Hon. Sec.*, Miss Isabella O. Ford.
NEWCASTLE-ON-TYNE.—*Hon. Sec.*, Miss Laing, 33 Hutt Street, Gateshead.
OXFORD.—*Hon. Sec.*, Mrs Arthur Sidgwick, 64 Woodstock Road, Oxford.
PLYMOUTH.— *Hon. Sec.*, John Adams, 14 St Lawrence Road, Plymouth.

---

## The Society of American Friends of Russian Freedom

has similar aims. The annual fee for membership is one dollar, and each member is sent the monthly paper, "*Free Russia*" (published in London).

Those interested in the object of the Society are invited to correspond with the Secretary, EDMUND NOBLE, 255 Washington Street, Boston, Mass., or if they desire to become members, they are requested to send their names and fee to the Treasurer—

FRANCIS J. GARRISON, 4 Park Street, Boston, Mass.

# INDEX OF NAMES AND SUBJECTS.

ABROGATION of Russo - American Extradition Treaty, [see Treaty.]
"Administrative Process" (imprisonment and exile by), 134, 194, 203-4, 211, 220-1, 232, 243, 250, 253, 254, 256-7, 262, 263.
Adrian (Patriarch), 45.
*Agents provocateurs*, 253, 255-6.
Agrarian difficulties, [see Land Question.]
Agriculture the almost universal occupation of the peasantry, 15, 181.
Ahmed (Khan), 38.
Aksákov, 213.
Alcohol (consumption of), 120.
Alexander I., 75, 77-9, 83, 159.
Alexander II., 83-5, 102, 104, 105-7, 110, 112, 140, 141, 175, 176, 179, 187, 189, 190, 195, 228, 229, 235, 240-1, 244.
Alexander III., 77, 96, 98, 102, 106, 110, 141, 152, 167, 175, 176, 179, 188, 204, 205-8, 218, 229.
Alexis (Emperor), 42, 61, 62, 82, 156.
Alexis (son of Peter the Great), 53-5.
Alliance between "nihilists" and Russian liberals, [see *Rapprochement*.]
Altai mountains, 18.
American Extradition Treaty with Russia, [see Treaty.]

Anarchists, 255-6, 268-9.
Anastasia Romanova, 39.
Anna (Empress), 63-5, 68.
Anna (daughter of Peter the Great), 67.
Anna Leopoldovna, Princess of Brunswick, 65, 66, 69.
"Annals of the Country" or "Annals of the Fatherland," 142, 210.
Anthony Ulrich, Prince of Brunswick, 65, 66, 69.
"Appanage" period, 34-7.
Approximation of climate in northern and southern parts, 4-6.
Arakcheiev, 79.
Aral Sea, 3.
Arbitrators respecting land redemption, *temp*. Alexander II., 93-4, 116-7, 120.
Archangel, 47.
Arctic or barren zone, 7.
Army, 185-6, 221, 226, 242.
Army Reform, 138.
Artisans, 48.
Aryan races, [see Indo-European.]
Assassination of Alexander II. (attempts at), 190, 195.
Assassination of Alexander II., 85, 195.
Assassination of Paul, 77.
Assassination of Mensenstev, 85.
Assemblies, [see Popular Assemblies.]

Assemblies of Nobles, [see Nobles (Assemblies of).]
Austerlitz (battle of), 77.
Austria, 70, 72, 81.
Autocracy, 36-7, 65, 84, 106-10, 207, 213, 238-45, 250, 261, 271.
Azov (town), 44, 47, 51.
Azov (ports frozen in winter), 5-6.

Baikál (lake), 3.
Bakunin, 268.
Balkash (lake), 3.
Baltic, 47, 52, 71, 227.
Baltic Provinces, 28, 73, 153, 169, 237.
Banks, 74.
Baptists (German), 158-9, 166-7.
Baptists (Russian), [see Stundists.]
Bar and barristers, 203-4.
Barbarous punishments, [see Punishments.]
Bariatinski, 74.
Basil, 37, 61.
Basil Shuisbki, 41.
Basmánov, 40, 41.
Beards (shaving of), 68.
Belo-Russ, [see White Russian.]
Beltchev, 254.
Belts, [see Zones.]
Berditchev, 174.
Berezovski, 190.
Berlin, 255.
Berlin Decree, 77.
Bessarabia, 237.
Bestuzhev, 80.
Bilinski (writings of), 103, 213.
Biren, 64, 65, 68.
Black earth or *Tcermoziom* zone, 8-9, 94, 119.
"Blacking out," [see Press and Press Censorship.]
Black Sea, 51, 52, 73, 227.
Bohemia, 23.
Borís Godunóv, 40, 91.
Borodino (battle of), 78.
Bosphorus, 228.

Brigandage, 67.
Bucharest, 253.
Bukovine, 24.
Bulgaria, 181-4, 189, 227, 254-5, 263.
Bureaucracy, [see *Tchin* and *Tchinovniks.*]
Bureaucracy and Autocracy, 107-10.
Bureaucracy and Peasantry, 110-19.
Burning of Moscow, 78.

Calendar reformed *temp.* Peter the Great, 45.
Canals, 52, 64.
Cantonal Chiefs, [see *Zemskii Natchalniks.*]
Carelia, 52.
Caspian Sea, 3, 53.
Catherine I., 47, 51, 63.
Catherine II., "The Great," 61, 62, 68-74, 75, 83, 159, 163.
Caucasus (mountains), 3.
Caucasus (region), 29, 160, 162.
Censorship, [see Press and Press Censorship.]
Charles XII. of Sweden (war with), 47-52.
Chekhs of Bohemia, 17.
Chernigov, 35, 42.
"Chiefs of the Rural Cantons," [see *Zemskii Natchalniks.*]
Christianity introduced into Russia, 34.
Christianity as a unifying force, 16.
"Christs," [see Sect of.]
*Christian World,* (articles in, [see in Index of Writers "Stundists (the); the story of a Great Religious Revolt."]
Church (Greek or Orthodox), 150, 151, 155-6, 166, 169, 207.
Civil Service, [see *Tchin.*]
Clergy, [see Priesthood.]
Clerk to the Village Commune or to the *Volost,* [see *Pissar.*]
Climate, 4-6, 5-6, 10.

## INDEX.

Code of Laws, 34, 38, 47, 73, 132-3.
Cold, 5-6, 50, 78.
Colonisation of South Russia, 12, 74, 190, 226.
Commercial Treaty, 64.
Communes, [see Village Communes.]
Comparison of condition of peasantry before and after the Emancipation, 120-3.
Conscription (general) for army, 138.
Constantine, 79.
Constantinople, 228.
Constitution proposed, *temp.* Anna, 64.
Constitution (struggle of the Decembrists for), 79.
Constitution adopted by Poland in 1791, 71.
Constitution of Poland cancelled in 1832, 80.
Constitution of Finland, 77, 208, 212.
Constitution of Bulgaria, 182-3.
Constitutionalism in Russia, 196-202, 225, 232-45.
Corporal Punishment, [see Punishments.]
Corruption amongst officials, 183, 186, 221-3, 235, 242-3.
Corvée, 91, 92, 93, 94, 96, 98, 100, 120-1.
Cossacks, 25-7, 38, 42, 44, 50, 72, 90, 153, 154, 208, 212.
Courland, 27, 28, 73.
Cracow, 72.
Crimea (southern coast of), 10.
Crimea Tatárs, 38, 39, 40, 42, 44, 72.
Crimean War, 81, 104-5.
Crown estates and crown peasants, 91-2, 99-100, 111.

Dantzic, 71.
Dardanelles, 228.
Decembrists (the revolt of the), 79-80, 86, 186, 228.

Declaration concerning his autocracy made by Nicholas II., 213, 238-45.
Delyanov (Minister of Public Instruction), 223.
Delyanov (dispatch to, from Dournovo quoted), 223-5.
Demetrius, [see Dmitri.]
Denmark, 67.
Desert region of South Russia, [see Ural-Caspian depression.]
Deutch (Leo), 136.
Dishonourable actions of Russian government, 250-8, 262-3.
District Commanders, [see Zemskii Natchalniks.]
Diversity of race, language, and religion on the Russian borders, 15.
Dmitri (son of Ivan IV.), 39, 40.
Dmitri : the first "false Demetrius," 40.
Dmitri : the second "false Demetrius," 41.
Dnieper, 23, 73.
Dobrogeanu, 253-4.
Dolgoruki (princes, *temp.* Peter II. and Anna), 63-4.
Domestic serfs, [see Serfs (domestic).]
Domiciliary visits, 253.
Don (river), 4, 10, 45, 51.
Don Cossacks, 25, 44, 72.
Doumas, 128, 131-2, 133, 144, 235.
Dournovo (Minister of the Interior), 223.
Dournovo (dispatch of, to Delyanov quoted), 223-5.
Drunkenness (alleged), 119-20.
*Dukhoburi*, 159-60.
*Dvorniks* (house porters), 195.

Ecclesiastical lands and property, 68, 70.
Education, 128, 129-30, 172, 174-5, 181, 183-4, 208, 211, 222-5, 232.
Education in the army, 138.

280  INDEX.

Elizabeth (Empress), 65-7, 110.
Emancipation of serfs, [see Serfs.]
Emigrants settled in South Russia, [see Colonisation.]
Emigration, 29.
Emigration of Mussulman Tatárs, 21.
England (Peter the Great's visit to), 44.
England (Commercial Treaty with), 64.
England (war with, *temp.* Paul), 76.
England (alliance with, at beginning of Alexander I.'s reign), 77.
England (Crimean War with), 81.
Espionage, 66.
Esthonia, 28, 52.
Ethnological groups, 16-18.
Ethnological descent of the Russians, 16-30, 225.
Ethnological descent of the Bulgarians, 182.
Eudoxia (wife of Peter the Great), 47.
Euxine, [see Black Sea.]
Executive Committee (Nihilist), 195 ; (manifesto of), 198.
Exile to Siberia, 80, 221.
Exile by "Administrative process," [see "Administrative process."]
Extent of the country and immensity of its natural features, 3-4.
Extradition, 136, 249-64.

"False Demetrius," (the), [see Dmitri.]
Family groups, 101.
Feodor I., 39-40, 90.
Feodor (son of Boris Godunóv), 40.
Feodor III., 42, 62.
Ferdinand of Bulgaria, 255.

Fertility of black earth zone, 8-9.
Finland (Gulf of), 47, 52.
Finland, and Finns of Finland, 18, 77, 82, 153, 207, 236.
Finns (ethnologic family), 16, 18-9, 23, 24, 225.
Flogging, 154, 259-61.
Forest and swamp zone, 7-8, 94.
Forged passports, 267.
Franco-Russian alliance, *temp.* Paul, 76-7.
Freedom (idea of appears), 83-5.
Frederick the Great, 66, 67, 70.
French invasion of Russia, [see Napoleonic invasion of Russia.]
French Revolution, 74, 181, 257.

Gallicia, 23, 24, 70.
Gendarms and gendarmerie, [see Political police.]
Georgia, 77.
Germans, 28, 207.
German provinces, [see Baltic provinces.]
Godunóv (Boris), [see Bóris Godunóv.]
Gogol, 229.
"Going amongst the people," 192-3, 233-4.
Golden Horde, 38.
Goldenberg, 194.
Golitsin (Basil), 42, 43, 62.
*Golos* (*The*), 141-2, 210.
Gordon (general, *temp.* Peter the Great), 43, 44, 45, 46.
Gortchakov, 213.
Governors of Provinces, 117, 129, 135.
Governors General, 142.
Great Britain, [see England.]
"Great man" theory of history, 55-6.
Great Princeship, 34.
Great Russia, and Great Russians, 15, 22, 23-4, 94, 169, 207.
Greek Church, [see Church.]

# INDEX. 281

Grodno, 27, 72.
Guilds (merchants'), 46.
Gurko (General), 195, 213

Hanseatic League (towns of), 35, 38.
Hegemony, 34, 36.
Henry (brother of Frederick the Great), 70.
Herzen (Alexander), 104, 208, 229.
Holstein, 67.
Holstein-Gottorp (Duke of), 67.
Holy Roman Empire of German Nations, 70.
Holy Synod, or Holiest Synod, [see Synod.]
Homogeneousness (ethnological): to what extent found in Russia, 11-16, 82.
Hospitals, 40, 52, 175.
Hungary and Hungarians, 18, 81, 225.
"Hunger strikes," 194.
Husbandry, [see Agriculture.]

Icons, 156, 157, 164-5, 166.
Identity of programme of nihilists and liberals, 190-202.
Ignatiev, 176, 213.
Immensity of extent of natural features of country, 3-4.
Imprisonment by "administrative process," [see "Administrative Process."]
Indirect representation, 238, 240.
Indo-European races, 17, 27, 225.
Inequalities of land endowments of peasantry, 98-9, 119.
Ingria, 52.
Inquisition, [see Secret Chancellerie.]
Insurance of cattle, 172.
Insurrection in Poland, [see Poland (insurrection in.)]
Interest (rate of), 171-2.
Invasion of Russia by Charles XII., 50-1.

Invasion of Russia by Napoleon, [see Napoleonic invasion of Russia.]
Irremovability of Judges, [see Judges.]
*Ispravnik* (police officer), 112, 117.
Ivan III., " the Great," 37, 38, 61.
Ivan IV. " the Terrible," or " the Cruel," 37, 38, 39, 61, 66.
Ivan (son of Ivan IV.), 39.
Ivan V., 42, 43, 62.
Ivan VI., 65, 66, 69.

Jacquerie, 72.
Jagolkovski, 255-6.
Japanese, 18.
Jews, 17, 28, 152, 169-76, 207, 208, 212, [see also Persecution of Jews.]
John, [see Ivan.]
Joseph II., Emperor of Germany, 70.
Judges (irremovability of), 134.
Judges appointed "on probation," 134.
Jury system, 133, 134, 136-7, 194, 257.
Justices of the Peace (elected), 128, 129, 133, 135.

Kakhovski, 80.
Kalenik, 260.
Kalmuks, 22.
Karakasov, 190.
Katkov (Michael), 141, 187-9, 208-11.
Kavalsky, 194.
Keltic races, 17.
Kharkov (revolt in central prison of), 194.
Kherson, 163, 169.
Kidnapping, 253, 263.
Kiev, 24, 34, 35, 36, 42, 163, 169, 174, 193.
"Kolokol" (The), Herzen's publication, 104.
Kosciuszo (Thadeus), 71, 86.

T

# 282 INDEX.

Koshelev, 213.
Kossuth, 81.
Kovno, 27, 78.
Kraievsky, 141-2.
Krapotkin (Prince), Governor of Kharkov, 194.
Krémlin, 38-9.
Krózhe massacre, 153, 212.
Kuban, 10, 25.

Ladislaus (King of Poland), 41.
Ladoga (lake), 3, 11, 64.
Land purchase, 94-100, 120-1.
Land question, 92-3.
Law (Russian), 132-3.
Lazarev (Egor), 203-4.
Le Fort, 46.
Legal reforms, 132-8.
Lemberg, 70.
Letters of Marque, [see Marque.]
Letts, 27, 28.
Liberals (the Russian), 189-91, 200, 230, 232, 244.
Liberalism at beginning of Alexander I.'s reign, 80.
Liberalism at beginning of Alexander II.'s reign, 84, 105-6, 244.
Liberty, [see Freedom.]
*Liberum veto* in Poland, 70.
Liège, 255-6.
Literature and the Emancipation, 103-4.
Lithuania, and Lithuanians, 27, 28, 29, 37, 80, 82, 94, 143, 237.
Little Russia, and little Russians, 15, 22, 24-5, 28, 29, 50, 72, 94, 101, 143, 163, 189, 213, 237.
Livonia, 27, 28, 52, 71.
Loans to peasantry from government for land purchase, 96-7.
Local government, 29, 127-32.
London, 255.
Löwenhaupt, 50.
Lutheran religion, 29, 153, 169, 208.
Lutski (Vladimir), 263.

Magyars, 18, 225.

Malo-Russians, [see Little Russians.]
Maria Theresa, 70.
Markov, 176.
Marque (letters of), issued by England, 76.
Marseilles, 255.
Marsh, 11, 29.
"May Laws" against the Jews, 176.
Mazeppa, Hetman of the Cossacks, 50.
"Mediators of Peace," [see Arbitrators respecting land redemption, *temp.* Alexander II.]
Melikov (Loris), 142.
Menshikóv, 46, 63.
Mezenstev, 194, 262.
Michael Románov, 41.
Migration of the Kalmuks, 22.
Migration, 29, 90.
Milan Decree, 77.
Military colonies, 79.
Miliutin (Dmitri), 138, 213.
Miliutin (Nicholas), 83, 85, 95, 99, 213.
Mingrelia, 160.
Minsk, 25, 71, 72.
*Mir*, [see Village Communes.]
Mixed marriages, 151.
Mohammedans, 20-1.
Mohilev, 27, 71.
Molokani, 150, 160-2.
Money-lenders and money-lending, 119, 121.
Mongols, 18, 21-2, 225.
Moraviov-Apostol, 80.
Moscow, 24, 36, 37, 39, 52, 66, 131, 132, 175, 203, 227, 228.
Moscow (comparative density of population in region of), 14.
Moscow (burning of, *temp.* Ivan IV.), 39; (and *temp.* Alexander I.), 78.
Moscow (retreat from), 78.
Moscow (mine at), 195.
*Moscow Gazette*, 141, 187, 209.

*Moscow Telegraph*, 142.
Motylióv, 254.
*Moujik*, [*see* peasantry.]
Mountains, (remarkable absence of except on outskirts of the country), 4-5, 11.
Mouraviev of the Amour, 109.
Münich (General), 64, 65, 66, 68.
Municipal Corporations, [*see Doumas.*]
Muscovite nation, 16.
Muscovite ascendancy established, 37.
Muscovite domination as a unifying force, 16.
Mussulmans, [*see* Mohammedans.]
Mysticism, [*see* Sects mystic and fantastic.]

Napoleon, 75-7.
Napoleonic invasion of Russia, 77-8.
*Narodnoe Pravo* Party (manifesto of), 201-2.
Narva (battle of), 48.
Narva (retaking of), 49.
Natchaiev (Sergius), 136.
*Natchalniks*, [see *Zemskii Natchalniks.*]
National Assembly demanded, 198, 202, 232, 233-6.
Naval construction under Peter the Great, 45.
Navorski (Stephen), 45.
Netherlands (Peter the Great's visit to), 44.
Neustadt (Peace of), 52.
Neva, 48.
Newspapers, [*see* Press.]
Nice, 255.
Nicholas I., 79-81, 83, 103, 109, 111, 123, 132, 139, 159, 228, 229.
Nicholas II., 211-13, 218, 238-45.
"Nihilism," and "Nihilists," 85, 191-202, 230.
Nikon (Patriarch), 42, 46, 66, 157.
Nobility of birth, 46.

Nobility of service, 46.
Nobles (assembly of), 94-5, 117, 127.
Nomad populations, 9.
Notoberg, [*see* Schlüsselburg.]
"Notes of a Sportsman," by Torguénev, 103.
Novgorod the Great, 20, 33, 34, 35, 36, 37.

*Obrok*, 91, 92, 93, 94, 96, 98, 100, 116.
*Obshchestvo*, [*see* Village Communes.]
Odessa, 73, 131, 132, 194.
Officialdom, [*see Tchin.*]
Oka (battle on the), 38.
Old Believers, 42, 156-8, 212.
Oligarchical Supreme Council, 64.
Onega (Lake), 3, 11.
Orenteln (General), 194.
Orlov (Alexis), 74.
Orlov (Gregory), 73.
Ostermann, 64, 66.
Orthodox Church, [*see* Church.]
Ottoman, (*see* Turk.)
Overcrowding in Jewish pale of settlement, 173-4.
Overcrowding of prisons, 221, 263.

Pacific Coast, 22-7.
Pale of Settlement (for Jews), 28, 173-4.
Panslavists, and Panslavism, 187-9, 208.
Paper Manufactories, 48.
Paris, 255, 269.
Partitionings of Poland, [*see* Poland, (partitionings of).]
Patriarchal family government, 101.
Patriarchate, 45-6.
Paul (Emperor), 68, 69, 74-7, 110, 159.
Paul (Emperor), and Napoleon, 75-7.

Paving of streets, 52.
Peasantry, 15, 88-123, 179-84, 226.
Peasantry (poverty of), [see Poverty.]
Peasantry in France before the Revolution, 181.
Peasantry in Bulgaria, 181-4.
Peasants' Insurrection, 72.
Peasant proprietary, [see Land Purchase.]
Permia, 5, 37, 90.
Persecution of Jews, 169-76, 208, 212, 242, 245.
Persecution of Lutherans, 153, 208.
Persecution of Raskolniks or Old Believers, 157-8, 212.
Persecution of Roman Catholics, 153, 208.
Persecution of Stundists, etc., [see Stundists and Sects of South Russia.]
Persecution of Uniats, 153-5.
Persia (Peter the Great's expedition against), 53.
Persia (Elizabeth's expedition against), 69.
Persia harasses Georgia, 77.
Pestel, 80.
Peter I., "The Great," 42-57, 61, 62, 82, 105, 107, 157, 187, 227, 245.
Peter II., 63, 110.
Peter III., 67-9, 74.
Petersburgh [see St Petersburgh.]
Petition of literary men to Nicholas II., 212.
Philaret, 45.
Pietism (formal), 66.
*Pissar*, 113-5, 119.
*Plet* (flogging with), 259-61.
Plot to assassinate Paul, 77.
Pobiedonostsev, 152-3, 167, 170, 176, 206, 208, 213, 245.
Poland, and Poles, 17, 23, 28, 29, 37, 40-1, 42, 48, 78, 79, 80, 82, 95-6, 143, 153, 170, 173, 189, 213, 236, 271.
Poland (comparative density of population in), 13.
Poland (partitionings of), 69, 70-2.
Poland (insurrection in), 80, 95-6, 102, 107, 190, 209-10.
Police, 52, 269.
Political police, 107, 134, 194, 203, 253, 255, 269.
Political offences, 134, 136.
Political prisoners, 136, 232, 256-8, 261-4.
Poltava (battle of), 50, 63.
Poniatowski, King of Poland, 70.
Popular assemblies, 35.
Popular right party, [see *Narodnoe Pravo* Party.]
Population, 4, 29.
Population (distribution of), 12, 14.
Population (rapid increase of), 13, 66, 226.
Population of *volosts*, 112.
Potemkin, 73.
Poverty, 119-23, 172.
Praga (suburb of Warsaw), 71.
Prairie (the Russian), [see Steppes.]
Prehistoric inland ocean, 9.
Press, and press censorship, 25, 139-45, 173, 208, 212.
Press (provincial), 143-4.
Priesthood, 204.
Prisons, 194, 221, 242-3, 258-9.
Pripet (river), 29.
Privileged classes, 174.
Procurator of the Holy Synod, [see Protasov, Tolstoi (Dmitri), and Pobiedonostsev.]
Professions (political attitude of), 204.
Protasov, 153.
Protestantism (influence of German), 158-9.
Prussia, 71, 72.
Prussia (war with, *temp*. Elizabeth), 66.
Prussia (peace with, *temp*. Peter III.), 67.
Pruth (battle on the), 51.

## INDEX.

Pskov, **35**, 37.
Public opinion, 144, 229, 259.
Public opinion and the emancipation, 105.
Public opinion of Western Europe, 168, 269, 270-1.
Pugachev, 69, 72.
Punishments (barbarous), 138, 258-61.

Racial descent of the Russians, [see Ethnological descent.]
Railways, 226, 228.
Rainfall (small), 5.
*Rapprochement* between "nihilism" and Russian liberalism, 197-202, 231.
Raskól (the) and the Raskólniks, [see Old Believers.]
Rationalistic sects, [see Sects of South Russia.]
Ratushni brothers, 165.
Reaction in the latter part of Alexander II.'s reign, 84, 102, 107, 126-44, 152, 179, 190, 196, 229-30, 241.
Red Russia, 24, 70.
Redistribution of lands, 101-2.
Red tape, 114, 220.
Redemption by the peasants of lands held by them, [see Land Purchase.]
Reformed sects, [see Sects of South Russia.]
Religious persecution, [see Persecution.]
Rent, 97, 120-2.
Representative Commission, 73.
Retreat from Moscow, 78.
Revision of Scriptures and Church Service books, 42.
Revolt of the Decembrists, [see Decembrists.]
Revolt of Pugachev, [see Pugachev.]
Revolutionary party, [see "Nihilists."]
Riazan, 38.
Riga (Gulf of), 47, 52.

Riga (town), **47.**
Rileyev, 80.
River system, 10-11.
Roman Catholic religion, 29, 80, 153, 155, 170, 208, 212.
Románov family, 41.
Rotation of crops; three years' system practised, 9.
Rouble (value of), 97.
Roumania, 253-4.
Rumantzev, 73.
Rurik, 33.
Russia as a sea power, 47.
"Russification," 27-30, 189, 207, 208.
"*Russian Messenger*," 209.
Ruthenians, [see Little Russians.]

Sacerdotalism, 165.
Saghalien, 260-1.
St George (feast of), 90-1.
St Gothard Pass (crossed by Suvórov), 76.
St Petersburgh, 52, 64, 131, 132, 149.
St Petersburgh (building of), 49, 227.
St Petersburgh (comparative density of population in neighbourhood of), 14.
St Peter and St Paul (fortress of), 194.
Saline Steppes, 10.
Salònica, 255.
Samarin (George), 95, **99.**
Sanitation, 128-9.
Saratov, 203-4.
Scandinavians, 18, 33.
Schism of seventeenth century in Orthodox Church, 42.
Schlüsselburg, 48, 66.
Schools (intermediate), 66.
Schuvalov (Ivan), 66, 213.
Seclusion of women broken through, *temp.* Peter the Great, 45.
Secret Chancellerie, 66, 68.
Sects, 156-69.
Sects mystic and fantastic, 158.

286  INDEX.

Sect of the "Christs," 158, 159.
Sect of the Uniats, [see Uniats.]
Sects of South Russia, 150, 152, 158-69, 208, 212.
Semetic groups of peoples, 17.
Separation of judicial from administrative power, 133, 134.
Serfs partially emancipated in Poland in 1791, 71.
Serfs in Russia, 89-92.
Serfs in Russia emancipated, 92-100, 103-7.
Serfs (domestic), emancipated, 95.
Settlement of South Russia, 12.
Servia, 17.
Short service in army, 138.
Shúishki, [see Basil Shúishki.]
Siberia, and Siberians, 15, 29, 38, 90, 160, 162, 203-4, 237, 259-61, 272.
Slaves, 89.
Slavs, 16, 17, 22-7, 225.
Slavophilism and Slavophils, 44, 186-9, 207.
Smolensk, 34, 35, 38, 42.
Socialism and Socialists, 192-201, 230.
Society (American) for abrogation of Russian Extradition Treaty, [see Treaty.]
Society of Friends of Russian Freedom, 267-8; Appendix, 273-6.
Soloviev attempts assassination of Alexander II., 195.
Soltykov, 142, 209.
Sophia of Anhalt-Zerbst, [see Catherine II.]
Sophia (half-sister of Peter the Great), 42-3, 63.
Spelling of Russian names, Preface, vii.
Spies, 253
Stambulov, 183, 255.
*Starosta*, 111, 112, 117-8.
*Starshina*, 112-3, 117-8, 119.
Steppes, 9, 94.
Sternberg (Baron Ungern), 255-6, 268.

*Streltsí*, 43, 44, 45, 90.
Strogonov, 37.
*Stundists*, 28, 150, 162-9, 170, 203, 212.
Suabian peasants (colonies of in South Russia), 163.
Succession to throne settled on hereditary principles, 75.
Suicide (wholesale suicide by Old Believers), 158.
Superficiality of changes introduced by Peter the Great, 57.
Suppression of Ukrainian literature, 25, 143.
Suvórov, 71, 73, 75, 76.
Suzdal, 35.
Suzerainty of the Tatárs, 36.
*Svod*, [see Code of Laws.]
Swamp, 11.
Sweden and Swedes, 18, 47-52, 69, 73, 77, 207.
Switzerland (Suvórov in), 76.
Synod, 46, 150.

Taganrog, 51, 52.
Tatárs, 16, 18, 19-21, 22, 35-37, 38, 90, 225. [See also Crimean Tatárs.]
Taxation, 90, 121, 128-9, 226, 243.
Tcherkaski (Prince), 95, 99.
Tchermozióm zone, [see Black Earth.]
*Tchin and Tchinoviks*, 46, 107-19, 130, 185-6, 203, 206, 217-25, 242-5, 261.
Terrorism, 193-6
Teutonic races, 17, 28.
Third section of Police, [see Political police.]
Three years' system of rotation of crops. [See Rotation, etc.]
Tilsit (Peace of), 77.
Toleration (governmental conception of), 149-52.
Tolstoi (Count Dmitri), 129, 153, 176.
Tolstoi (Count Leo), 162, 180, 209, 270-1.

## INDEX. 287

Tomsk forwarding prison, 221.
Torture, 55, 154.
Tourguénev, 103, 192, 209, 229.
Towns (growth of large), 181, 226.
Trade, 35.
Transcaucasia, 10, 82.
Treaty (Russo-American for extradition), 251, 261-4, 267-8.
Trepov (General), 137.
Tsebrikova (Madame), 231-2.
Turanian groups of peoples, 17.
Turanian races, 16.
Turkestan, 19.
Turks, 19, 20, 44.
Turks (Peter the Great's war with), 51-2.
Turks (Elizabeth's war with), 69.
Turks (Catherine II.'s war with), 71, 72.
Turks (Alexander III.'s war with), 188, 193, 221.
Tver, 37.
Tyranny of old lords, 123.
Tyranny of local officials, 115-6, 243.

Ukázes, 100, 132, 134, 135, 140.
Ukraine, and Ukrainians, [see Little Russians.]
Ungern-Sternberg, [see Sternberg.]
Uniats, 80-1, 153-5.
United States, 255.
University of Moscow, 66.
Urál mountains, 5, 18.
Urál (region of), 237.
Urál river, 10.
Urál Cossacks, 25.
Urál-Caspian depression, 9-10.
Uro-Altaic group of Turanian peoples, 18.
Usury, [see Interest.]

Valdai hills, source of the principal rivers, 10-11.
Vassiliéff, 260.

Veto (right of), 118.
Viatka, 35, 37.
Vienna (Congress of), 79.
Village Communes, 15, 101-2, 118, 127-8, 130.
Vilna, 27, 72.
Vistula, 23.
Vitebsk. 27, 71.
Vladimir (Prince), 34.
Vladimir (town), 36.
Volga (river), 4, 10.
Volga (region of), 237.
Volhynia, 72.
*Volost*, 111-2, 113, 117, 118, 128.
Vulkovitch, 254.
Vyburg, 52.

Warsaw, 71, 72, 79.
Wheelbarrow (chaining prisoners to), 259-60.
White Russia, and White Russians, 15, 22, 27, 28, 29, 237.
Winter Palace (explosion at), 195.
Wool, 48.
Wyburg, [see Vyburg.]

Yaroslav (Prince), 34.
Yaroslav (town), 37.
Yermák, conqueror of Siberia, 38.

Zasúlitch (Vera), 136-8.
*Zemskii Natchalniks*, 117-8, 134.
*Zemstvo*, and *Zemstvo* Assemblies, 118, 127-32, 133, 135, 144, 184, 190, 211, 222, 231, 235, 238, 239, 240.
*Zemstvo* (sessions of), 130.
*Zemstvo* (permanent committee of), 130-1.
*Zemstvo* (franchise for election of), 131.
Zones (Arctic or barren) 7 ; (Forest and swamp), 7-8 ; (Black earth or Tchernozióm), 8-9 ; (Steppe), 9.

# INDEX OF WRITERS AND BOOKS
## TO WHICH REFERENCE IS MADE.

Barrow (Sir John), "Life of Peter the Great," quoted 48, 49, 52-3; referred to 57.
"Burning Question," (The) (pamphlet), referred to 201.
*Century Magazine* (article from), quoted 145.
*Contemporary Review* (articles from), quoted 150-2, 209-11.
*Daily Chronicle* (newspaper), quoted 223-5, 255-6, 259-60.
De Quincey, "The Revolt of the Tatárs," referred to 22.
Dicey (Edward), "The Peasant State : an account of Bulgaria in 1894," quoted 184 ; referred to 182-4, 213, 254, 255.
"Distinguished Persons in Russian Society," translated from the German by F. E. Bunnétt, referred to 213.
Errera (Leo), "The Russian Jews: Extermination or Emancipation?" referred to 172, 173, 175, 176.
*Evening Standard* (newspaper), quoted 260.
*Fortnightly Review* (article from), referred to 255.
*Forum* (articles from), quoted and referred to 261-4.
Fowler (George), "Lives of the Sovereigns of Russia," quoted 74 ; referred to 36.
Freeman (E. A.), "General Sketch of European History," referred to 86.
Frederic (Harold), "The New Exodus : a study of Israel in Russia," quoted 205-6, 208 ; referred to 65, 173, 176.
*Free Russia* (newspaper), quoted 108-10, 211-2, 251-2, 255, 257-8; referred to 253, 254, 255.
Herzen (Alexander), "My Exile," quoted 8, 123, 252.
Kennan (George), "Siberia and the Exile System," referred to 203, 221, 245. "Blacked out" (article in the *Century Magazine*), referred to 145. "The Russian Extradition Treaty" (article in the *Forum*) quoted 261-4 ; referred to 264.
Kostomárov (Nicholas), "Russian History in Biographies of its great Actors," quoted 57 ; referred to 55.
Lanin (E. B.), "Russian Characteristics," referred to 120, 180.
Leroy-Beaulieu (Anatole), "The Empire of the Tsars and the Russians," quoted 4, 105, 112-3, 121, 136-7, 139, 141-2, 143, 144-5, 154-5, 187, 191-2, 197, 219, 229, 233-7 ; referred to 3, 30, 57, 85, 116-7, 117-8, 123, 133, 145, 176, 193, 213, 219, 245.
Lowe (Charles), "Alexander III. of Russia," quoted 188, 207-8.

Moore (John Bassett), "The Russian Extradition Treaty" (article in the *Forum*), referred to 264.
Morfill (W. R.), "Russia" (The Story of the Nations Series), referred to, 57, 85.
*New York Evening Post* (newspaper), quoted 257-8.
Noble (E.), "The Russian Revolt, its causes, &c.," quoted and referred to, 142, 193-5.
Novikoff (Olga), "A Cask of Honey with a Spoonful of Tar" (article in the *Contemporary Review*), quoted 150-2.
Peter the Great (letter from, to his son Alexis), quoted 54.
Petition to Congress by American Society for Abrogation of Russian Extradition Treaty, quoted 251-2.
Potapenko (J. N.), "A Russian Priest," referred to 204, 213.
"Revelations of Russia: or the Emperor Nicholas and his Empire in 1844, by One who has seen and describes," quoted 220.
Royal Commission on Labour (Report of) (Bluebook), Russia, quoted 122-3.
Roylance-Kent (C. B.), "Russian Intrigues in South-Eastern Europe" (article in *Fortnightly Review*), referred to 55.
Samson-Himmelstierna (H. von), "Russia under Alexander III. and in the preceding Period," referred to 213.
Schuyler (Eugene), "Peter the Great," quoted 25-7, 35, 36-7, 41, 46, 50, 51; referred to 53, 57.
Soloviev (Sergius), "History of Russia," referred to 67.
Stead (W. T.), "The Truth about Russia" (review of), quoted 150-2.
Stepniak (Sergius), "The Russian Peasantry: their Agrarian Condition, Social Life, and Religion," quoted 15, 113-5, 115-6; referred to 111, 123, 176. "Russia under the Tsars," quoted 222-3; referred to 245, 264. "The Russian Storm Cloud: or Russia in her Relations to neighbouring Countries," referred to 213, 221, 245. "Underground Russia: Revolutionary Profiles and Sketches from Life," referred to 137. "Nihilism as it is," quoted 199-201; referred to 213. "What can the Tsar do?" (article in *Free Russia*), quoted 108-10.
Stretton (Hesba) and an anonymous collaborator, "The Highway of Sorrow," referred to 163.
"The Stundists: The story of a Great Religious Revolt," (anonymous), quoted 163-5, 166-67, 167-8; referred to 159, 163, 176.
*Times* (newspaper), quoted and referred to 238-44.
Tsakni (N.), "La Russie Sectaire: Sectes Religieuses en Russie," quoted 159, 160, 161-2; referred to 158, 176.
Tsebrikova (Maria), (open letter from, to the Tsar), quoted 231-2.
Wallace (Sir Donald Mackenzie), "Russia," quoted 155-6, 156-7; referred to 123, 145, 176, 245.
Weber and Kempster (special commissioners of U. S. Government) (Report of), referred to 173.
Windt (H. de), Letter to *Evening Standard*, quoted 260.

# NEW BOOKS.

## THE HONORABLE PETER STIRLING.
A Novel. By PAUL LEICESTER FORD. 12mo. $1.50.

"A very good novel ... so strongly imagined and logically drawn that it satisfies the demand for the appearance of truth in art ... telling scenes and incidents and descriptions of political organization, all of which are literal transcripts of life and fact —not dry irrelevancies. ... Mr. Ford is discreet and natural."—*Nation*.

## TEN BRINK'S LECTURES ON SHAKESPEARE.
Translated by JULIA FRANKLIN. Contents: *The Poet and the Man; The Chronology of Shakespeare's Works; Shakespeare as Dramatist, as Comic Poet, as Tragic Writer; Index to Works Mentioned.* 12mo. $1.25.

## A HISTORY OF THE NOVEL Previous to the Seventeenth Century.
By Professor F. M. WARREN. $1.75.

## KALIDASA'S SHAKUNTALA; or, The Recovered Ring.
Translated by Professor A. H. EDGREN. 12mo, gilt top, $1.50.

## HEINE'S LIFE TOLD IN HIS OWN WORDS.
Edited by KARPELES. Translated by ARTHUR DEXTER. 12mo. $1.75.

"On every page there is an illustration, worth reproduction, of the wit, the sentiment, and the romantic charm which flowed without an effort from the author's brain."—*New York Tribune*.

## HEYSE'S CHILDREN OF THE WORLD.
An intense romance of German life that has become a classic. 12mo. $1.25.

## THE DAYS OF LAMB AND COLERIDGE.
An Historical Romance. By ALICE E. LORD. 12mo. $1.25.

## JEROME K. JEROME'S NOVEL NOTES.
Stories, tragic and comic. With 140 illustrations. 12mo. $1.25.

"We have here Mr. Jerome at his best."—*London Athenæum*.
"Many of them are extremely amusing."—*Evening Post*.

### SARAH BARNWELL ELLIOTT'S NOVELS.
Uniform edition. 12mo, cloth. $1.25 *per volume*.

## JOHN PAGET.
"A story very far above the ordinary."—*Buffalo Commercial*.
"Is vivacious and humorous, ... evidently drawn from life."—*The Churchman*.

## JERRY: A STORY OF A WESTERN MINING TOWN.
"Opens on a plane of deep emotional force, and never for a chapter does it sink below that level."—*Life*.

## THE FELMERES.

---

**HENRY HOLT & CO., 29 West 23d Street, New York.**

# BUCKRAM SERIES.

18mo, with frontispieces, 75 cents each.

"These dainty specimens of the bookmaker's art have nothing superfluous about them."—*Bookman.*

"The novels of Henry Holt & Co.'s Buckram Series have met with success surprisingly uniform. . . . This dainty little volume contrived to look like a tall folio in miniature. . . . The series of Buckram 16mos that include so many charming stories, and none that we remember that are not far above the ordinary. . . . That admirable Buckram Series—to which a dull book is never admitted."—*N. Y. Times.*

"The publishers of the Buckram Series are uncommonly fortunate in their books."—*Critic.*

"The most important of all the 18mo fiction libraries."—*Review of Reviews.*

"Successful, . . . convenient, and dainty."—*N. Y. Commercial Advertiser.*

"A very pretty volume."—*Life.*

"The form which has become so popular and well known lately."—*Yale Courant.*

"It is as a rule perfectly safe to say a good word in advance for any story announced to appear in the Buckram Series."—*Buffalo Commercial.*

"A dull book is never admitted to Holt's Buckram Series."—*Boston Herald.*

A MAN AND HIS WOMANKIND. A novel. By NORA VYNNÉ.

SIR QUIXOTE OF THE MOORS. A Scotch romance. By JOHN BUCHAN.

LADY BONNIE'S EXPERIMENT. A quaint pastoral. By TIGHE HOPKINS.

KAFIR STORIES. Tales of adventure. By WM. CHAS. SCULLY.

THE MASTER-KNOT (2d Edition.) And "Another Story." By CONOVER DUFF.

THE TIME MACHINE. The story of an invention. By H. G. WELLS.

THE PRISONER OF ZENDA. (26th Edition.) By ANTHONY HOPE. A stirring romance.

THE INDISCRETION OF THE DUCHESS. By ANTHONY HOPE. (9th Edition.)

TENEMENT TALES OF NEW YORK. By J. W. SULLIVAN.

SLUM STORIES OF LONDON. (*Neighbors of Ours.*) By H. W. NEVINSON.

THE WAYS OF YALE. (6th Edition.) Sketches, mainly humorous. By H. A. BEERS.

A SUBURBAN PASTORAL. (5th Edition.) American stories. By HENRY A. BEERS.

JACK O'DOON. (2d Edition.) An American novel. By MARIA BEALE.

QUAKER IDYLS. (5th Edition.) By Mrs. S. M. H. GARDNER.

A MAN OF MARK. (7th Edition.) A South American tale. By ANTHONY HOPE.

SPORT ROYAL. (3d Edition.) And other stories. By ANTHONY HOPE.

THE DOLLY DIALOGUES. (8th Edition.) By ANTHONY HOPE.

A CHANGE OF AIR. (9th Edition.) By ANTHONY HOPE. With portrait.

JOHN INGERFIELD. (5th Edition) A love tragedy. By JEROME K. JEROME.

**HENRY HOLT & CO., 29 W. 23d St., New York.**

www.ingramcontent.com/pod-product-compliance
Lightning Source LLC
Chambersburg PA
CBHW022054230426
43672CB00008B/1166